THE
CHEMISTRY
OF
FEAR

THE
CHEMISTRY
OF
FEAR

HARVEY WILEY C. 1910

THE
CHEMISTRY
OF

FEAR

HARVEY
WILEY'S
FIGHT FOR

PURE FOOD

JONATHAN REES

JOHNS HOPKINS UNIVERSITY PRESS
BALTIMORE

Johns Hopkins University Press
2715 North Charles Street
Baltimore, Maryland 21218-4363
www.press.jhu.edu

Library of Congress Cataloging-in-Publication Data

Names: Rees, Jonathan, 1966– author.
Title: The chemistry of fear : Harvey Wiley's fight for pure food /
Jonathan Rees.
Description: Baltimore : Johns Hopkins University Press, 2021. |
Includes bibliographical references and index.
Identifiers: LCCN 2020013524 | ISBN 9781421439952 (hardcover) |
ISBN 9781421439969 (ebook)
Subjects: LCSH: Wiley, Harvey Washington, 1844–1930. | Food—
United States—Safety measures. | Food additives—Safety regulations—
United States—History. | Food supply—United States.
Classification: LCC RA601 .R42 2021 | DDC 363.19/260973—dc23
LC record available at https://lccn.loc.gov/2020013524

A catalog record for this book is available from the British Library.

*Special discounts are available for bulk purchases of this book. For more
information, please contact Special Sales at specialsales@press.jhu.edu.*

Johns Hopkins University Press uses environmentally friendly book
materials, including recycled text paper that is composed of at least 30
percent post-consumer waste, whenever possible.

CONTENTS

WHO WAS

HARVEY

WILEY?

ON DECEMBER 22, 1902, six young men sat down for breakfast in the basement of a US Department of Agriculture (USDA) building in Washington, DC. This area of the building would become the site of a series of experiments to test the effects of common food preservatives on human health. The men all pledged to eat every meal (in fact, every bite of food or drink) at this table for the duration of this first experiment. On this day, the participants ate significant amounts of borax, a common preservative for meat and dairy products. The first six experimental test subjects, along with the six who quickly followed them, all worked for the USDA.[1] Furthermore, so that their food intake could be controlled and their habits observed, all the subjects temporarily lived there too.[2]

Staff carefully weighed all the food they fed the subjects before giving it to them. Then they weighed what remained on the men's plates afterward. Most important, scientists recovered, weighed, and analyzed the subjects' urine and feces so they could determine how much of the borax remained in their bodies at the end of the experiment. These were hardly the first experiments designed to test the effects of chemical preservatives on human health, but previous experiments had involved animals. This was the first such test to use a large group of human subjects. Six similar experiments testing other preservatives would follow over the next five years.

These experiments attracted an enormous amount of media attention because they involved feeding so much of these seemingly dangerous substances to people. The subjects quickly came to be known as the Poison Squad. The Poison Squad experiments were a new approach to studying an old issue: food adulteration. Food producers had been tampering with food—most notably, adding cheaper ingredients without the purchaser's knowledge to increase profits—for centuries by the time the Poison Squad

FIGURE I.I Subjects of the infamous Poison Squad experiment eating a meal with Dr. Harvey Wiley standing over them. The sign in the corner reflects the kind of humor generated by the experiment among both its participants and the general public.

Courtesy US Food and Drug Administration

experiments began. We tend to think of adulteration in terms of obviously dangerous chemicals getting slipped into everyday foods, but this picture reflects the modern perspective associated with tragic industrial mistakes. During the late nineteenth century, as the mass production of food took off, adulteration as a form of deception was far more common.

The industrialization of food manufacturing made the problem of food adulteration particularly pressing for two reasons. First, the increasing physical distance between the manufacturers and consumers of food and the opaque nature of the production process made it far easier for producers to cheat consumers by mixing in cheaper, and sometimes dangerous, ingredients to save on production costs. Second, the demands associated with industrialization—particularly the need to preserve foods as they traveled to markets farther from their point of production—meant that producers increasingly added ingredients to preserve these foods for much longer time periods, even though these preservatives had never been in food products before. These additives gave the Poison Squad its name, even though most of them were not really poisonous at all.

The Poison Squad experiments, which lasted from 1902 to 1907, were designed to help scientists make definitive conclusions about the effects of common preservatives on human health.[3] Despite these hopes, the results of these experiments offered no easy answers. Different scientists in many different countries came to different conclusions about most of the preservatives tested at the Department of Agriculture because the standards for evaluating whether a food ingredient was harmful had not been established. Or, to put it another way, society had not yet determined how much risk any particular ingredient could impose on the people who consumed it and still be allowed in the food supply. Not even the passage of the Pure Food and Drug Act of 1906 (PFDA), the landmark Progressive Era law that forms the basis of US food safety legislation to this day, could adequately resolve these issues.[4]

The man behind the Poison Squad experiments was Dr. Harvey Washington Wiley (1844–1930). A native of Indiana, Wiley was a chemist, a medical doctor (though he never practiced), an author, and a civil servant who ran the Division (later Bureau) of Chemistry at the USDA from 1883 to 1912.

This office was the forerunner of the modern Food and Drug Administration.[5] The Poison Squad experiments were Wiley's attempts to demonstrate that preservatives should be treated as unwelcome adulterants—even poisons—rather than necessary additives needed to make the mass production of food economically viable.

The experiments on the Poison Squad were a turning point in Wiley's life and career. They convinced him of the paramount importance of health and safety with respect to food adulteration of any kind. Those experiments also transformed him from a follower to a leader inside the broader pure food movement of that era. Initially, Wiley's well-publicized findings scared much of the public into believing that new food additives like borax and sodium benzoate were threats to their health. This fear generated support both for the passage of the PFDA and for a strict interpretation of that law, which Wiley favored. The work of the Poison Squad made Harvey Wiley one of the most famous men in America. Before long, newspapers could simply mention "Dr. Wiley" in a headline, and everyone in America knew to whom they were referring. Wiley would be associated with the fight for pure food for the rest of his long life.

From the passage of the PFDA in 1906 until he resigned from the Department of Agriculture in 1912, Wiley engaged in a series of fierce bureaucratic battles to determine which additives should be considered acceptable under the law. Then, as an editor and columnist at the magazine *Good Housekeeping* from 1912 to his death in 1930, Wiley continued to exercise enormous influence over what Americans ate. While it is common to think of the fight for pure food as a single struggle, Wiley fought many battles to determine what purity meant in foods and drugs of all kinds. Although Wiley came to believe that he had lost the overall fight for strict enforcement of the pure food law, his arguments and actions while enforcing the act nonetheless changed how manufacturers made and marketed a wide range of foods and drugs.

Harvey Wiley led an unconventional life. He was well over fifty years old when the Poison Squad experiments made him famous. He did not marry until he was sixty-six, when he wed a suffragette half his age. He worked constantly, putting in long hours at the office, followed by long hours at lavish parties, football games, or elaborate banquets. He traveled constantly too, visiting Bureau of Chemistry facilities all over the country and giving paid speeches at universities and at dinners of all kinds in support of his cause. Wiley worked at this breakneck pace long after most men would have retired.

"Dr. Wiley is built on large lines," explained one otherwise flattering 1910 profile. "He is tall and massive of stature, with a big head firmly poised above a pair of titanic shoulders. His hair never stays in order, but masses itself forward on both sides of the forehead, giving him at times a somewhat uncouth appearance. The penetrating glance of his rather small eyes, the large and roughly modeled nose, and the severe lines of his mouth add to this impression."[6] While he could wear formal wear as well as anyone who needed such clothes, his ordinary wardrobe was often a poorly cut suit that was seldom laundered.[7] A 1910 *Los Angeles Times* story about Wiley observed, "There is something suggestive of the cleric in his aspect. He might be a bishop. As it is, he is a bachelor—which is strange, because he likes women immensely."[8] Indeed, many women fought fiercely to gain access to him during his always-rare leisure time.

Wiley was charming, gregarious, and lovably eccentric. He had a wide circle of adoring friends. One former associate remembered Wiley as "a prince of good fellows. He loved a good story and always told a better one."[9] Another associate recalled that Wiley commanded loyalty through the "sheer force of his marvelous personality."[10] His popularity is reflected in his enormous correspondence with scientists, food manufacturers, and many other acquaintances made during his travels throughout the United States and Europe. Wiley's personality emerges clearly in his many writings for the general public—essays about food, nutrition, and diet issues published in a wide range of the new and highly popular muckraking magazines. Though his background was in chemistry and, to a lesser extent, medicine, he became a recognized expert on all food-related subjects.

Yet in retrospect the experiments that made Wiley famous are problematic, for a couple of reasons. First, there was the moral problem of testing potentially dangerous chemicals on human subjects. Second, many of the preservatives that Wiley condemned during the first decade of the twentieth century would later be recognized as safe when subjected to modern scientific analysis. Still, the experiments were remarkably successful in one way: they scared people about what was in their food enough to cause them to support the passage of the PFDA.

Wiley had clear ideas about the risks posed by preservatives and other food additives, and those ideas only hardened over time. As he grew more famous, he often switched sides on important food-related debates, invariably by strengthening his degree of opposition to food additives. In some cases, both his private and public statements about the health effects of particular additives or foods changed drastically over a few short years. He cared more about getting attention, and the political support that came with that attention, than he did about consistency. Over time he became increasingly willing to draw broad scientific conclusions about additives he had never tested and about food-related subjects on which he had little knowledge. What stayed constant was Wiley's supreme confidence in his own judgment, which created more enemies, but also attracted more attention.

———————

This book is organized primarily around a series of Wiley's struggles over how various foods and drinks were made and marketed. For a man who merits a biography organized primarily around foodstuffs, Wiley seldom expressed any extracurricular interest in eating or cuisine to the general public. "Too much stress is laid on the gastronomic function of food," Wiley argued in 1915.[11] In his public persona he assumed the dispassionate approach of the scientist, but in fact he loved to eat and cared deeply about the taste of food even if he seldom wrote about it. "To hear Dr. Wiley discourse on diet is an inspiration," one of his many friends once said. "To see him eat an eight course dinner is an exaltation." At one point during a banquet in his honor, a friend later remembered, Wiley corrected the master of ceremonies by saying, "Mr. Toastmaster, I am not a star. It would be more appropriate to liken me to the moon, for the fuller I am the brighter I shine."[12] Wiley's substantial paunch in his later years testified to the size of his appetite. Protecting the purity of food meant more than just protecting the safety of an activity that was important to everyone's day-to-day existence. It meant protecting the sanctity of something Wiley loved. While he seldom admitted it in public,

Wiley's ideas about how a particular food should taste often affected whether or not he thought that food was healthy and pure. Whether arguing with distillers over the definition of whiskey or with ketchup makers over whether they really needed to use preservatives, Wiley wielded the idea of purity as a cudgel against his enemies based upon his impressions of what ingredients or manufacturing processes created the best-tasting products.

The chapters that follow focus on the struggles that attracted the most public attention and took up most of Wiley's time and energy. These were also the struggles that tended to last beyond his years of government service because he came to believe in them so strongly. Many of the chapters center on individual foodstuffs, showing how Wiley's ideas about these substances evolved across the years. The chapters cover overlapping periods, but the organization here remains roughly chronological: the struggles that Wiley began earlier in his life come earlier in the book, even if they played out over years or even decades.

In many instances, the struggles described here cover events from the period 1907–1912, when the federal government and the judiciary gradually determined the standards under which the Department of Agriculture could enforce the Pure Food and Drug Act. Looking at these fights topically rather than strictly chronologically (as in a conventional biography) makes it easier to see the evolution of Wiley's general ideas about food as applied to particular struggles. It also becomes easier to see when Wiley changed his mind about particular additives, something he was always loath to admit in writing and especially in public.

Taken together, the fights covered here touch upon every stage of Wiley's career as a pure food advocate: his early years researching food adulteration in Washington before he became a leader in the pure food movement; the years immediately preceding the Pure Food and Drug Act of 1906, when Wiley was a major leader working toward the passage of that bill; the intense period after the bill's passage, when he engaged in open bureaucratic warfare over how that law should be enforced; and the long period at the end of his life when he worked for *Good Housekeeping*, expressing his ideas about food while simultaneously looking back on his career and often writing about the people who prevented him from making the pure food law as effective as he thought it should have been. It does not include every single prolonged public struggle over food in Wiley's long career, but it does include the most important ones.

Chapter one examines Wiley's childhood and early career in Indiana, including his time at Purdue University. Wiley's early days resembled those of other farm kids born in the mid-nineteenth century. Many signs of his rural Midwestern roots, like his taste in food, surfaced throughout the rest of his life. Some of his main character traits were also apparent: his intelligence, his dedication to his work, and (less admirably) his devotion to making money so that he could escape the relative poverty of his rural childhood.

Wiley's work in food chemistry began at Purdue during the 1870s and mostly involved sugar. Wiley learned how to determine the chemical composition of sweeteners when taking study leave in Germany during his time at Purdue, and he employed those skills as soon as he arrived in Washington to work for the Department of Agriculture. Besides telling the story of his early research and academic career, chapter two focuses on honey. Wiley angered beekeepers across America by questioning the purity of their honey, and the fallout from that fight lasted for decades. Chapter three examines work that had little to do with food purity but much to do with the mission of the Department of Agriculture—Wiley's search for a domestic source for America's growing demand for sugar. Wiley found that source in sugar beets, and his research made possible that entire industry.

Before the turn of the twentieth century, Wiley's work in the pure food movement was limited to examining the extent of adulteration rather than fighting for legislation to prevent it. Chapter four describes his 1890s research on the extent of adulterated food in the United States, comparing it with the more forceful efforts of other pure food advocates at that time. Chapter five covers the growth of Wiley's division within the Department of Agriculture in light of the publicity attracted by the first Poison Squad experiment. Wiley's research on borax not only had a major impact on how meat was preserved in the United States but also convinced Wiley that pure food legislation should be one of the country's top priorities.

In the eyes of most contemporaneous observers and historians, Wiley's primary legacy was his role in the passage and enforcement of the PFDA.

Chapter six considers exactly what Harvey Wiley did to support passage of that law through Congress, focusing on the period immediately before its final approval. Wiley's lobbying efforts, vocal support for the cause of pure food, and—most important—publicizing of his Poison Squad experiments all contributed significantly to the law's eventual passage. By isolating these activities, it becomes possible to separate Wiley's actual contributions from his later attempts to claim near-exclusive ownership of a law that was the work of many people. Chapter seven examines Wiley's fight with a large segment of the country's whiskey distillers. This struggle predated the passage of the Pure Food and Drug Act, but it eventually inspired opponents of government regulation in the manufacture of foods and beverages of all kinds.

Chapter eight considers the bureaucratic struggles Wiley faced when trying to enforce the act with respect to a wide variety of foods. To temper Wiley's power, his superiors appointed two different boards to review his decisions—the Board of Food and Drug Inspection and the Board of Consulting Scientific Experts (better known as the Remsen Board after its chair, the chemist Ira Remsen). The mere existence of these two institutions, one of which duplicated his work and both of which sometimes questioned his judgments, infuriated Wiley. Nevertheless, neither board hindered significant progress on behalf of consumers toward the cause of pure food. On many food-related issues, Wiley and his bureaucratic antagonists actually agreed. Chapter nine considers the argument over sodium benzoate, an additive that was a key ingredient in both ketchup and the popular artificial sweetener saccharin. This was the first, and most important, fight between Harvey Wiley and the Remsen Board.

Chapter ten addresses the complicated fight over the purity of drugs. While many critics have charged that Wiley was more concerned with the purity of foods than drugs, this chapter examines the PFDA's distinct treatment of food and drugs and describes Wiley's more subtle strategy to combat impure drugs. In the years immediately preceding his resignation, Wiley's most famous struggles over food no longer involved preservatives; instead he took strong stands in longstanding fights over the safety of particular foods. Chapter eleven looks at Wiley's role in the prolonged dispute over the safety of alum in baking powder. This struggle had begun long

before Wiley's tenure in Washington, even if it did not attract his attention until late in his government service. It also examines Wiley's campaign
against bleached flour, which ultimately led to a Supreme Court case and
had disastrous results for Wiley's cause.

Chapter twelve covers Wiley's well-publicized but lonely attempt to
prosecute the Coca-Cola Company for adulterating its product with caffeine—a substance Wiley considered an addictive drug, like cocaine.
Although it took many years for this case to be resolved, Wiley's position
won out in the end. Chapter thirteen examines the circumstances surrounding Wiley's resignation from the Department of Agriculture. Wiley liked
to depict his resignation as a selfless act designed to make it easier for him
to tell the truth about food adulteration, but it also increased his ability to
make money.

Chapter fourteen considers his postgovernment career as an editor and
columnist for the magazine *Good Housekeeping*. When not writing, Wiley
spoke on multiple lecture circuits and wrote books and columns about his
earlier struggles over pure food. The concluding chapter analyzes Harvey
Wiley's complicated legacy, particularly his impact on the foods that people still eat today. That legacy goes beyond the composition and patterns
of consumption for foods of all kinds and touches upon how Americans
think about food in general. Right or wrong in his conclusions, Wiley was
a pioneer in advocating for healthier foods and better diets for all Americans—whether they wanted to follow his advice or not.

———◆———

Wiley may have started his career as a chemist, but he became something
else. He wasn't really a nutritionist, but he was deeply concerned with maintaining the healthful natural qualities of the foods people ate. He wasn't
really a food scientist (no such discipline existed at that time), but he was a
scientist with a deep and abiding interest in and love of food. By looking at
Wiley's entire life, it becomes possible to see that his early career in chemistry helped him pioneer his later role as a consumer advocate even while he
still served as a federal employee. It is important to remember, however, that

Wiley did not take on that role until the Poison Squad experiments made him famous. Fame gave him public support, allowing him to be far more openly political than he had been up to that point in his government career. That support influenced the positions he would take on food additives of all kinds for the rest of his life.

Toward the end of his life, Wiley self-published a memoir (apart from his autobiography) that detailed his efforts to get the federal government to enforce the PFDA as strictly as possible. His argument is apparent from the title: *The History of a Crime against the Food Law*.[13] Wiley thought the enemies of pure food had already destroyed the law that he by then claimed as his legacy. However, to believe that Wiley's legacy was destroyed requires forgetting the chemist's other obvious victories, like the banning of formaldehyde or the end of the use of borax as a preservative for meat. Consumed by what had become his absolutist position on pure food, Wiley himself failed to recognize the huge range of small improvements for which he alone could plausibly take credit.

Thanks to Wiley, many manufacturers changed the way foods were made and marketed under pressure from the Department of Agriculture and threat of prosecution by the federal government under the PFDA. Some changes happened voluntarily because producers didn't want to attract Wiley's ire. In a few cases Wiley's pressure led to changes in the way Americans ate or drank that neither Wiley nor the manufacturers themselves ever anticipated. By employing the term "pure food" in different ways across many struggles, Wiley greatly influenced how a surprisingly wide range of foods were made and marketed during a crucial turning point in the development of the modern American diet. The scope of the effects of Wiley's ideas and actions upon what Americans ate is described in almost every one of the following chapters.

Wiley's vast influence on food itself does not mean that the chemist's role in the passage of the Pure Food and Drug Act was unimportant. The PFDA was the first major national legislation of the Progressive Era. Wiley's lobbying and coalition building helped pull a bill that had been proposed in every Congress since the early 1890s over the finish line to final approval. This is by itself a significant achievement, as recognized by all previous scholarship on Wiley and every Wiley biography. Yet Harvey Wiley is a familiar figure among food historians for many more reasons than just his role in the passage of that one law. In effect, Wiley has two legacies: one is his impact on the politics of food purity, and the other is his impact on precisely what Americans ate. The few existing biographies of Wiley (including his own autobiography) focus overwhelmingly on the first.[13] This one focuses primarily upon food itself.

By doing so, this book makes a different case for the chemist's long-term historical significance than Wiley did himself. With more than a hundred years of perspective on how Americans have coped with modern forms of food production, it is now easier to recognize Wiley's impacts on how foods were made and marketed. In many cases, this is because these impacts have endured. While some of these changes are more historically significant than others, taken together they form a significant historical legacy for Wiley independent of his role in the passage of a single law. They also demonstrate Wiley's own ideas about food far better than that particular piece of compromise legislation does.

In a practical sense, any suggestion that food should be "pure" ought to be the beginning of the discussion rather than the end. To Wiley, pure food was always less processed and therefore safer than the mass-produced alternatives. This position is, of course, highly debatable. "The treadmill of purity," argues the anthropologist Melanie DuPuis, "is a threat to life and health. Romantic notions of pure food create unrealistic purification projects that, in some cases, lead to conundrums—continued attempts at creating boundaries that cannot be achieved."[14] Wiley ran up against these boundaries constantly during his time at the Bureau of Chemistry and after. He faced this problem because, to him, purity was never a defined quality. Instead, it was a rhetorical device he used to inspire fear in consumers, which in turn generated political support for whatever struggle he happened to be engaged in at that time.

Invoking notions of purity across a wide range of struggles over food helped Wiley attract attention but did nothing to resolve the contradictions in his own positions when he argued with other government bureaucrats who were trying to balance many complicated competing interests. Wiley's usual response to these contradictions was to land on whichever side seemed to limit the risk for consumers, doing nothing to acknowledge that his position had changed. After the Poison Squad experiments began, he continually advocated for the federal government to take positions on the healthfulness of particular foods even when those positions had no support among important political constituencies. While he always argued in the name of consumers, Wiley never recognized that consumer opinion on the definition and importance of purity was far from uniform.

Plenty of consumers welcomed changes that Wiley opposed because they liked the convenience that baking powder offered or the low price at which distillers sold rectified whiskey. Other struggles involved the manufacturing process itself. Wiley wanted to change the government's approach to enforcing the Pure Food and Drug Act to make most chemical additives and preservatives illegal. By taking this position, the chemist was taking a stand against industrialized food production of all kinds. This approach proved both impractical and, in some cases, unpopular with the very consumers that Wiley wanted to protect.

Unlike Wiley, his superiors in government had to balance a variety of factors when fighting over exactly how food was made and marketed in the United States. Over the course of a long struggle in which Wiley represented only one side, the Roosevelt and Taft administrations gradually negotiated an effective compromise between the interests of corporations and multiple political constituencies, including people who valued the purity of food above any other consideration. While the question of safety always received the most attention, they were really debating the question of how much risk was acceptable for American consumers. Tipping the scale opposite that risk were issues like price, convenience, and taste. This same weighing process remains highly relevant to modern consumers. Wiley's many struggles on behalf of his conception of pure food still resonate because his ideas still reflect our fears about what's really in our food.

While Harvey Wiley did not win every struggle in which he choose to engage, his efforts had two important results. First, even if some foods never measured up to his own standards of purity, Wiley still managed to improve the safety or quality of everything from ketchup to Coca-Cola as a result of the pressure he wielded against food manufacturers. Second, he drastically changed public opinion about whether some additives were unsafe or healthy to consume. In many cases, his influence on public opinion was greater than his influence upon the federal regulatory apparatus, which left Americans fearful of foods that its government believed to be safe. To see Harvey Wiley's impact on exactly what we eat and how we think about foods of all kinds requires a detailed look at the chemist's most public arguments with other interests who disagreed with him. It also requires some understanding of where Harvey Wiley came from and how his interest in food developed at a young age.

CHAPTER ONE

INDIANA

HARVEY WASHINGTON WILEY WAS BORN** on October 18, 1844, near the village of Kent, Indiana, close to the Kentucky border. At that time, Indiana was still overwhelmingly rural. Just a few years earlier, it had been at the frontier of North American settlement. When Wiley was born, the area was full of hills and heavily forested. The unpaved roads were impassable in bad weather, and the nearest railroad station was ten miles away.[1] Although the earliest rural settlers had lived a self-sufficient existence, the generation preceding Harvey Wiley had experienced the beginnings of a market revolution that provided even the most rural Americans with the kinds of goods (including foodstuffs) that made their lives easier. Still, Indiana was underdeveloped compared with much of the country. It lagged behind the East Coast in developing both markets for the agricultural goods it produced and consumer markets for manufactured goods from the New England and Mid-Atlantic states.

Harvey Wiley's father was descended from Irish Protestants who had first landed in Maine in 1658. Wiley's great-grandfather went west to Kentucky either during or immediately after the American Revolution. His son Joseph brought Wiley's father, Preston, to Indiana when the child was five years old, before Indiana had become a state. Harvey's mother arrived in Indiana under similar circumstances: Lucinda Maxwell came from a Scotch-Irish Presbyterian family that moved to Kentucky and then Indiana during the early nineteenth century as the state opened up for settlement. Preston Wiley married Lucinda, a year-and-a-half his elder, in 1830. A farmer and day laborer, Preston earned barely enough to support his large family. Harvey was the sixth of the couple's seven children—four boys and three girls.[2]

The women surrounding Wiley during his childhood greatly influenced him, and later in life he was a feminist. "In my early years, my knowledge and the influence of women so far as it affected my character and career, was based chiefly on my own mother," Wiley wrote in 1925. He thought he bore a stronger physical resemblance to his mother than to his father. Lucinda had great conversational powers, which Wiley developed himself as he grew older. He described her as a religious woman who was funny enough to get her neighbors to convulse with laughter.[3] Lucinda was literate but had attended only three months of school—all before she turned ten. "My whole time and strength was devoted to my children by day and night," she wrote Harvey in 1887, long after he had moved to Washington.[4]

Preston and Lucinda Wiley educated all of their children, including their daughters.[5] On his own initiative, Wiley's father asked professors from nearby Hanover College to lend him the books necessary to study Greek. Preston learned it well enough to read the New Testament in the original.[6] Harvey Wiley gave special credit to Indiana's state-funded traveling libraries for his education. This library system guaranteed that at least a hundred new books would arrive in his rural township every few months.[7] Although they occupied him with many chores, Wiley's parents also gave Harvey plenty of time to read. Wiley's father was his first schoolteacher at the local schoolhouse, paid for by subscriptions from local farmers. Harvey not only had a flair for reading but also proved particularly adept at math from a young age.[8]

Wiley's family lived in a log cabin when Harvey was born and moved to a two-story farmhouse when he was a small child. The family's farm consisted of 125 acres, but much of the land was virgin forest or otherwise untillable during Wiley's childhood, with the result that his family had to work extremely hard to make a living. The Wileys raised and sheared sheep and made their own clothes. They grew wheat and corn and brought the grain to the miller, who ground it, taking some and placing the rest into the burgeoning stream of nationwide commerce. At home, the family ate graham flour—the whole-grain product preferred by the physician Sylvester Graham, the well-known food faddist of that era. They sold butter and eggs in exchange for sugar, which they supplemented heavily with whatever syrup they could tap from the farm's large maple grove.[9]

Wiley often remarked that his diet growing up consisted of the plain and simple foods available on a southern Indiana farm at that time. These included homegrown fruits and vegetables, cornmeal, and plenty of milk. For sweets, there were sorghum and molasses. In winter the family subsisted on skim milk, hot mush, and fried mush for breakfast, along with a variety of nuts and winter vegetables. The family never even had pork, a fairly common meat at that time.[10] Nearly the only product the Wileys bought from outside the farm was coffee. Almost everything else they ate came from the farm itself.[11] Their diet, like that of most people in this period, was generally monotonous; it was a typical rural American diet with plenty of calories but little flavor.[12] Wiley would recommend this simple, old-fashioned diet his entire life.

What separated Wiley from most from other rural Americans of the mid-nineteenth century was his proximity to the outside world. The Wiley farm was only five miles from the Ohio River. Under the right conditions he could hear the whistles of steamboats on the river and sometime see smoke from their stacks.[13] Thanks to his father, publications like the *Atlantic Monthly*, the *New York Tribune,* and the *National Era* (an anti-slavery newspaper published in Washington, DC) arrived at the farmhouse by mail once a week, on Friday afternoons. The *National Era* serialized the anti-slavery novel *Uncle Tom's Cabin* after its release in the early 1850s. Preston would read the latest installment to the entire family by the fireside after dinner. When the Civil War arrived, there was no doubt which side Harvey, raised as he was by an abolitionist, would join.[14]

Harvey Wiley had never expected to go to college. While he had learned a great deal from his father, Wiley had had only four winters of formal schooling when he entered Hanover College in April 1863.[15] Founded in 1827, Hanover College sat on a high plateau above the Ohio River. It was a Presbyterian liberal arts school that had grown out of the local secondary school in the town of Hanover. In its early years the school had had severe financial troubles, and when Wiley arrived, the college was less than a decade from a major fund-raising campaign to construct a new building and create an endowment large enough to keep the college running indefinitely.[16] Even by the standards of the day, the school was small: Wiley's graduating class in 1867 consisted of just nine students.[17]

Wiley paid for college with money from his father and from his earnings from summertime work on neighboring farms. He walked home every Friday afternoon, helped around the farm on Saturdays, and returned to Hanover on Sundays carrying his food for the week. The room he rented in a farmhouse at the edge of Hanover with his brother Ulric cost fifty cents a week, and he brought his furnishings from home. This would be the only time in his life that he did his own cooking. His meals during college consisted mostly of mush, molasses, and boiled potatoes—typical rural fare. Still, now that Wiley was better connected to the wider world, there were new foods to try. Indeed, he later spoke of his first food experiments as those he conducted in his farmhouse room, where he and Ulric rated the relative merits of different new foods.[18]

In 1864, while still at Hanover, Wiley interrupted his education to enlist in the Union Army. The previous year, both Harvey and his father had joined a home guard unit in an attempt to ward off Confederate raiders, and in May 1864 Wiley joined the Indiana volunteer infantry. He went to train in Indianapolis that month and was shipped south in June. Wiley's unit was tasked with guarding a railroad depot at Tullahoma, Tennessee, a vital link in the support structure for the offensive led by General William Tecumseh Sherman. In October, Wiley was discharged with a severe case of what he later recognized as hookworm. (It was misdiagnosed at the time because the affliction was not yet fully understood. Most people thought he had tuberculosis.)[19]

FIGURE 1.1 Dr. Harvey W. Wiley as a young man. This photo was taken in 1863 as he entered the freshman class at Hanover College.

Courtesy of the Library of Congress

Ironically, Wiley ate better in the army than he did at home. "I get fat on Uncle Sam's bread, meat and coffee and like it better every day," wrote Wiley in his diary while still in camp in Indianapolis. He found it particularly noteworthy that he got all the food he wanted—a situation completely unlike what he had faced either at college or at home. Upon arriving in Tennessee, he began to complain about the coffee but still admired the vast array of different foods. At one point, Wiley wrote about a picnic of "pies rasberry, pies blackberry, pies huckleberry in profusion, rusks, butter, canned peaches, fresh berries, cream, white sugar, [and] lemon."[20] Yet many years later Wiley insisted, "During the Civil War I lived on cornmeal mush, milk, and sorghum molasses and felt perfectly satisfied."[21]

Wiley's time as a soldier was mostly uneventful. Given that he spent most of his time in Tennessee sick—first with the measles, then with hookworm—he never made it to the front. By his own description, Wiley was discharged in late October 1864 "more dead than alive." He weighed a mere 119 pounds, a frightening weight for a man his size. Wiley returned to Kent, where his parents nursed him back to health. Wiley studied hard during his convalescence so that he could pass his freshmen exams and return to Hanover as a sophomore.[22]

When Wiley returned to Hanover, he joined the Philalethean Society, one of two literary societies on campus devoted to speech and public affairs.[23] On June 20, 1865, he delivered a speech expressing his views on digestion. The speech was highly technical for a twenty-one-old college student; notably, it contains elements that point to his future career. "Not only does physical beauty and symmetry depend upon the kind and quantity of food," Wiley told the crowd, "but also moral power and moral excellence."[24] These words foreshadow the ideas that would influence his judgments about which ingredients belonged in food during the years following the start of the Poison Squad experiments.

His values came partly from his apparent fear of death at his then-young age. "Life is short enough at longest," he explained near the beginning of his speech, "and that knowledge that will add ten years or even a year to human existence can not be valued."[25] In other words, knowledge about the health effects of one's diet was priceless. These sentiments hint at Wiley's later view that it was worth cutting off access to consumer goods that would do some people harm, even if other people happened to like them, since nothing was more valuable than the chance to spend more time on earth. Yet Wiley, by his own description, indulged himself "too freely or rather servilely" when hungry and given the opportunity to eat a good meal.[26] In later years, Harvey Wiley became well known in the circles in which he traveled for polishing off a ten-course meal when he was so inclined.[27] In short, here was a man who, starting at a rather young age, was conflicted about what he ate.

———

By 1868 Wiley had decided that he wanted to go to medical school, but he could not yet afford to pay for it. He took a job teaching secondary school in Lowell, Indiana, a small community in the northwestern corner of the state. After a year he received an appointment to teach Latin and Greek at Northwestern Christian University (now Butler University) in Indianapolis. The following year, he was promoted to adjunct professor of languages but taught anatomy, algebra, and physiology as well. This appointment gave him a salary large enough to pay for medical school. Indiana Medical College (now the medical school at Indiana University) opened in Indianapolis in 1869, and Wiley became a member of its first class. Wiley left Northwestern Christian in 1871, the year he graduated from medical school.[28]

Medical education in mid-nineteenth-century America was generally rather poor. While the first medical schools were tied to long-established universities, newer proprietary schools established by groups of physicians accepted just about anyone capable of paying tuition. Medical students did not work in laboratories. Instead, they sat and listened to lectures. Neither the government nor the profession oversaw licensing; given the severe shortage of doctors at the time, they didn't want to deny anybody care by restricting the flow of new doctors.[29] The best indication that Indiana Medical College was not producing particularly knowledgeable doctors at this time was that the school appointed Wiley himself chair of its chemistry department immediately after his graduation. He got this plum position even though his entire medical school education consisted of two four-month terms in 1869–70 and 1870–71. Such short medical educations were common in those days.[30] The real education came from an apprenticeship with a practicing doctor. Wiley spent two summers working under S. E. Hampton, a fellow veteran who had helped him read anatomy books while they were both stationed in Tennessee.[31] Because he never actually practiced medicine, however, Wiley never considered himself a medical doctor.

Wiley's recognition of the problem with medical training helps explain his budding interest in chemistry over medicine. In an 1873 speech at the Academy of Medicine in Indianapolis, Wiley emphasized the role of chemistry in educating doctors about the mechanisms behind the healing practices they learned and observed. "It was the study of chemistry for medical purposes which gave the grand impulse which has made, and is still making, chemistry the glory of science," Wiley explained.[32] Doctors, however, bore the brunt of his criticism. "It seems to me that we make doctors too easily," Wiley declared in another speech the next year. "They come up like the spring floods."[33] Little wonder that he ultimately preferred chemistry over medicine.

The fact that Wiley never chose to practice medicine despite earning a medical degree spoke volumes about the kind of work he most valued. Time and again Wiley chose to teach or learn other subjects rather than helping patients directly. His real expertise was in chemistry—a subject in which he never did the classwork for an advanced degree. Yet for the rest of his life Wiley would be referred to as "Dr. Wiley." Given his medical degree, the title was more than justified. People undoubtedly interpreted his pronouncements on health as coming from a medical doctor, thereby giving them far more weight than they probably deserved.

By the early 1870s Harvey Wiley had proved that he had a remarkable aptitude for a wide variety of subjects. He had studied chemistry in college and at medical school and was now employed to teach that subject. He could teach classical languages and mathematics. He had even picked up a master of fine arts degree at Hanover. Wiley had selected chemistry as both his discipline and his vocation, but he knew little about it at this stage of his life. In 1872 he borrowed $500 from a neighbor and set off for Cambridge, to fulfill a lifelong dream of studying at Harvard.[34]

In September 1872 he enrolled at the university's Lawrence Scientific School and quickly got a job working as a laboratory assistant to help cover his expenses. This was his first experience doing real laboratory work and quantitative analysis.[35] Both would serve him well in future endeavors. "I did not give my whole time to lectures and work in the laboratories of Harvard College," Wiley later remembered, "but from five to eight hours a day I attended lectures and worked in the laboratories of qualitative and quantitative analyses."[36] He also studied mineralogy, biology (under the famous Professor Louis Agassiz), and French. He bought his first suit of formal evening wear so he could socialize with his famous professors. He attended the opera and developed a lifelong love of baseball by watching college games.[37]

Compelled to return to Indianapolis to teach a term at the medical college, he came back to Harvard as quickly as possible in the spring of 1873. At that point one of his professors invited him to stand for a bachelor of science degree, something he had not contemplated doing. Wiley began an intensive course of study in the school's new program in engineering and practical science, and in just five weeks he took exams in chemistry, quantitative analysis, qualitative analysis, mineralogy, French, and German, thereby earning his degree.[38] Wiley became an honorary member of the Harvard class of 1873 and would continue to attend the functions of that class for the next fifty years.[39]

Returning to Indiana from Harvard in 1873, Wiley expected to practice medicine in Indianapolis and serve as a professor of chemistry at the Indiana Medical College, from which he had recently graduated. He was also elected chair of chemistry at Northwestern Christian University, where he had earlier taught classical languages. At first he delayed practicing medicine to teach at both schools simultaneously. Overworked as a result of this heavy load, he fell so sick that he nearly died. Upon recovery he learned that a new school, Purdue University, wanted him to teach chemistry there. He maintained his medical professorship, giving three lectures a week in Indianapolis.[40] However, Purdue is where Wiley began to develop his reputation.

Purdue University was established under the terms of the Morrill Land Grant Act of 1862. Competition over where to place this new public institution delayed its opening, but a $150,000 gift from John Purdue led the state to situate the school in Lafayette, Indiana. The university was then named for its benefactor.[41] The first class arrived in 1874. There were forty-six students and just six faculty, including Wiley.[42] "In so far as I know, no one of the faculty ever had any experience in a technical or agricultural school," Wiley later remembered. "We might say it was a case of the blind leading the blind; everything had to be discovered."[43] One case in point was the failure of anyone to write an entrance exam for students. Wiley wrote Purdue's first entrance exam the evening before the school opened.[44]

When Wiley arrived on campus, a building was designated to house the chemical laboratory, but it had no fixtures, chemical supplies, or equipment. Wiley's philosophy—rare among chemists at the time—was to put students directly to work doing chemical research. In service of that philosophy, the chemical laboratory contained student desks rather than just chairs.[45] Wiley lectured, but the students were charged with following along with the experiments he described and filing reports on what they had done. Wiley covered less ground this way, but he was convinced that students would better retain the material he did cover.[46]

Despite such novel teaching methods (or perhaps because of them), few students chose to take the entire three- or four-year array of chemistry courses that Wiley (the only chemist at the university) offered.[47] In an annual report to the university administration, he claimed that his students devoted twice as much time to their chemistry work as was actually required of them.[48] Those students who stuck with him learned not just about chemistry, but about how they might conduct their lives too:

> Wherever there is want, there is your place to supply; wherever
> ignorance, there is your place to teach; wherever sickness, there
> is your place to heal; wherever oppression, there is your place
> to relieve; wherever injustice, there is your place to vindicate;
> finally, wherever in the battle of life there is need of hands or
> nerve or brain, there amidst the carnage and desolation in the
> middle of the sulfurous smoke and the hail of death and the
> tempest of passion and hate, is your place to stand or fall fight-
> ing with your face to the foe.[49]

Presumably, Wiley tried to live his own life by the same credo.

Although Wiley had few students, the university equipped his chemistry lab quickly and well. Of the $2,500 budget for equipment, $1,400 went to Wiley's department.[50] Wiley used the result to power his philosophy of chemical research. According to Wiley, "It is a mistake to wait until a man has been trained in the technic of chemistry until he is taught that there are things to be discovered which are yet unknown. His success in discovering these things, of course, depends largely upon his technic, but the fact that the unknown exists may be thoroughly grasped by the young chemist at the very beginning of his career."[51] This is precisely the approach that Wiley, who had had little formal training in chemistry when he began teaching at Purdue, took.

Wiley's report to the president of the university detailing his work for the first two years of the school's operation illustrates the range of activities in his laboratory. Wiley described analyzing the soil from the university's farm; determining the exact composition of local woods; determining the fat content, cream percentage, and water level in milk from the university's cows; comparing those results to milk produced along the River Tweed in England; beginning to assay gold, silver, and lead ores with new equipment in his laboratory; examining soil brought in from Dallas, Texas; examining the composition of cosmetics purchased in San Francisco; and analyzing the composition of the water from the local enginehouse well.[52] In short, Wiley both contributed to Purdue's local agricultural mission and began to operate in the context of a wider world eager for analysis of many new products that people did not entirely understand.

Starting in 1876 Wiley also taught physics, a field at Purdue that until then had received substantially fewer resources than most other departments at the university.[53] Wiley would quickly change that imbalance. His first mission was to build a new laboratory for physics, virtually from scratch, on the top floor of the building housing his chemistry laboratory.[54] With this goal in mind, he convinced to the university to purchase one of the two electric generators on display in the French Pavilion at the 1876 Centennial Exhibition in Philadelphia. The dynamo (as it was then called) arrived at the university in October 1876, right after the fair closed.[55] Wiley purchased a lantern from Philadelphia and used it with the dynamo to project lantern slides for his chemistry lectures. This practice was unique enough in Indiana at that time to merit an exhibit at the Indiana State Fair.[56]

Besides his teaching and research, Wiley was generally recognized as the father of Purdue University athletics.[57] In addition to serving as pitcher on the baseball team, Wiley played some role in organizing every sport on campus.[58] He also set up the first Purdue militia, as required under the Land Grant Act that had established the college. Elected captain of that squad until they could attract a West Point graduate to fill the role, Wiley led the militia in regular drills two or three times a week in the center of campus based on what he had learned while training for the Civil War.[59] At one point, he helped publish a college magazine.[60]

During his early life, Harvey Wiley demonstrated many of the traits that would serve him well in his long career both as a chemist and as a public figure. He had strong intellectual interests and could learn a varied body of knowledge quickly. When he began higher education, he quickly developed an interest in science that overshadowed his early devotion to religion, even though the moral lessons of the Presbyterian faith in which his father had instructed him never disappeared. Along these same lines, he developed an enduring sense of duty to the greater good.[61] With his success, he developed a supreme confidence in his own ability that affected his future career for both good and ill.

Harvey Wiley was an ambitious and forward-looking young man, but his temperament and his drive did not always combine favorably. Early during his time at Hanover College he wrote in his diary, "As present time is only a relative term and not a reality, we can not live in it. And as we can not live in the past or present time, there is only one place where we can live and that is the future."[62] Within the next few years Wiley would survive the Civil War and become a doctor, a scientist, and a professor. Yet he remained unhappy with his achievements. "Today I am 28," he wrote in his diary on his birthday in 1872. "What have I done? Not one whose early manhood has passed can boast of. I have failed to do what would make one famous. I see clearly, as everyone can see, my errors. They have not been ruinous or of great magnitude, but many. I will try more earnestly for excellence."[63] Despite all his success to that point, Wiley was unsatisfied.

Here was the source of the drive that got him through Hanover College despite his work schedule and enabled him to earn a degree from Harvard so quickly. Wiley had work to do, places to go, and great confidence that he was smart and hard-working enough to achieve his ambitious goals. "I could go to Heidelberg and take a degree very easily," he wrote in his travel diary while studying in Germany in 1878. "The examinations are not as hard as I passed at Harvard but *then I can't stay a year.*"[64] Wiley turned down his opportunity to pursue a doctorate in Germany because he wanted to keep his job at Purdue. After all, he was already a practicing chemist and probably believed the Germans had nothing else useful to teach him about what he already did.

Along with all the work he did to improve his knowledge base in his chosen field and to keep the job at Purdue, Wiley found time to romance many young women. Writing about Wiley in the 1908 Purdue yearbook, an undergraduate from that era explained, "A prize can be safely offered to any young eligible young lady in the county at that period who was not engaged to the Doctor one or more times."[65] This reputation hindered his advancement at a place where most professors had married and settled down. However, not everyone at Purdue was as conservative as the men who ran the university. Others recognized that Wiley's lifestyle reflected the changing times. "I think you should not get a Wife and stop playing ball," wrote one letter from an unsigned correspondent preserved in Wiley's files. "Go have a good time generally."[66] Yet he expressed unhappiness about being alone. "Why do I sadden my whole life by an imperious passion?" he asked in a diary entry from 1872.[67]

Sarah H. Fletcher—whom he addressed as "Dovie" in letters—was about ten years younger than Wiley. She had been his student when he taught philosophy at Northwestern Christian University. She signed her first surviving letter to Wiley from 1869 as "Your Little Friend." While Wiley pursued other women at the same time, he was particularly smitten with Sarah yet not particularly clear about his feelings for her.[68] "I feel now in the silence of my room that what I said to you tonight was broken and incoherent for . . . I was intoxicated with the strong wine of your secret presence," he wrote in 1870.[69] He was also more than a little melodramatic. "There are times in the lives of men where decades are concentrated in a single hour. Such an hour has come to me," he wrote to her in 1871. "I am old. My hand trembles as with age. My throat and lips are dry but not with fever; my head throbs but not with pain. . . . Oh my God! I am *dead! dead!! dead!!*"[70] Somehow, with a couple of decades of life experience under his belt, Wiley found that this air of desperation had evolved into the kind of charm that made pursuing multiple women at one time a luxury rather than a necessity.

Unfortunately for Wiley, Fletcher heard about his interest in other women. "Father has been told by *some one* (I know not by whom) some very absurd things, such as this;—that you write to twenty girls at once telling each one she is the only person you love." Despite the rumors (and the truth of those rumors), Wiley managed to convince her to maintain the relationship for a time. In a later letter she wrote, "I know [what Father told me is] not true—but—now I do not control my own actions. I do not really belong to myself for I am so closely watched and guarded." In that letter, she stated that her feelings had not changed, but her parents' wishes won out and she cut off the courtship.[71] The fact that she returned Wiley's letters to him and that he kept at least some of hers suggests the state of the relationship at its end.

Throughout the late 1870s he flirted often in letters with "Bertie," a woman he probably met at Harvard. While charmed, she could also become deeply annoyed with the young Dr. Wiley, writing at one point, "If you are not one of the most provoking men—to ask me again if I wanted you to spend vacation with me—Haven't I asked you, teased [and] begged you . . . because in my eyes to come and now very deliberately ask me if I really want you to. I refuse to answer that question again because if you don't come —." She let the end of the sentence trail off for effect.[72]

At the same time he was writing to Bertie, he was also wooing a distant cousin, Mamie Hall. "I believe that you think that all such intimacies between people who love are right and proper," she wrote near the end of their relationship, "and I would sooner die than think that you signal impure motive when you won my confidence and trust so wholly. I am sure you were *tried* to the limits of any man's endurance, yet you never yielded to the strong temptations. How can you ask me to live over again this thing, will you ever ask me? If you do I shall hate you." At the very least, these sentiments strongly suggest that Wiley was deeply conflicted between his desires and his moral code. Like so many other relationships that Wiley pursued, this one did not end well. "I never believed that you loved me, Harvey," Mamie wrote at the end, "and I never believed you when you said you would like for me to be your wife. I don't know why but I couldn't believe you, and I *don't* now."[73] Finding a wife with whom he wanted to settle down would take Wiley another thirty years—leaving him plenty of time to study and advance his ideas about purity with respect to a wide range of foodstuffs.

CHAPTER TWO

HONEY

I N 1879, **HARVEY WILEY BOUGHT** a high-wheel bicycle and recruited a few Purdue students to help him learn to ride it. Bicycling was just becoming popular as a mode of transportation, but it was not yet widely accepted or used by cultured people. His decision to purchase a riding uniform with knee breeches did not help his image around Lafayette.[1] Even worse, his strategy for avoiding falls while learning to ride was to crash into bushes.[2] As one of the students at that time later remembered, "The daily contests between the Doctor and the machine to determine which would remain on top of the other were the joy of large and enthusiastic street audiences."[3]

While a bicycle craze was hitting the nation at this time, undoubtedly only a small number of the participants were employed as supposedly respectable college professors. "One day," Wiley later recalled, "when riding . . . up a long hill on the road to Frankfort, we came near some children playing in a yard. The mother standing in the doorway, seeing that apparition appearing over the crest of the hill, called in a terror-stricken tone to the children,

'Come in quick, the devil is coming.'"[4] Nevertheless, he wrote, "Sitting on this vehicle made one feel as if one were riding through thin air."[5] Despite the scandal it caused, he continued riding.

The purpose of the bike, Wiley later recalled, was to provide himself with easy, accessible transportation. This made sense as he lived more than a mile from campus and had no horse at the time, but the trustees of the university thought riding around on a high-wheel bicycle an undignified activity for a member of their faculty.[6] When ordered one day in 1880 to appear before that body, Wiley expected to hear that his salary was being increased. Instead a trustee said:

> The disagreeable duty has been assigned to me to tell Professor Wiley the cause of his appearance before us. We have been greatly pleased with the excellence of his instruction and are pleased with the popularity he enjoys among his pupils. We are deeply grieved however, however, at his conduct. He has put on a uniform and played baseball with the boys, much to the discredit of the dignity of a professor. Professor Wiley has bought a bicycle. Imagine my feelings and those of the other members of the board on seeing one of our professors dressed up like a monkey and astride a cartwheel riding along our streets. Imagine my feelings when some astonished observer says to me, "Who is that?" and I am compelled to say, "He is a professor in our university!" It is with the greatest pain that I feel it my duty to make these statements in his presence and before this board.[7]

As Wiley later summed up the case against him, "In short, I was irreligious, frivolous and undignified."[8] Wiley's response to this hearing was to plead guilty to all of the charges made against him and tender his resignation. The next day, the board sent him a letter refusing the offer.[9]

Wiley would remain at Purdue for three more years even though he came "to look upon myself as an almost hardened criminal" because of this ordeal.[10] The bicycle would end up in a museum on campus under the label, "This is the Bicycle Professor Wiley rode at Purdue." In his autobiography

Wiley wrote, "I fear the fact that I started the first chemical laboratories at Purdue and presided over them for nine years will gradually fade from the memory of man. I feel inclined to pin my hope of immortality at Purdue to the old bicycle in the museum!"[11] When he arrived in Washington to join the US Department of Agriculture, he found different ways to get his exercise.

———

In the early 1880s the chief chemist at the US Department of Agriculture was Peter Collier, who was working to determine at what stages the sorghum plant contains the most sugar. Collier's work stimulated Wiley to become involved in developing sorghum as a cash crop—both as a researcher and as an entrepreneur. In 1882 Wiley and some friends created a company and built a refinery to process sorghum and thereby attracted the attention of the US commissioner of agriculture George B. Loring. Loring and Collier had been fighting over the future prospects of sorghum in the United States. Loring was much more skeptical than Collier, and when this difference of opinion became personal, Loring needed to find a competent sugar chemist to serve as Collier's replacement.[12]

In March 1882 the Indiana Board of Health appointed Wiley to the position of state chemist.[13] The law creating that office specified that it would be held by the professor of chemistry at Purdue, and he was the only one. When Wiley attended a meeting of Mississippi Valley sugar producers in St. Louis in 1882, he met Loring for the first time. At another meeting, Loring invited Wiley to come to Washington to speak at the National Agricultural Convention. Wiley's speech, "True Relations of Science to the Industries and Arts," dovetailed nicely with the division's purpose. Most important for Loring, despite Wiley's interest in a sorghum-processing factory, he was appropriately skeptical about the prospects of the sorghum industry. Loring soon after offered him the job of chief chemist. Unhappy at Purdue, Wiley quickly accepted and began work in mid-1883.[14]

Wiley's perception that Purdue was mistreating him rested not just on his character but on his salary. In an anonymous letter he got published in the *Nation* just after he left Lafayette, Wiley wrote, "Nearly all the college professors I have known have been men of fair ability and devoted to their work.... Without exception they have all felt the burden which the meagre salary of the Western college professor places on them. With all of these honest and able men life has been a constant struggle, embittered by the thought that the urgent demands of the present permit no preparation for old age."[15] Wiley was still under forty years of age when he wrote these words. His struggle to make money would last throughout his tenure in the federal government.

——•——

In 1878 and early 1879, Wiley, on leave from Purdue, spent about six months in Europe, mostly in Germany. His goal was to improve his knowledge of chemistry, and even though he did not receive a graduate degree for his work, the trip proved pioneering. Only a trickle of scholars had begun to make the trip to Germany for graduate education in the late 1870s, so even a short sojourn set a path for others to follow in later decades.[16] Wiley spent most of his time at the German government's Imperial Health Office, studying sugars under a polariscope. The polariscope (also known as a polarimeter or saccharometer) dates from the early nineteenth century. Related to the microscope, a polariscope measures the polarization of light as it passes through a substance. Developed to study minerals (and to determine the authenticity of jewels), it has also been used to study the strength of glass. As early as 1814, scientists were beginning to examine parts of the animal kingdom under polarizing light in an attempt to reveal their chemical makeup.[17]

In his work at the Imperial Health Office, Wiley helped pioneer the use of a polariscope to determine the purity of sugar crystals. Under a polariscope, crystals with a higher concentration of sugar polarize light passed through them more than crystals with a lower concentration of sugar. He bought two of the instruments, hoping Purdue would compensate him for the purchase when he returned to Indiana. Later he would buy a superior French model to improve the quality of his research on sugar.[18] In subsequent years, he sought to improve its operation and effectiveness in his work on sugars of all kinds, and he wrote a book explaining how to use the polariscope for agricultural chemistry.[19] Indeed polariscopes are used to determine the quality of honey to this day.[20]

When Wiley returned to the United States, the Indiana State Board of Health asked him to examine sugars and syrups sold in Indiana to see if they were adulterated. "The State should protect its citizens in the consumption of sugar . . . and require every sugar exposed for sale in the State to bear its proper name and a label setting forth its composition," Wiley wrote in his report on that research. "Each purchaser would then know the exact character of the article he proposed buying. If then he preferred to purchase the cheap and adulterated articles, he would do so with full knowledge of the character of the transaction."[21] This was the first report on food adulteration that Wiley ever wrote.[22]

In June 1881, while still teaching at Purdue, Wiley published an article entitled "Glucose and Grape Sugar" in the magazine *Popular Science Monthly*. The vast majority of the article concerned how glucose was then manufactured and its role as an ingredient for commercial table syrup, a major sweetener at that time. However, there was one line about the honey industry. "In commercial honey," Wiley wrote, "which is entirely free from bee mediation, the comb is made of paraffine, and filled with pure glucose by appropriate machinery. This honey, for whiteness and beauty, rivals the celebrated real white-clover honey of Vermont, but can be sold at an immense profit at one half the price."[23]

Wiley later admitted that this was a statement "which I had not personally investigated, but which I made on the authorities of others," but it was not entirely wrong.[24] Some apiarists were using artificial combs and feeding their bees glucose. Wiley's error was the idea that no bees were involved and—at least from the perspective of the beekeepers—that the resulting honey was adulterated by glucose, artificially colored, yet somehow as good as the pure article.[25]

What Wiley wrote about honey slowly but steadily began to spread around the world. When the *American Bee Journal* denounced a "Professor Riley," Wiley wrote to a different magazine, the *Indiana Farmer*, to defend himself. "'Glucose' has the same effect on the BEE JOURNAL man that a red rag has on an infuriated bull," Wiley joked. Wiley continued, taking quotes from the *Bee Journal*'s articles on the affair that might have been mistaken for maligning someone else's reputation at Purdue: "As I am probably the person meant by the 'Prof. Riley' alluded to in their mellifluous effusion, I think it but just to the eminent entomologist of the agricultural department that I should relieve him of all responsibility for the 'recklessness' which seems about to destroy his 'posthumous reputation as a scientist.'"[26] When called out on his pronouncement by people in the honey industry, Wiley's response was to make more pronouncements of questionable accuracy. This course of action would become a theme in Wiley's career: Never apologize, only attack. Never retract, only revise.

Wiley called the line about honey a "scientific pleasantry," passing off the error in the original *Popular Science* article to something that he had heard from a colleague, E. J. Hallock.

In reply to Wiley's response, the Honey Producers' League expressed its disgust by attacking Wiley personally:

> Do scientific men indulge in pleasantries which will cast a gloom over thousands of honest producers throughout the country, and depreciate the value of their product by creating a prejudice against it? For nearly a year this scientific joker saw his fabrication published in nearly all the papers in the country, and reiterated from across the ocean, and yet he lacked the manhood to affirm it a joke until the "BEE JOURNAL man" counteracted its influence by showing the falsity and absurdity of the article. Whether it be true, as has been often intimated, that the story was instigated by parties interested in the glucose traffic, in retaliation for the hostility of the bee men to their frauds, we cannot affirm; but we do believe it originated with no honest intention.[27]

Some politicians feared that what beekeepers now called the "Wiley Honey Lie" would harm American exports of all kind across the globe. For an industry also reeling from rumors that its product was poisoned, charges of widespread adulteration were difficult to bear.[28] Beekeepers, perhaps overly sensitive because there was extensive adulteration in the honey Americans bought at that time, hounded Wiley for years afterward. Wiley considered bringing a civil suit against the many beekeeping journals that repeatedly called him a liar but ended up merely continuing to investigate the adulteration of honey in America.[29]

Wiley had started researching how to detect the adulteration of honey while he was still at Purdue, but he knew little about how the honey industry actually operated.[30] His expertise was chemistry, not beekeeping. Nevertheless, he was willing to make sweeping assertions about the industry. The real dispute between Wiley and the honey industry was over exactly what constituted adulteration. Wiley believed that anything less than the natural process—in which bees fed on pollen produced honey extracted by hand—created an adulterated product. Honey producers, just then ramping up what could pass for mass production in the late nineteenth century, thought otherwise. During the late 1880s and 1890s Wiley was prone to find adulteration more often in honey than in any other article. The attacks on his character by honey producers probably contributed to this tendency. By 1900 Wiley would use the adulteration of honey as a jumping-off point to argue for national pure food legislation.

———————

Honey is, of course, a sweet, sticky substance created by bees from the nectar of the flowers they visit. Humans have tended bees for thousands of years to get easy access to this common sweetener. Besides its relative accessibility (compared with beet or cane sugar at this time), honey was an important sweetener because it could be kept indefinitely without refrigeration.[31] Nevertheless, beekeepers were relatively rare in mid-nineteenth-century America. Most were small producers who raised bees for the little extra cash that their honey provided. Perhaps honey's greatest advantage compared with other foods was that it required no processing to be ready to eat. Many producers filtered out bits of honeycomb and the like, but beyond that, honey was (and is) ready to eat straight from the hive. Apiarists could simply put it into jars and sell it.[32]

During the late nineteenth century, beekeepers began to organize, creating trade groups and publications to share essential information.[33] This organization facilitated the spread of three inventions that improved productivity. The first was the artificial hive. Instead of having to reach into the natural hive, apiarists started raising bees in boxes with sliding walls so they could easily look in on their bees and get honey out. The second invention was the artificial comb, which saved the bees the trouble of producing a natural comb and gave them more time to produce honey. The third invention was the honey extractor, which allowed beekeepers to remove honey more easily and efficiently.[34]

As these inventions increased the amount of available honey, wholesalers emerged to market the product of small producers nationwide. At this time, they sold liquid honey in jars. Makers had different brands that generally represented different grades of honey. At the top of the line was pure honey. Other brands would be cut with a mixture of glucose and cane sugar. Honey went from a product that was produced and distributed locally—beekeepers with extra product selling to friends and acquaintances—to a one that was distributed by wholesalers, some of whom were more ethical than others.[35] However, when Wiley exaggerated the extent of adulterated honey, small producers and wholesalers both took offense. The "Wiley Honey Lie" threatened to destroy the reputation of the entire industry, including that of the ethical actors.

Around 1880 glucose production was just starting to become a major industry. Glucose, best known at this time as a cheap artificial sweetener made from cornstarch, was produced and sold as a thick, colorless syrup. While not nearly as sweet as honey, when glucose was mixed with honey the resulting substance could pass as pure honey to those who did not know better.[36] For some consumers, cutting sugar with glucose likely made honey affordable. Wiley was not opposed to glucose per se; he opposed its use to cut other kinds of sugar and syrup that were more expensive to produce.[37] In the early 1870s, for example, honey cost sixteen cents a pound. Glucose, in contrast, cost five cents a pound. Each pound of glucose added to a barrel of honey, therefore, netted the producer eleven cents profit.[38] Unsurprisingly, the National Academy of Sciences found in 1884 that glucose was being used extensively as a substitute for cane sugar and as a replacement for barley malt in the brewing of beer. It was a major component in most of the table syrups available at that time, as well as in popular penny candies.

People who thought they were buying pure cane sugar during this era often got 80 percent cane sugar mixed with up to 20 percent glucose.[39] Glucose had been identified as a common adulterant in cane sugar as early as 1874. New technologies developed later that decade made it easier for small companies to make sugar out of corn, and it was increasingly found in sugar of all kinds.[40] In 1880 Wiley visited a glucose factory in Peoria, Illinois, for two or three weeks to learn production methods that were then still considered a "trade secret."[41] In 1881 he told an audience in Crawfordsville, Indiana, to grow corn, the source of glucose, because better honey could be made from glucose than the stuff made by bees. Only when Wiley put such sentiments in print did the beekeepers of America attack him, yet Wiley proved reluctant to change his mind or retract his statement in public.

Toward the end of the nineteenth century, sugar prices dropped, making adulteration of sugar less lucrative and the cutting of sugar with glucose less prevalent. Yet even when other sweeteners, like molasses, fell to about the same price as glucose, manufacturers still liked to cut honeys and syrups with glucose because it tended to give the product an attractive color and texture. These mixtures undercut the prices that producers of pure honey could charge for their product. Sometimes beekeepers fed their insects glucose to save on production costs, creating a honey full of glucose that was certainly sweet, but not natural.

It was by railing against adulterated honey that Wiley got his start fighting food producers over the quality and healthfulness of their products. In 1889 Wiley brought honey with a dead bee on top of it to a congressional hearing to suggest the lengths that adulterators would go to make their honey look authentic.[42] He argued that his chemical testing proved that the honey was adulterated. Wiley and honey producers had a long-running argument over whether chemical tests could prove whether honey had been adulterated at all because they did not agree over what exactly adulterated honey was. Apiarists knew exactly how they produced their honey. They did not know what wholesalers did with that honey after they sold it to them.

FIGURE 2.1 Harvey Wiley (*standing, front*) and his colleagues at the Division of Chemistry, 1889.

Courtesy of the Library of Congress

When Wiley attacked adulterated honey, he did not know exactly at which stage of production the honey had been adulterated, or even if it had been adulterated at all.

This battle had begun in the scientific and trade literature a few years before in response to the "Wiley Honey Lie." In 1885 Wiley published a paper on "Honey and Its Adulterations." That same year he publicly challenged Charles Muth, one of the most respected beekeepers and wholesale honey dealers in the country. Wiley tested samples of Muth's honey and suggested that they were probably adulterated—if not by Muth himself or the apiarists he bought them from, then by the bees' feeding on glucose without the knowledge of their beekeepers.[43] Muth later responded:

> I gave the professor, at his request, a number of samples for analyzation. All of it was pure honey, without any doubt about it, i.e. if there is any pure honey at all. I do not know what standard Prof. Wiley has for pure honey, but I verily believe that my samples could have served the Professor as a standard. Prof. Wiley reported at the next annual meeting, in person, in substance, as follows, that most of the samples were adulterated, and that one was probably pure.[44]

The follow-up study from the USDA Division of Chemistry, written by Wiley (its head), came in 1892. All of this work found a significant amount of adulteration in America's honey supply.[45]

A more careful scientist would not have been nearly so definitive. The composition of honey, like many other natural products, varies greatly depending on numerous factors, such as the species of bee, the pollen the bees feed upon, and the time of year it is produced.[46] Completely natural honey contains a substantial amount of glucose, which can range between 23 and 32 percent of the product.[47] Even in 1892, Wiley admitted, "At the present time it is quite difficult and sometimes impossible, to decide in a given case whether pure honey is present or whether it is largely adulterated with inverted sugar."[48] For Wiley to make definitive declarations about the adulteration of honey while privately doubting his own methods speaks volumes. The real problem—namely, the wide variation of glucose amounts in honey itself—stood beyond the test of chemistry.

Still, Wiley never publicly withdrew his original assertion about honey, and for years afterward he continued to malign the honey industry as producing mostly a seriously adulterated product. Wiley's 1892 conclusions on honey were definitive because of the standard he set rather than tests he conducted. "Honey made by feeding bees glucose, sugar, invert sugar or other saccharine substances is not pure honey," Wiley explained. "Nor is that pure honey that is made by adding to any empty or partially-filled honeycomb glucose or any other saccharine substance."[49] To Wiley, anything that did not fit his conception of a natural substance or a natural production process was adulterated. Beekeepers vehemently disagreed with this standard, which would have made the industrial production of honey impossible had it ever been widely adopted.

As Wiley became more interested in passing a national pure food law, his rhetoric about adulterated honey grew increasingly severe. In a well-attended 1897 speech before a Washington audience, Wiley claimed to have examined 500 samples of honey from the market and found 60 percent of them to be adulterated. Wiley also charged that bee parts were put into the honey to help carry out the fraud (since the presence of bee parts suggested the presence of bees).[50] Testifying before an arm of Congress, the Industrial Commission on Agriculture, in 1901, Wiley said that the adulteration of honey had grown so extensive that it had driven many producers into bankruptcy, especially in California, where adulteration was indeed common at the wholesaler level.[51]

Wiley understood that his original lie about honey was incorrect. In 1904 he wrote in a private letter, "In point of fact I believe that the artificial comb and honey have only been made in an experimental way and have never been placed upon the market. . . . It has always been a matter of regret to me that an article which I had written with such innocent intentions should have produced so much disturbance." In 1903 Wiley had explained this in an address to a gathering of beekeepers and thought they had forgiven him for his mistake.[52] Yet the "Wiley Honey Lie" became one of the arguments used by opponents of the Pure Food and Drug Act to discredit the chemist's support for the legislation around the time that Congress considered it for final passage.[53]

Unable to convince beekeepers or consumers that fraud in the production of honey, or any other food product, was of sufficient concern to justify national legislation, Wiley began to argue that adulteration presented a health risk that demanded a national pure food law. While there are hints of this focus on health in the struggle over honey, Wiley did not make this argument explicitly until after he began the Poison Squad experiments on borax. Equally important from Wiley's perspective, after the Pure Food and Drug Act passed in 1906, the focus on the health effects of adulteration helped ensure that the authority for determining what constituted adulteration would remain the Bureau of Chemistry—in other words, his office. Wiley would remain in the limelight, which by then he had grown to love.

———

In the case of honey, Wiley decided that adulteration was unhealthy because he thought the most common adulterant of honey was unhealthy. That adulterant was glucose. This was not his original position on the matter. In 1880, while still at Purdue, he wrote, "I do not anticipate that mixed sugars [sugars mixed with glucose] will jeopardize the public health. When well made they are certainly palatable and harmless."[54] Later, in 1902, Wiley insisted, "A mixture of glucose with food products, I maintain, is not injurious to health. Neither is it a fraud."[55] Extraordinarily, before making this statement Wiley had spent about twenty years arguing that adulteration with glucose was a fraud rather than a health hazard. Later, after leaving government, Wiley argued that glucose was both a health hazard and a fraud. This is something Wiley did many times during the years immediately before and after the passage of the Pure Food and Drug Act—namely, strengthen his position against various food products that he thought somehow unnatural.

The isolation of glucose as a separate sugar dates to the late 1700s. Often referred to as grape sugar, it could actually be derived from a variety of natural sources. What ruined its reputation in pure food circles (and likely with Wiley too) was the fact that it had to be made in a laboratory. Laboratories, to pure food enthusiasts, were like factories—sites of unnecessary human interference in natural processes that existed entirely to fool consumers.[56] Nevertheless, this characteristic did not stop the increased use of this product. Between 1904 and 1914, the total value of glucose produced in the United States increased by 61.2 percent. While the number of producers dropped as glucose manufacturing became more industrialized, the size of those producers increased remarkably.[57] What made glucose particularly irksome for Wiley was that it had spread from being an adulterant for honey to all sorts of other food products where he believed it did not belong. For example, it started to appear in beer, in mincemeat, and in jams and jellies. Wiley called glucose "the universal adulterant" and blamed glucose manufacturers for opposing the food law and its proper enforcement at every step.[58]

After the turn of the twentieth century, glucose became a product in itself rather than merely an ingredient in other foods. It was no coincidence that this transformation accompanied a major consolidation in the glucose production industry.[59] In 1902 the Corn Products Refining Company—a trust backed by John D. Rockefeller's Standard Oil Company—began selling "Karo Corn Sirup" directly to consumers. Wiley objected vehemently to this rebranding even before the pure food law passed Congress. After the passage of the law, Wiley sat on the committee in charge of enforcing that law, and he claimed that relabeling glucose as corn syrup was deliberate misbranding.[60] The members of the committee quickly agreed with Wiley's position, but the glucose manufacturers and corn producers heavily lobbied the White House to thwart Wiley's interpretation of the law. Under political pressure, the members of the committee reversed themselves to allow glucose to be renamed.[61]

President Theodore Roosevelt had the final say on this question, and he sided against Wiley. In his autobiography, Wiley explained that the secretary of agriculture passed on what TR had told him about the product: "Archie [Roosevelt's son] spent a week-end down in Virginia, and they had this stuff on the table, and Archie says it was good. If the makers want to call this product 'corn syrup,' why, that's the name by which it shall be known." Wiley refused to sign the decision approving the name change, but his resistance did not stop the spread of glucose as a sweetener throughout the American diet.[62]

While the glucose debate was about much more than honey, it affected the honey market all the same. Wiley never ran tests on the safety of glucose, yet in 1912 he claimed that it was "a well known fact that bees die if fed glucose."[63] A report from the Bureau of Chemistry made the same assertion.[64] This argument was wrong. Some sugars do indeed poison honeybees, but modern research has shown that glucose for bees is both "safe and nutritious."[65] When Wiley claimed that beekeepers fed glucose to their bees as part of what became known as the "Wiley Honey Lie," he saw that practice as an adulteration. To Wiley, any food that did not occur naturally was adulterated. Ultimately, the public did not agree. Wiley's decision to switch gears and question the safety of glucose demonstrated his recognition of that fact, setting a pattern that Wiley would repeat in many struggles over the purity of different foods.

Wiley's campaign against adulteration had only a limited effect on the honey industry. In his autobiography, Wiley claimed that his strong stand against adulteration with glucose translated into support from members of the beekeeping industry, claiming that they became his "most enthusiastic supporters."[66] Nothing could be further from the truth. In 1904, twenty-three years after his infamous *Popular Science Monthly* article, the National Honey Producers' League published the pamphlet *The Wiley Honey Lie*, which embedded that term into the discourse over honey. Still later, Wiley angered apiarists by opposing the use of glucose to feed bees even when the government wanted to use this strategy to greatly expand honey production after World War I.[67] As late as 1940, the journal *Gleanings in Bee Culture* complained that "the Wiley lie is not dead, even yet."[68] And mixing glucose and honey persisted as a standard industry practice.

The persistence of glucose in honey may demonstrate Wiley's failure to leave his mark on this industry, but it also shows the problems inherent in the mass production of honey. Consistency is an important benefit of mass production. Modern consumers like the fact that the jars and packages they buy from the supermarket tend to be the same from item to item and from season to season. Honey, however, varies in both taste and appearance depending upon the environment where the bees produce it. Nevertheless, Wiley became convinced that the purity of honey was an absolute standard and explicitly argued that adulterated honey "defied detection" outside of a chemical laboratory.[69] Natural honey has so many natural compositional varieties that it is difficult even today to determine whether or not it is adulterated. Moreover, even attempting to do so requires a substantial amount of expensive equipment. For many governments, confronting this problem simply is not worth the effort.[70]

Honey adulteration remains a serious problem. High-quality honey is an expensive product that can be easily and convincingly adulterated with cheaper sugars—not only glucose but high-fructose corn syrup or even molasses. Other adulterations involve hiding the geographic origins of the honey by removing the pollen associated with its point of origin so that it can be marketed as coming from somewhere else where the honey is known to be better.[71] Honey from China, for example, might be misbranded as expensive Manuka honey from New Zealand. In 2013 some samples of imported Chinese honey were demonstrated to be entirely corn syrup. At least this was better than the adulterated Chinese honey, discovered in 2002, that contained chloramphenicol, an antibiotic that can cause a potentially fatal bone marrow condition.[72] The problems created by technology in Wiley's era have only worsened in this globalized economy.

Since Wiley's time, the US Department of Agriculture has introduced a grading system—A, B, or C—to help consumers judge the quality of their honey. In theory this system would be a welcome compromise for honey producers who resist the idea that their product has been adulterated; if adding glucose to honey causes taste to suffer, then mixed honey would be sold at lower prices. Yet because there is no enforcement mechanism for this entirely voluntary system, plenty of adulterated honey is still being sold to consumers.[73] In 2011 more than 75 percent of the honey in grocery stores had added ingredients. While Harvey Wiley would have called this honey adulterated, American consumers are apparently willing to sacrifice taste for convenience and price when it comes to this product.

Wiley's willingness to jump to conclusions about honey mirrored his lackadaisical attitude toward studying the effects of food adulteration in general. In short, Wiley believed he knew more about honey than the bee-keepers did. This same dynamic would work against him in future struggles over foods like whiskey and flour. Harvey Wiley trained as a sugar chemist. His expertise was in determining the composition of sweeteners, not detecting or stopping adulteration of foods more broadly. But as he embarked on his study of food adulteration, he maintained his research on developing new sources of sugar for the American market. Outside of food adulteration, his work on the American beet sugar industry was easily the most important accomplishment of his career, and it had a substantial impact on what Americans eat, all the way to the present day.

CHAPTER THREE

SUGAR BEETS

I T WAS NOT UNTIL 1889 that the United States Department of Agriculture achieved cabinet status. Before then, it was a division of the Patent Office, within the Department of Interior. The purpose of the newly designated department then was to collect information about agriculture and to distribute seeds and information to help farmers grow more crops.[1] The tiny number of crops grown by American farmers at the time was a huge problem. Since nearly everyone grew just corn or wheat, prices dropped so low that few farmers could grow them profitably. This situation contributed to the bland meat- and cheese-centered American diet. The United States was industrializing, and farming had to change with it. To help with this transition, and to keep farmers happy, the Department of Agriculture grew much larger during this period.[2]

Before launching his work to combat food adulteration, Harvey Wiley devoted most of his time at the Division of Chemistry to helping develop a domestic sugar industry. Wiley recognized that, in contrast to other foods, sugar from any source was chemically identical, or at least similar enough that he had no taste preference about which plant from which American sugar should originate. He developed an interest in sugar beets, correctly believing that this crop could eventually become a source of sugar to satisfy most of the country's growing demand. With his work on sugar beets, Wiley almost single-handedly created a new source of sweetness for American consumers. Though it was not until after his death that his research led to an entirely domestic source of sugar, Wiley's work changed the industry forever and constitutes one of his most important contributions to the American diet.

Before Harvey Wiley helped make sugar commonplace, human beings would taste sweetness only in the occasional piece of fruit or bit of honey. Except for the very rich, they got their calories elsewhere. Cane sugar, the only source of sugar in the United States during the mid-nineteenth century, came from the Caribbean. Before the development of a sugar beet industry, the United States depended on these sugarcane imports for the vast majority of sweeteners. By Wiley's time, the US Department of Agriculture was seeking to promote new domestic sources of sugar. There had been a sugar beet industry in Europe since shortly after the turn of the nineteenth century, and the forerunner of the USDA had started experimenting with sugar beets during the Civil War. But the sugar shortage created by the embargo of the South during that conflict convinced officials that the lack of homegrown sugar was a significant economic vulnerability for the United States.[3]

Sugar beets contain vastly different amounts of sugar depending on how and where they are grown, and this is why the Division of Chemistry got involved. Wiley helped establish and coordinate infrastructure for testing the sugar content of beets grown around the country. The division's goal was to help farmers grow beets with more sugar efficiently enough to allow production of this crop to expand. Success depended sometimes on the particular climate where beets were farmed and sometimes on farmers' practices for growing and harvesting beets.

During Wiley's childhood, a large maple tree had supplied his family with the sweetener they needed.[4] Having regular access to any kind of sugar put his family in the minority of Americans. In 1857 the first sorghum seeds appeared in the United States. Sorghum is a tall, leafy plant of African origin that resembles corn in the field. Wiley's father obtained sorghum seeds in the late 1850s through southern Indiana's member of Congress. He had little interest in planting the seeds himself, so he gave them to Harvey, who grew a bit at the edge of the garden. When he first tasted it, he found the cane of the plant "deliciously sweet." Wiley's success with the crop convinced his father to build a sorghum mill during the Civil War, when the usual shipments of molasses from New Orleans disappeared. Wiley retained an interest in sweeteners for his entire life.[5] As long as they grew naturally and remained unadulterated, his research supported their production. Breeding better sugar beets and teaching beet farmers and processors how to grow and treat beets properly formed a large part of his research during the 1880s and 1890s.

While still in Indiana, Wiley investigated the adulteration of sugar and sugar syrups, finding 90 percent of them adulterated with glucose.[6] By the 1880s the problem had changed. The price of sugar was so low that few people bothered to adulterate it anymore. Although the purity of sugar was no longer an issue, the government wanted to encourage domestic sugar production to protect consumers against price hikes during potential future shortages. Wiley's charge was to raise domestic sugar production. Introducing European sugar beets into the United States was the most obvious approach. Beets produced sugar just as sweet as that from sugarcane, and they could grow in temperate areas where sugarcane could not.

Wiley's earliest experiments at the Division of Chemistry involved three sources of sugar: sorghum, sugarcane, and sugar beets.[7] His initial goal was to determine which of these crops could be built up to serve the domestic sugar market so that Americans could wean themselves from foreign sources. The lack of competition in the domestic sugar-refining industry was another problem. On the one hand, technological advances in refining drastically drove down the price of sugar between 1840 and 1870 and lowered barriers to entry. As a result, it cost only $500,000 to build a modern sugar refinery.[8] However, in 1887, a large conglomerate of sugar refiners concentrated in New York City became another concern. Henry Osborne Havemeyer merged his company with seventeen other concerns to form the

Sugar Refineries Company. Most people called it simply the Sugar Trust. The Sugar Trust's operations epitomized the industrial production methods of that era. At the turn of the twentieth century, its factory in Brooklyn employed 2,218 people.[9] While the Sugar Trust controlled the processing of sugarcane into cane sugar, it did not control the processing of sugar beets into the chemically identical product beet sugar. This created a commercial opening for beet sugar and other alternatives.

Sorghum is often milled and cooked down to create a sweetener. Although the final product resembles molasses, sorghum syrup does not come from sugarcane; it is an entirely different source of sweetness.[10] Peter Collier, Wiley's immediate predecessor as head of the Division of Chemistry at the Department of Agriculture, had been examining sorghum as a possible domestically produced sweetener since 1877. Thanks in part to his research, the sorghum industry grew sharply during Collier's tenure at the division, even if it had not expanded enough to satisfy America's entire demand for sweetener.[11] Wiley, despite having planted sorghum back in Indiana, was not inclined to keep up the sorghum research when he joined the division.[12] "All that is nasty and green and sticky and rancid in the sugar vocabulary is associated with it," he explained in 1883. "Sorghum is surrounded by an ocean of prejudice which is well nigh unnavigable."[13] To make matters worse, a series of experiments designed to extract more sugar from sorghum all failed.[14]

In 1885 Wiley had some success with experiments designed to improve the extraction of sugar from the infant domestic sugarcane industry (then based primarily in Louisiana). After studying the milling process in Europe in 1885 and 1886, the Division of Chemistry established two facilities in the United States using those methods.[15] Wiley's experiments showed how processing techniques could make sugarcane refining much more efficient.[16] While these experiments had little impact in the short term, the processing innovation Wiley introduced into the United States—known as the diffusion process—eventually encouraged the domestic sugarcane industry to move away from the traditional method of simply crushing the cane that it had depended upon for hundreds of years.[17] Wiley also demonstrated that the soils in Florida around Lake Okeechobee were fertile enough to support sugarcane cultivation. No one would make use of this information for many years, but it would eventually prove important to the creation of a domestic sugarcane industry.[18] In the interim, Wiley oversaw a long series of experiments designed to promote the growth and consumption of sugar from sugar beets.

———

Before Wiley joined the Division of Chemistry, William McMurtrie, an assistant chemist in the department, had traveled to Europe to examine European sugar beet cultivation methods. He had concluded that experiments with sugar beets in America had failed because farmers and farm workers had not given enough attention to the careful cultivation this crop required, there had not been enough capital available to build factories, and no one in the United States understood the climate in which sugar beets needed to grow.[19] Despite this assessment, in 1881 Congress had appropriated $10,000 to import English and French equipment to cultivate beets. The funds went to a single company in Delaware.[20]

In late 1884 Wiley traveled to the West Coast to study its nascent beet sugar industry, and the following year he went to see Europe's sugar beet industry, which was already mature enough to supply most of the sugar consumed there. When Wiley made his initial efforts to jump-start the American sugar beet industry, political considerations demanded that the initiative include every region of the country. The Department of Agriculture bought European seed and sent samples to agricultural stations and farmers all over America. The farmers then sent their samples back to Washington for testing. While popular with congressmen, this approach did little to prove the value of the industry because of the farmers' failure to follow instructions. Many of the beets produced were too large, which meant that they did not contain enough sugar. Some farmers grew smaller beets with higher sugar content, sacrificing yield and profitability. Farmers often failed to clean the beets well, posing a threat to refiners' machinery.[21]

When Congress included enough money in the fiscal 1889 budget to establish a special experiment station to study different methods of sugar

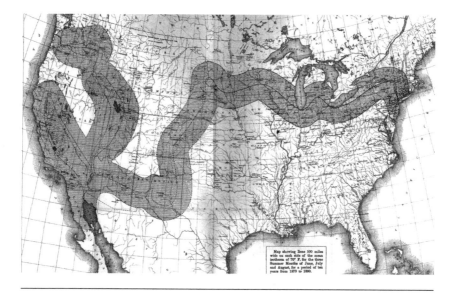

FIGURE 3.1 Map delineating the 100-mile-wide zone where rain and temperature conditions were best for growing sugar beets in the United States. Though the map was subsequently revised, even this first version was basically accurate.

H. W. Wiley, The Sugar Beet Industry, US Department of Agriculture, Division of Chemistry, Bulletin No. 27 (Washington, DC: Government Printing Office, 1890), 169

manufacture, it did not specify whether that station should concentrate on sorghum, Louisiana sugarcane, or sugar beets. Wiley used the money to set up a lab at a Grand Island, Nebraska, refinery specifically to study sugar beets. "There is now a fair prospect," he wrote that year, "that the manufacture of sugar from the sugar beet will become a financial success in the United States, and our desire is to further this subject as much as possible."[22]

What convinced most people that sugar beets could serve as a domestic sugar supply was a map Wiley included in his 1890 report to Congress. That map highlighted a large swath of the United States, about a hundred miles wide from the Canadian border in the Northeast to the Mexican border in the Southwest. This was the area where—at least theoretically—the sweetest sugar beets could be grown.[23] Before Wiley's experiments, no one understood under what conditions the sugar beet would grow best. Through his experiments, Wiley identified the temperature and rainfall conditions under which sugar beets were most likely to grow within the ideal size range for processing. The necessary average summer temperature range formed a narrow band across the country, passing from the New England states through the upper Midwest, down to Colorado, and out to California, although only the places with enough rainfall could support a sugar beet crop. This map gave a huge impetus to the industry's growth, and all the eventual successful sugar beet factories would be built there.[24] In the 1890s, however, the problem was to get people to grow beets in those areas.

Farmers could certainly grow beets throughout the zone that the Division of Chemistry (under Wiley's supervision) had identified; the issue was whether they could grow beets profitably. There was a market for the sugar, but the beets they grew had to yield enough sugar and the labor to tend and harvest them had to be available. Perhaps most important, there had to be a processing station nearby so that the beets could be turned into sugar. For that to happen, there had to be enough farmers to supply the station with beets. During the 1890s Wiley tried to tackle all these problems at the same time.

The Division of Chemistry's research on sugar beets was spread around the country. The goal was to develop different varieties that could grow best in the different beet-growing regions. As time passed and the breeds improved, the industry would presumably grow to match the success of sugar beets in Europe.[25] These research stations, established with money from Congress, provided both farmers and beet-processing firms with information, but they could not do the farmers' and processors' jobs for them. Unfortunately, the beet farmers seldom followed the division's instructions to the exacting degree that sugar beet cultivation required. Potential sugar beet farmers "are so busy with other work," Wiley wrote, "that as a rule, they are not able to give attention to the experimental details. They do not have the time to properly prepare the soil for beet culture nor do they give the growing beet proper attention." Faced with other crops ready for harvesting, farmers tended to wait to harvest their beets, another problem in a lengthy list of problems. While sugar beets could in theory be grown all over the country, Wiley could only guess where they would do best based on highly imperfect results.[26]

Then there was the problem of finding wageworkers to do sugar beet labor. Tending, picking, and transporting sugar beets was hard work. In the early decades of the industry, sugar beets had to be planted in close to one another as this practice produced the most usable specimens. This approach required considerable hand labor, both for weeding and for removing the plants in a clump that would not produce the best results. While this work could be done with a hoe, most people found the labor excruciating. As Wiley explained in 1886, sugar beet labor "requires a bowing of the back and a holding of the hoe which is repugnant to the American farmer. The man who rides on a sulky-plow and cuts and binds his wheat with a machine is likely to despise the manual labor which a beet field requires."[27] Before conveying beets to the processing facility, farmers had to cut off their tops, which are full of salts and cannot be processed.[28] This required more hard labor, usually with a large knife. It took still more labor to remove tons of soil from tons of sugar beets.

Beet processors often had trouble finding an adequate supply of labor for the fields from which their sugar beets came.[29] The only people willing to perform such hard labor were the most desperate Americans—often immigrants and children. Few of them cared how well they did their jobs (since they didn't directly benefit from the quality of the crop), and the quality of American sugar beets suffered as a result. In the late nineteenth century, Eastern European immigrants constituted much of this labor. As the Eastern Europeans saved enough money to become farmers rather than farm workers, Mexicans and Mexican Americans gradually replaced them in the fields. Because of the difficulties associated with this work, labor costs accounted for between 60 and 75 percent of the cost of the beets.[30]

This labor had to be done well in order to produce the best beets for processing. Sugar refiners could not process just any beet. As before, beets that were too big did not have enough sugar in them to make them worth processing. If farmers grew beets that were too small, they would be rich in sugar, but the overall yield would not be large enough to justify the expense needed to grow them.[31] These considerations explain why farmers, and even growers at the Department of Agriculture's own experiment stations, required so much instruction.

In 1898 Harvey Wiley delivered a special report to Congress about the state of the American sugar beet industry. This report was the culmination of years of experiments during which Wiley had sent seed to the department's agricultural experiment stations so that staff at these stations could try to grow beets as well as redistribute beet seeds to individual farmers. While the document included many optimistic findings, Wiley reported that the main barrier to greater success was the stubbornness of his volunteer farmers. "We found, as a rule," the report explains, "that the farmers were going more upon their own experience and knowledge of growing field crops than they were upon the directions given to them by the Department and experiment stations." Farmers simply could not understand how to raise commercially viable sugar beets that factories could process because the requirements of the crop were completely foreign to their previous experience.[32]

———

One of Wiley's jobs at the Division of Chemistry in the 1890s was to direct the Sugar Laboratory at the Department of the Treasury. To collect tariffs on imported sugar, the government had to determine its quality, which in turn dictated its price; hence, Treasury needed a sugar lab. Here Wiley's expertise in the use of the polariscope came in handy, as the degree of refraction shown by the instrument could be used to determine the purity of sugar. Sellers and buyers often got different readings of sugar purity, but Wiley's laboratory had the final say in how much money the government could collect.[33] For example, raw sugar and refined sugar were taxed at different rates, and the laboratory sometimes had to run tests to see whether sugar had been processed.[34] That laboratory also tested samples of beet sugar to help farmers judge the results of the various farming practices they were experimenting with.[35]

Wiley was far more interested in one these tasks than in the other. "It is a pitiable spectacle to see a great nation," he declared in 1898, "the largest sugar consumer in the world, confiding the standard of its revenue from this great staple to an irresponsible foreign broker!"[36] That irresponsible foreign broker was Spain, which controlled Cuba, the largest sugar producer in the world at the time. Cuba produced cane sugar, a labor-intensive crop, but one that had been economically viable for centuries. Wiley's experiments with sugar beets were, therefore, nationalistic. The earlier association of beet sugar with the anti-slavery cause may also have played to his pro-Union sentiments from his Civil War days. Tariffs were the only way to protect American sugar beet farm labor from cheap competition. While there was enough room for both cane sugar and beet sugar in the growing American market, this competition from cheap foreign sources prevented sugar beets from becoming more important sooner.

Between 1880 and 1884 Americans consumed 38 pounds of sugar a year per person, more than any other country except Great Britain. By 1887 that number had increased to 60.9 pounds a year, and it only rose from there.[37] Many Americans, including Wiley (at least at this juncture), considered rising sugar consumption a sign of progress; the notion that sugar was harmful developed only decades later. With steady growth in demand, not only Wiley but domestic sugar producers in general wanted a sugar tariff to help grow the domestic sugar beet industry. In theory, tariff protection would last until the industry became established. In fact, such protections seldom worked this way. For sugar, the tariff fluctuated wildly.

Wiley's work with sugar and the polariscope made it possible for the US government to grade sugar for the first time. The instrument was used to determine which sugars were of the highest quality and were thus subject to a higher tariff.[38] In 1890 Congress decided that foreign sugar could enter the country duty free but American sugar producers would get a bounty of two cents for every pound of domestic sugar they produced. The Dingley Tariff of 1897 was supposed to give domestic sugar a leg up. In fact, it only increased the price of foreign sugar by twenty-nine cents for every hundred pounds.[39] At that price, foreign sugar still competed well against sugar from the United States.

To complicate matters for sugar producers, new domestic production of cane sugar came online after the Spanish-American War. Initially Harvey Wiley opposed the Spanish-American War because of the impact that bringing Cuban sugar under domestic control would have had on the market for beet sugar, but he quickly changed his mind. In fact, the impact of

American imperialism on the domestic sugar market proved considerable. When the United States annexed the Hawaiian Islands in 1898, 420,000 tons of cane sugar could enter the country duty free each year. When the United States took over Puerto Rico that same year, an additional 217,000 tons of cane sugar could enter the country each year. A reciprocity agreement with the Philippines and a Cuba newly freed from Spain led 1,440,000 more tons of cane sugar annually to enter the country at a reduced price,[40] largely from modern US-built sugar plantations in Cuba.[41]

———

Although food adulteration gradually replaced sugar research as the most important of Harvey Wiley's professional priorities over the course of the 1890s, he remained interested in sugar for the rest of his life. In 1889 Wiley had tried to make government experiments with sugar permanent when he suggested the establishment of an agricultural station devoted entirely to sugar, but Congress wouldn't fund it. Between 1880 and 1890 Congress had appropriated $424,500 to get the American sugar industry going and had little to show for it. In 1894 the secretary of agriculture in the second Cleveland administration, Sterling Morton, cut off all funds for government-sponsored sugar experiments.[42] At this juncture Wiley promoted the production of domestic sugar of all kinds—cane sugar, sorghum sugar, and beet sugar. However, his lasting contribution to American agriculture was his research on sugar beets. While it took time and still more research for sugar beets to become popular in the United States, the beet sugar industry eventually grew despite its problems with labor and competition from cane sugar. By 1905 many new processing plants had been erected and beet sugar production had reached about two-thirds of the level of cane sugar. Wiley's map had showed investors where beets could grow best so they could build processing plants nearby.[43] "It is a remarkable fact that every beet sugar factory is located in the area marked out by the Bureau of Chemistry twenty years ago," Wiley told a reporter in 1911. "This work saved many millions of dollars from being invested in localities not favorable to the production of beets of the highest character."[44]

Although the sugar beet industry did not during his lifetime become the ubiquitous source of sweetness that it is today, one sign of Wiley's success is that by the time he wrote *Foods and Their Adulteration* in 1907, he noted that because of the increase in production of sugar of all kinds, sugar had become so cheap that nobody bothered to adulterate it any more.[45] In contrast, adulteration of most other foods increased over the course of Wiley's long career, and Wiley's fame increased as he took on more and more of these adulterations over time.

Long before the sugar beet industry became economically viable, there were efforts to make sugar beet tending and harvesting less labor intensive. Europeans and Americans made many attempts to automate each step in the process, especially harvesting. Unfortunately, none of the foreign or domestic machinery designed to save sugar beet labor did the job.[46] No such harvester would be found until World War II, after improvements had been made in the breeding of the beets themselves.[47] During his lifetime, the primary effect of Wiley's work on sugar was to improve the production of cane sugar since the improved presses used to refine beet sugar found their way into cane sugar processing and made that practice more efficient.[48]

Today Harvey Wiley is generally credited as the father of the sugar beet industry in the United States.[49] In early 2017 the US Department of Agriculture reported that 55 percent of US domestic sugar production came from sugar beets.[50] If Wiley were around to see this success, he would probably be more upset about how sugar gets sold than he would be about how much of it was beet sugar. Americans now consume large amounts of sugar derived from high-fructose corn syrup, and few of them bother to read the label of any food product to examine what kind sugar they happen to be consuming.

In his autobiography, Wiley makes little mention of his considerable work on sugar beets. The topic doesn't even merit a mention in the index, perhaps because of his later fame for pursuing the cause of pure food. Part of this attitude can be explained by the corporatization of beet sugar production after the turn of the twentieth century. Starting in 1902, the Sugar Trust entered the beet sugar industry as a way of maintaining control over the sugar-processing market, and it became the largest investor in the product. Another important investor in consolidated western sugar beet–processing firms was the Mormon Church.[51] When the opportunity to both make money and help Americans get cheaper sugar disappeared, Wiley largely lost interest in the whole industry. In 1909 there were still only 58 sugar beet–processing facilities in the entire country.[52] Sugar beet firms like the Great Western Sugar Company (based in Colorado) now did their own research on improving the quality of their product rather than relying on the work of the US Department of Agriculture, which was engaged with other food issues.[53]

Wiley tried to increase domestic production of sugar for most of his career, and nobody played a bigger role in making sugar in America cheaper, but eventually, as with glucose, Wiley started to question his own handiwork. After he retired from government, the best thing he could say about the sugar beet industry was that it operated like a normal school for farmers since sugar beets were so difficult to grow to the exacting specifications required by refineries.[54] Speaking in Oklahoma City in 1913, Wiley declared, "The effects of excessive sugar consumption are more injurious in many ways than those of alcohol. . . . We eat sugar on everything except meat and honey. . . . We put it on our breakfast foods. We mix it in the dough with which we make our bread. We put it on the fruit we eat."[55] In 1919 he called sugar "rank poison to human systems."[56] Of course, the problem Wiley highlighted would only grow worse after his death. Wiley would have been particularly concerned to learn that beet sugar has become a common adulterant for orange juice.[57]

Although sugar refining was controlled by a trust, the price of sugar never again rose high enough for it to be regularly adulterated. Nonetheless, sugar companies capitalized on consumers' interest in pure food. The Sugar Trust, for example, advertised that their heavily refined white product was purer than brown sugar (even though it wasn't).[58] Historian Benjamin Cohen explains the cultural dimension of this relationship, noting, "Beet-sugar advocates would advertise the racial dimensions of their product"; investors in this nascent industry wanted "to offer sugar untouched by dark hands," referring to the labor of ex-slaves who harvested and processed Caribbean sugarcane.[59] The influence of Wiley's racial thinking on his food preferences would be clear only later in his career, but the racism inherent in any quest for "purity" in this era is worth noting.

Wiley was attracted to beet sugar because he thought it was just as good as cane sugar.[60] The ability to substitute one for the other was one of many factors that holding down the price of sugar. If one sugar was inferior to another, producers would have introduced substitutions, which Wiley would have considered adulterations. Instead, Wiley worked to increase the supply of sugar in a natural way. Artificial sweeteners raised Wiley's hackles just for being artificial, and he came to believe that most of them were unhealthful too. Having fathered an entire industry during his early days in Washington, Wiley would go on to spend his later days in Washington trying to hinder the expansion of what many other people considered progress—namely, the industrialization of food processing of all kinds, because of the health effects of the additives this required.

———

Throughout the 1890s, Harvey Wiley had attempted to organize investors in new lands where sugar beets could grow to expand the domestic sugar supply. Unfortunately for Wiley, uncertainty about the tariff on imported sugarcane limited his success. In 1900 a Chicago company invited him to join an investment consortium for growing sugarcane in Cuba and Puerto Rico. He responded, "I believe that with the proper kind of management and energy, profitable returns would be certain to come from investments of the kind you mention. With American machines, American methods and American push, I am certain that the output of sugar in these islands will soon be double." He went on to recommend one of his former assistants at the Division of Chemistry to oversee operations there and offered to invest "a few thousand dollars" in this arrangement because he was "not a millionaire."[61]

The sentiments in this letter were remarkable for a number of reasons. For one thing, Harvey Wiley's job for many years had been largely to promote the domestic sugar industry. While the Spanish-American War had put Cuba and Puerto Rico under American control, any investment in sugarcane there hurt the sugar beet farmers he had been charged with assisting. In other words, such an investment was an extraordinary conflict of interest. It was also a vote of no confidence in the future of the American sugar beet industry. Had Wiley had faith in the future of American sugar beets he never would have contemplated such an investment because it would not have paid off for him. Moreover, Wiley's recognition that he was "not a millionaire" offers a tiny window into his extraordinary drive to make money throughout his career in government service.

Wiley made a series of investments in Washington, DC, area real estate during his early years in that area that would pay off handsomely over the next few decades. He also began to invest successfully in stocks and bonds.[62] The most complete records that remain in Wiley's papers cover his private investments in the production of the foodstuffs he researched starting in the early 1890s. In 1894, for example, Wiley proposed going into business with his friend John Arbuckle, of the coffee importer Arbuckle Brothers in New York, to grow coffee in California.[63] His office had investigated adulteration in coffee two years earlier.[64] High-end firms like Arbuckle Brothers were unlikely to adulterate as a matter of daily business, but Wiley's willingness to work so closely with an industry that was the subject of his investigations suggests the limits of his commitment to becoming a crusader at this time. This episode does not mean that his interest in pure food was a scam, but it does show that Wiley saw this cause as a way to become rich while serving the public good.

Wiley's letters from the time show that he saw his involvement in the pure food movement as one way to achieve that goal. It can be difficult to tell where Wiley's government work ended and his private work began. During the 1890s Wiley made personal loans to individuals (charging 7 or 8 percent interest), invested in real estate, and engaged in private chemical analysis for firms in industries he helped regulate. Wiley and four other scientists formed a syndicate to develop fifty acres of land in Chevy Chase, Maryland, and he participated in another syndicate to develop land near College Park, Maryland.[65]

One sign of improvement in Wiley's lifestyle was his decision, in October 1900, to buy an automobile—the second one ever purchased in Washington, DC. While Wiley's correspondence does not reveal the make and model, it does say that his car was steam driven.[66] This was extremely early in the history of America's fascination with cars. At that time, no one had heard of Henry Ford, and automobiles were toys for rich people rather than a regular means of transportation. In December 1900 Wiley crashed the car.[67] It was the city's first automobile accident.[68]

Of all Wiley's efforts to supplement his salary during this time, the most important involved the Marsden Company of Philadelphia. Its purpose was to make usable products out of cornstalks, most notably cattle food. Thanks to Wiley, the firm would branch out considerably. Shortly after its formation in 1897, Wiley became the firm's chemist while also holding his government job. The company moved its chemical laboratory so that Wiley could work there in his spare time. Wiley received two patents for his work with Marsden, one for the manufacture of alcohol (which Wiley thought would fuel "the autocar of the future") and the other for the use of that alcohol to sterilize food-manufacturing equipment. In December 1897 Wiley signed a contract with Marsden giving the company a half interest in those patents in return for promoting them and using them to manufacture what Wiley considered to be pure food. Marsden took no action along those lines, and the arrangement ended in acrimony. This episode illustrates the way in which Harvey Wiley often mixed his official business with activities meant to improve his own bottom line. Obviously, if the passage of a pure food law had occurred before this arrangement was disbanded, it could have worked to his financial advantage.[69]

This conflict of interest did not dim Wiley's support for the cause of pure food. He didn't want to sell out. Rather, Wiley wanted to become both rich and loved. "I am anxious to develop this matter both because I think it is a good thing, and also because I want to make some money out of it," he wrote to a friend when the deal with the Marsden Company began to go south. "I am getting old and would hate awfully to die poor."[70] In those last days before the arrival of muckraking journalists, government service didn't have to mean a vow of poverty; no one was checking on where officials invested their money. Yet even after the turn of the twentieth century, as the climate for the enrichment of government officials grew less friendly, he persisted in pursuing various moneymaking strategies, even as he became an increasingly prominent spokesman for the cause of pure food. However, he was far from that movement's prime force in the years before the Poison Squad experiments began.

CHAPTER FOUR

ADULTERATED FOOD

UNTIL HE BEGAN THE FIRST Poison Squad experiment, Harvey Wiley was not a significant factor in the pure food movement. Indeed, even after that experiment began, he remained agnostic about the extent of the danger posed by food adulteration. "Personally, I had never gone so far as my associates in the pure food congress and other movements relating to injurious substances in food," he explained before he started the series of experiments that changed his life. "I have always been of the opinion, and still am . . . that it is entirely sufficient to place upon a food label the nature of any substance that has been added . . . and leave to the consumer him-self . . . the determination of whether or not that substance is injurious to him."[1] While a truth-in-labeling law would have been a significant improve-ment over the situation that existed before the passage of the Pure Food and Drug Act (PFDA), this position was hardly at the vanguard of calls for reform at that time. Therefore, it is an error to read the activism of Wiley's later career backward into the late nineteenth century.

Looking back over his life, Wiley made precisely this self-serving mistake. In his autobiography he wrote, "It took many years of education on the part of my Bureau and other agencies interested in protecting the health of the people before the vast and effective weight of public opinion swung in behind the passage and enforcement of a general food and drugs act."[2] This was an exaggeration. Starting during the late 1880s, Wiley and his colleagues at the Division of Chemistry published research examining the extent of deceptive adulteration in the food supply. At that point, he saw his role in the movement as providing scientific information that others could use as they saw fit.

Wiley held on to this perspective for a long time. As late as 1904, Wiley could still tell an audience, "I am not one of the people who think there is a very great increase in the attendance at the graveyard due to the practice of food adulteration. In other words, the injury to public health, in my opinion,

FIGURE 4.1 Harvey Wiley, looking through an optical instrument in the laboratory at the US Department of Agriculture Bureau of Chemistry, 1902. The picture dates from the period when the Poison Squad experiments were just beginning.

Courtesy Library of Congress

is the least important question in the subject of food adulteration, and it is one which should be considered last of all. The real evil of food adulteration is deception of the consumer."[3] This sentiment was wildly out of step with the cause of pure food legislation. Throughout the 1890s there had been multiple attempts to pass pure food legislation in Congress. Harvey Wiley supported these efforts, but his work at the Division of Chemistry was of only minor assistance to that cause, in large part because of Wiley's conservative attitude toward reform.

During the 1880s and 1890s Wiley had found adulteration in all kinds of foods and beverages, but only at the turn of the twentieth century would he claim that adulteration was universal.[4] More important, not until the start of the Poison Squad experiments did he assert that these adulterations harmed the health of consumers. Until then, his research on adulteration centered on the damage it did to people's pocketbooks rather than their health. The publicity surrounding the Poison Squad experiments scared enough people to make Wiley the apparent leader of the once-disjointed pure food movement.

Another explanation for Wiley's role in this issue involves his being based in Washington. During the 1890s the pure food movement was strongest at the state level, but as time passed local leaders became increasingly interested in seeking a national law to combat adulteration. The first bill introduced into Congress to prevent the adulteration of food came in 1879.[5] Then, between 1879 and 1906, Congressmen proposed 190 pure food bills.[6] In 1892 a pure food bill first passed the house only to be stymied in the Senate.[7] Nevertheless, that bill marked the beginning of pure food as a major national issue. That same basic bill kept getting introduced in Congress and then stalling from 1892 all the way to 1906, when the PFDA finally emerged.[8] In the early days of this struggle, Wiley's self-appointed role was to conduct research to determine the extent of adulteration in the American food supply, not to shepherd those bills through Congress. That role changed once Wiley obtained a public following.

The problem of adulterated foods goes back many hundreds of years. The Law of Moses includes rules to combat food adulteration. Ancient Chinese literature describes adulteration practices. Records from Medieval Britain recount the punishments inflicted upon dishonest brewers who watered down their beer and butchers who short-weighted their customers. During the age of European colonial expansion, governments throughout Europe began to regulate the purity of bread and the potency of wine in response to food adulteration. Much of the tea that traveled from China to Great Britain during America's colonial period was adulterated long before reaching its intended destination.[9]

Despite this long history of adulteration, there was no concerted effort against this problem until Frederick Accum published his *Treatise on Adulterations of Food and Culinary Poisons* in 1820.[10] That book covered the European situation, and specifically Great Britain. At that time many Americans produced much of the food they ate on their farms and had no fear of impure food. As industrialization picked up over the course of the nineteenth century and more people depended on outside sources for an increasing portion of their diets, the problem of adulterated food became worse. In 1861 Thomas Hoskins published the first important book on adulteration in the United States.[11] As food adulteration became more frequent and changed in nature in the late nineteenth century, it began to draw increased attention. While earlier adulterations were mostly deceptive but harmless to people's health, the advent of industrial-scale food processing saw the introduction of the first coal tar chemicals into the food supply. As a result, people became increasingly afraid that their food was slowly poisoning them.

By the late nineteenth century disparate pure food efforts had coalesced into a movement. Among its members were grocers, consumer advocates, domestic scientists like Ellen Swallow Richards, and a large group of industrial chemists. The American Society of Public Analysts, a coalition of health officials, convened in 1884 to coordinate their efforts against food adulteration and food fraud. Even the Women's Christian Temperance Union, famous for its fight against alcohol, devoted enormous effort to the cause of pure food. In 1886 some chemists started producing a trade journal called *American Analyst*, devoted to the "suppression of adulteration."[12]

The first results of these anti-adulteration efforts came at the state level. New York State passed an anti-adulteration bill in 1881. Nearly identical bills became law in New Jersey and Massachusetts shortly thereafter.[13] Both state and local efforts to promote pure food faced a problem with inconsistent standards of purity and inconsistent enforcement of those standards that did pass, and in response respectable businesses and their trade organizations tried to promote national pure food legislation as early as 1880. By 1900 legislatures in just about every state had passed some kind of law combating adulteration.[14] These laws rested on the domestic police powers of the respective states to protect their citizens, but they did not apply to foods transported in the stream of interstate commerce.[15]

The earliest state laws therefore tended to concentrate on particular foods rather than foods in general. As scientists like Wiley developed ways to determine the chemical composition of foods of all kinds, pure food laws became more general too. Provisions in many of the resulting state laws were incorporated into the federal Pure Food and Drug Act when it finally passed. Standards developed by Wiley and others explaining exactly what constituted the normal state of particular foods helped states that wanted to amend and broaden their statutes.[16] After the passage of the Pure Food and Drug Act, this same research helped federal investigators determine which foods were adulterated so they could enforce the act accordingly.[17]

At the federal level, bills designed to prevent adulteration were targeted mostly at classes of products and made much slower progress. Congress passed the first federal pure food law around 1850. It set standards for imported teas and blocked any tea that didn't meet those standards from entering the country. That law deemed that artificially coloring tea leaves to avoid this restriction was an "adulteration."[18] The first federal law regulating any food produced inside the United States was aimed at oleomargarine—a butter substitute charged with being deceptive, unhealthful, or both—and was not enacted until in 1886.[19]

In the 1880s, when Wiley arrived in Washington, the problem of adulterated food was serious but not critically so. Most food production in America was just beginning to industrialize, and only a small share of those adulterations were life threatening. Wiley remembered adulteration in the days before he took office differently: "There was universal misbranding, universal exaggeration of qualities, and universal adulteration. Honest manufacturers were forced by fear of bankruptcy to follow the example set by the dishonest ones. Strawberry jam, for instance, with artificial coloring, ethereal salt for flavoring, and a few seeds of hay to imitate the berry seeds. What was true of foods was also true of beverages and drugs. And the misstatements on the labels concerned not only the contents but also the place of manufacture and the identity of the manufacturer." Asked what this meant for the average consumer, Wiley responded, "Why, universal dyspepsia, of course," referring to the common name for stomach trouble in the late nineteenth century. "And also an enormous increase in kidney diseases."[20] Contemporary research by state food commissioners at that time makes apparent that Wiley's assessment was exaggerated but not entirely off base.[21] It also raises the question of why Wiley didn't fight food adulteration harder and sooner.

One industry that attracted enormous attention from the pure food movement was bread making. Between 1850 and 1900, the number of commercial bakeries in America grew by 700 percent. Once women had baked the vast majority of bread loaves at home. Now it was done mostly in small, one-oven, commercial bakeries.[22] These new ventures could sell bread at prices so low that it no longer made economic sense for most families to bake at home.[23] Industrially produced, store-bought bread not only was convenient but also offered consumers far more variety than they ever could have hoped to produce themselves.

Unfortunately, many of the small local bakeries of the late nineteenth century were filthy. Factory inspectors and investigative journalists revealed unsanitary conditions in the bakeries in New York City. Union bakers described the conditions that prevailed when workers labored such long hours that they no longer cared about sanitation.[24] These conditions inspired pure-food reform. One attempt to regulate bakers' hours in New York State gave rise to the landmark Supreme Court case *Lochner v. New York*.[25] Although Harvey Wiley's chemical testing methods were designed to reveal adulteration rather than filth, in this era the pure food movement was as much about cleanliness as it was about deception.

Much of Wiley's government research during this period appeared in Bulletin No. 13, a series from the US Department of Agriculture's Division of Chemistry that was published gradually in many parts between 1887 and 1902.[26] The purpose of this and other reports that appeared during the 1890s was to reveal the extent of adulteration. If they found adulteration to be severe, Congress would presumably legislate against it eventually. Yet just determining whether a product was adulterated was difficult at that time.[27] Nonetheless, plenty of people in the late nineteenth century were willing to legislate against adulteration before they understood the full extent of the problem. Wiley's attitude was research first, legislate next—a stance that put him far from the forefront of the pure food movement. "It is hardly necessary to call attention here to the fact that the public ideas of adulteration of food are in many cases very much exaggerated," wrote Wiley in a prefatory note to a general report on food adulteration published in 1894, "and this, perhaps, is the cause of the many extravagant assertions which are made."[28] At this point, in other words, Wiley was hardly on a crusade.

The division's report *Lard and Lard Adulterations*, written by Wiley himself and published in 1889, shows further evidence of this conservative attitude. Lard, of course, was hog fat used as grease for cooking, separated from the animal's tissue by high heat. In the late nineteenth century it was commonly cut with less expensive substances like cottonseed oil, beef tallow, or other tissues from the animal that couldn't be sold separately. Wiley figured out how to detect the presence of these adulterants through chemical analysis even though the physical differences between pure lard and adulterated lard could be essentially invisible to the naked eye. Indeed, the entire study proved inconclusive in the sense that Wiley could not determine the degree of adulteration for any particular sample of lard that he and his chemists examined.[29]

The scope of the lard study clearly demonstrates Wiley's priorities with respect to pure food. "It is not within the scope of this report," he wrote, "to consider whether lard or olive oil, when adulterated with cottonseed is necessarily unwholesome. The vital fact is that in paying from 40 to 50 cents per kilogram and 30 [percent] duty on American cottonseed as olive oil, the people of the United States are submitting to a wholesale fraud, the proportions of which are increasing year by year."[30] Deception angered Wiley. If the threat to the health of the consumer concerned him then, he could have considered that too, but he didn't.

When Wiley's long series of bulletins about adulteration were released, they attracted little press attention. Their chief contribution to the debate was to convince the Association of Official Agricultural Chemists, which Wiley himself had founded in 1884, to join the movement for reform.[31] Summary articles appeared in a few newspapers on occasion, but the real action of the pure food movement remained elsewhere. For example, in 1896 Professor W. E. Stone of the Chemistry Department at Wiley's old employer, Purdue, told one audience that "nearly every article of food was systematically adulterated" and that "most all green goods were covered with poisonous metals."[32] These scare tactics did more to expand the pure food movement at this stage of its development than Wiley's measured research did. Wiley adopted such scare tactics only later, after he began his Poison Squad experiments.

Despite Wiley's relative conservatism, his research during this period served as an important foundation for future legislation: without understanding the extent of the problem, Congress might never have acted. Apart from the Division of Chemistry's findings, Wiley created the research techniques needed to investigate the purity of food. Wiley's work both standardized and improved the methods of chemical analysis for agricultural products. He created new equipment and developed new methods. He spread the word about his innovations in a pathbreaking multivolume study of the subject, *Principles and Practice of Agricultural Analysis*.[33]

It would have been difficult for Wiley to have been as militant as the rest of the pure food movement in the 1890s; his government job in a then poorly staffed office involved many other agricultural chemistry problems besides food adulteration. The Division of Chemistry had to do analysis for the rest of the Department of Agriculture. It remained closely involved in the development of a domestic sugar beet industry for much of this decade. Wiley himself was interested in analyzing soil samples from around the country to aid farmers. The Division of Chemistry even started an extended study of the nature of America's sewage.[34] The reports Wiley wrote or directed included many complaints about the work involved in producing them and the delays caused by lack of funds or personnel.

In the 1890s the Division of Chemistry was too small to be much help to the national pure food movement. In 1888 there was one chemist (Wiley), two assistant chemists, seven laboratory assistants, and three other employees. In 1897 the division employed twenty people.[35] While this size was impressive compared with other government departments during this era, Wiley had no reputation among the general public. He was an important chemist by virtue of his position with the Department of Agriculture, but he was by no stretch of the imagination the leader of an important social movement.[36] Harvey Wiley remained a relatively obscure government bureaucrat for most of his first two decades in Washington. Once Wiley's position on food adulteration became more militant, new employees were in place to do the research needed to encourage passage of the PFDA and help enforce the law when it became operational. But when Harvey Wiley turned fifty years old in 1894, all of his fame still lay ahead of him.

Some evolution in Wiley's thinking about pure food is apparent in his public speeches from the 1890s. At first he was overwhelmingly concerned with identifying adulteration so that consumers could avoid such goods if they so chose. By the end of the decade, while that concern remained his primary one, he nonetheless expressed far stronger support for a national pure food law. Still, it was not until after he began the Poison Squad experiments in 1902 that he even considered that adulterations could be unhealthful. At no point did he take the radical positions that he would after the Pure Food and Drug Act passed in 1906. In other words, throughout the 1890s Wiley remained a follower in the pure food movement rather than a leader.

Wiley's primary emphasis on the deceptive qualities of adulteration was particularly prominent in an 1894 speech he delivered at the Franklin Institute in Philadelphia. For much of the lecture, Wiley reviewed the various state laws in place at that time, describing their effectiveness in limited areas. Near the end of the speech, however, he emphasized the dangers of exaggerating the problem of adulteration, quoting the *Philadelphia Star*, which had raised the prospect of poisons in candy and attributed this information to the Division of Chemistry. "The above startling facts in regard to adulteration," he declared, "which are attributed to the Department of Agriculture, are worthy of especial notice because not one of them was ever abstracted from any report of the Department. . . . Thus it is seen that the popular idea of adulteration is really very much at fault and this has been due largely to the exaggerated statements of presumably honest men who desire to call attention to the fraud and prevent it by exciting the popular mind against it."[37] There is no better evidence of Wiley's initial conservatism on the pure food issue than this speech. This sentiment sounds like someone cautioning against Wiley's hysteria after the Poison Squad experiments began rather than Wiley himself.

Wiley remained relatively conservative about the risks of food adulteration even closer to the start of the Poison Squad experiments. In 1898 the National Pure Food and Drug Congress met in Washington, DC. The call to that congress, as reproduced in its proceedings, read, in part, "Adulteration, misbranding, sophistication, substitution and imitation undoubtedly exist to an alarming extent, to the detriment of health, legitimate business and sound morals, and it becomes needful to secure legislation that will check this growing evil and permit an honest man to do an honest business." One speaker at the congress, a US representative from Pennsylvania who had introduced his own pure food bill during the previous session, called the effort against adulteration part of a "holy war."[38]

Another speaker at this congress was Harvey Wiley. His speech stood out for its moderation, focusing far more on the scope of the problem than on its danger.[39] "Right at the start I may say there is an exaggerated idea with regard to food adulteration," he told the crowd. "We heard it stated that almost every article in the pantry, every article of food that goes to our table is adulterated." In fact, Wiley explained, although every article of food could in theory be adulterated, he estimated that only 25 to 30 percent of what people ate had actually been adulterated. With respect to a pure food law, Wiley stated, "I believe prohibitory measures never prohibit. If we are going to prohibit things we are going to fail." Wiley went as far as to suggest that he was willing to ingest additives like salts of copper or salicylic acid, substances that in just a few years he would work strenuously to ban entirely.[40] He also suggested that adulteration sometimes made food taste better.[41]

By 1901 Wiley's thinking had still not quite caught up with the rest of the pure food movement. "When a public audience hears a discussion on food adulteration it is likely to form wrong notions in regard to the extent of this evil," he wrote in the journal *The Medical Age*. "Exaggerated impressions are formed, and expression is often given to them. One would think from some of the articles which have appeared in the newspapers that it would be quite impossible to secure a pure food in any of the markets of the United States. Nothing could be more erroneous than this idea."[42] Ironically, a little more than a year later, Wiley himself would be providing the copy for such articles. This change came because of his experience with the Poison Squad.

———

Besides the other work in his office, Wiley's interest in socializing kept him from becoming a bigger force in the movement. In 1883, long before he became famous, Harvey Wiley joined the Cosmos Club, then located in downtown Washington, DC. Founded in 1878, the private club had a membership consisting of men devoted to science, literature, and the arts. It was a good place for Wiley to socialize with other scientists who found themselves working in a town devoted almost exclusively to politics.[43] Wiley was sponsored for membership in the club by the chemist Frank Clarke (whom Wiley later described as the only man he knew in Washington) and the explorer John Wesley Powell. Wiley later called Powell "the best one-armed billiard player I ever saw."[44]

Over time Wiley became one of the most important members of this organization. He chaired its House Committee, which oversaw food, drinks, and entertainment. He ordered its milk, meat, and even water so that he could be certain that they entirely pure. He arranged for the milk to be periodically tested to ensure that the dairy delivered only the pure article. He later served as president of the club. Most important, at least in Wiley's later view, he used his knowledge of alcohol to select the Cosmos Club's liquor supply: "At the end of my service on the House Committee the Cosmos bar was famous all over the world. One beverage which became quite popular bore the name of Wiley scotch."[45]

Early in its history the club had a number of different locations, moving around Washington as the club expanded and better buildings became available, but all were close enough that Wiley could walk there for lunch almost every day that he was in town. "I was so well satisfied to be a member of this club that I didn't take time to get married until I was sixty-seven years old," Wiley remembered. "In those days, as I had no place to go, except to the club, I used to spend all my evenings [there], when not otherwise occupied, and sometimes I stayed until the wee small hours."[46] Despite such sentiments, Wiley's failure to get married was not for want of trying, and his attempts, at the time he made them, appeared both scandalous and a little sad.

In 1900, before his role in the pure food movement really took off, the trustees of Purdue University, his former employer, considered Harvey Wiley to fill the job of university president. Obviously, the job was prestigious and would have paid well, and he told a friend he would consider taking it if asked. However, rumors of religious infidelity prevented the opportunity from getting past the initial stages. "I believe in the church and its work," Wiley wrote when informed of this threat to his reputation, "but am no longer a member because of my inability to believe in dogma. I consider a hypocrite as a thousand time worse than an infidel."[47] While this was not a surprising stance for a scientist, it was for a public servant.

After all this time the source of those rumors is impossible to identify, but it seems quite possible that they derived not from Wiley's lack of church attendance, but from his behavior with women—both at Purdue and in Washington, where he maintained his status as a notorious ladies' man.[48] Wiley may have seen many women during these years, but he proved just as unlucky in love as he was in Indiana. In 1884 Wiley was engaged to Myla Charles, a woman half his age. That romance broke up about four years later in mutual acrimony, and his former fiancée died soon afterward. Wiley was also involved with a successful female chemist from Philadelphia, Helen Abbott. She cut the relationship short because of his efforts to control her. By the 1890s Wiley saw a wide range of women rather than pursuing one with marriage specifically in mind.[49] "The chemist's friends accused him of having a regiment of the prettiest girls in Washington," wrote Wiley's first biographer. "He did not deny the charge."[50] Given that Wiley's residence from 1886 until his marriage in 1911 was a rented room in the modest Washington home of Mr. and Mrs. R. V. Belt, much of Wiley's social activity likely occurred in public, a situation that would have fed more rumors.[51]

One of the women he met during the 1890s became his wife ten years later. Anna Campbell Kelton, whose father had been adjutant general of the US Army, was a librarian at the Department of Agriculture. A later description of her as "extremely slight, with a quick color in her cheeks and [the] frank manner of a nevertheless shy child" probably applied even more in her early twenties.[52] Wiley, who later claimed that he had been instantly smitten with her, had her transferred to the Division of Chemistry, where she served for two years as his private secretary.[53] When he proposed, she considered the offer but ultimately rejected it because her parents disapproved and she thought he was too old for her. (Their age difference was thirty-three years.)[54]

While Wiley was on his way to Europe for one of his usual summer trips, she transferred to the Copyright Office at the Library of Congress. "When I left for Paris I had a perfect understanding with her but I had not been here long before I received a very sensible letter from her saying that she had concluded that our agreement had better be terminated," he wrote to a friend around that time. Despite their age difference, he concluded, "I have yet to learn that loving a pretty girl in a proper way and being loved by her in return has anything blameworthy in it." Anna's decision to break off their engagement by letter, along with her failure to respond to Wiley's response to that letter, suggests how persuasive the chemist could be when given the opportunity to make his case.[55]

Wiley's personal life is just one of the wide range of distractions that kept him away from organizing on behalf of national pure food legislation. Wiley was a research chemist, and many of his publications dealt with the practice of agriculture rather than food per se. Wiley had founded the Association of Official Agricultural Chemists in 1884 as part of his work at the Department of Agriculture. His success in that work helped inspire the restructuring of the American Chemical Society along national lines during the early 1890s, and in 1892 he became its president.[56] Wiley also assumed local leadership roles in two other professional societies. He attended numerous congresses of chemists from around the world, no matter where they happened to be held. Starting in 1893 Wiley held a part-time job as a professor of agricultural chemistry at the Columbian University, now known as George Washington University, where he taught an evening class and read graduate theses.[57]

Wiley's boss, James Wilson, began his service as secretary of agriculture in 1897. He would continue in that job until 1913, making him the longest-serving cabinet secretary in American history. Wilson was a Scottish immigrant and an Iowa farmer who understood little about chemistry. A firm believer in applied agricultural science, he wanted government scientists to improve the lives of American farmers by solving the specific problems they faced. Wiley greatly benefited from this attitude during Wilson's early years, expanding his division (later his bureau) and gaining increasing attention from a press that was genuinely interested in reporting on his research.[58] In 1901 the Division of Chemistry became the Bureau of Chemistry, netting Wiley an extra $500 per year in salary to spend on his various pursuits.[59]

The following year Wiley began his work on what would be dubbed the Poison Squad experiments. These experiments changed how the problem of food adulteration was discussed in Washington and across the country. The experiments captured the public imagination in a way that scientific papers never could, and the attention they stimulated promoted Wiley's chosen cause, flattered his ego, and helped expand his power within government, all at the same time. As his media skills improved, Wiley would become a household name. The experiments began with boric acid, or borax, a common preservative for meat, which was then, as it is now, at the center of nearly every American meal.

❖ CHAPTER FIVE ❖

MEAT

IN 1899 THE UNITED STATES ARMY began investigating the meat that large Chicago packers had provided to soldiers fighting during the Spanish-American War of the previous year. General Nelson A. Miles had charged that the product was so full of chemical preservatives that it was essentially "embalmed." Secretary of agriculture James Wilson instructed Harvey Wiley to examine the canned and refrigerated meat from the same sources that had provisioned soldiers during the war. Wiley found no evidence of harmful chemical preservatives and cited inadequate refrigeration in the tropical climate of the Caribbean as the main source of the problems with the food.[1] A military investigation that included public testimony from Wiley himself corroborated this finding. In truth, the accusations of tainted beef came from a single source, a Pittsburgh physician serving as a volunteer surgeon who was a friend of Miles. The beef was of poor quality, not poisoned. Nonetheless, the scandal stayed in the popular press for many months,[2] demonstrating consumers' fears of industrial food production.[3] Just a few years later, after the beginning of his infamous Poison Squad experiments, Wiley would exploit these same fears.

Even before those experiments had run their course, the "embalmed beef" controversy led to passage of several pure food laws at the state level.[4] Newspapers greatly increased their scrutiny of preservatives in foods of all kinds.[5] In 1899 Congress began a series of hearings on the issue of food adulteration chaired by Senator William Mason of Illinois. Testifying at these hearings, Wiley claimed that 5 percent of all foods were routinely adulterated, and he singled out coffee and spices as foods where the practice was particularly prevalent. The press repeated Wiley's claim that 90 percent of these two kinds of food were invariably adulterated but incorrectly applied that figure to all foods.[6] In this climate of fear, Congress allocated $5,000 to the Department of Agriculture so the Division of Chemistry could investigate the exact effects of chemical preservatives on human health.[7]

This allocation was part of Wiley's concerted effort to raise the profile of the Division of Chemistry itself. As late as 1897, Wiley's bureaucratic area had had significant problems. With a secretary of agriculture committed to austerity, the department had closed four agricultural experiment stations around the country. Many of Wiley's assistants had left for jobs in private industry because of their low salaries. Wiley had trouble finding good assistants who could do what he wanted them to do and who would work as hard as he did.[8] Yet even before his lobbying on behalf of the Pure Food and Drug Act (PFDA) picked up, Wiley managed to reverse this trend. In 1897 the Division of Chemistry had 20 employees. By 1902 that number had risen to 70, and in 1906 it was 110. In 1897 the Division of Chemistry's entire budget had been $29,500. By 1906 it had risen to $155,000.[9]

By 1905 Wiley had reorganized his division, by then called the Bureau of Chemistry, into nine divisions that reflected the scope of its work: Division of Foods, Sugar and Starch Laboratory, Dairy Laboratory, Drug Laboratory, Contracts Laboratory (which conducted chemical tests for other government departments), Plant Analysis Laboratory, Microchemical Laboratory, and the Leather and Paper Laboratory. The final laboratory, the Miscellaneous Laboratory, investigated products like insecticides and cattle food.[10] All of this growth in activity came before the PFDA, and once the Department of Agriculture set up the infrastructure to enforce that law's provisions, even greater growth followed.

After the turn of the twentieth century, the effects of food additives on human health—a question of safety rather than morality—moved to the center of the pure food debate, and Wiley moved with it.[11] In July 1902 Wiley told a new subordinate, "There has been too much argument about the effect of chemical preservatives on health. I propose to find out by scientific experimentation what is the truth about a question of such vital concern to the consumers of the nation. Some day we will have a law."[12] In the larger context of his life, Wiley went from researching ways to detect food adulteration to the effects of that adulteration on the people who ate

FIGURE 5.1 William Carter served as both cook and waiter during the Poison Squad experiments. His willingness to talk to reporters when Wiley wouldn't brought enough publicity to the experiment that Wiley changed his mind about talking to the press. Wiley's skill at bringing attention to his causes kept him famous for the rest of his life. Carter went on to become a lab technician, retiring from the agency then known as the Food and Drug Administration in 1946.

Courtesy US Food and Drug Administration

those products. By studying the safety of preservatives, Wiley helped to build enough pressure on Congress to get a pure food law passed (although whether those studies were accurate is another question). Moreover, Wiley would employ the lessons he learned about manipulating the media to advance his own career through the rest of his life. The Poison Squad experiments turned Harvey Wiley from an obscure government scientist into a household name.

Wiley began the Poison Squad experiments with boric acid (or borax), a preservative often used on meat and dairy products in the years before refrigeration became widespread. Wiley started with this preservative because it was the easiest one for chemists to detect in human tissue. Although the chemists in his bureau knew chemistry, they had no experience conducting this kind of study, so it was important to start with a preservative that was easy to detect chemically.[13] Borax, which has almost no taste, was commonly used to preserve fish, butter, and meats of all kinds. Mixed in with other foods, it was impossible to distinguish.[14]

The design of the Poison Squad experiments depended upon being able to document everything that the subjects ate, including the amount of any chemical that Wiley happened to be testing. The methods that Wiley developed during the borax experiment became the model for every subsequent study. At first, the cook hid the borax in the butter. The young men, suspecting the location of the borax, stopped eating butter. When the cook tried placing the borax in the subjects' coffee, they stopped drinking coffee. As a result, the subjects were compelled to swallow the borax in pill form in the middle of the meal. After a few days, several of the subjects began to experience stomach trouble. Those troubles grew worse over time. While everyone survived the experience, nobody escaped the exercise without some form of distress, ranging from loss of appetite to an inability to do any work at all.[15]

Before the borax experiment had even begun, Wiley frequently talked about it to the press, and reporters took a keen interest. Shortly after the first experiment started, all the subjects' names leaked to the press. The initial press reports attracted more reporters. While the public's strong interest in the subject of pure foods meant that reporters visited Wiley often, a series of *Washington Post* articles by a young reporter named George

Rothwell Brown single-handedly turned the experiments into a public sensation. According to Wiley, Brown frequently visited the participants in this first experiment and published some kind of anecdote or story about them nearly every day.[16]

In his initial articles, Brown reported the events in a neutral tone, describing how the experiments would be conducted and quoting Wiley on the scientific importance of these efforts. By Christmas, however, the stories had taken a humorous turn as Brown started to interview Wiley's "boarders." One of the participants allegedly told him that the cook wanted more money because he used to be the head chef for the Queen of Bavaria.[17] Indeed, a spirit of levity overhung the entire experiment. "Only the brave dare eat the fare" became the unofficial but posted motto of the Poison Squad shortly after the experiment began.[18]

Brown's frequent use of the term "poison" in his articles explains why the group came to be known as the Poison Squad, despite Wiley's initial opposition to the name. Putting the word "poison" in the headlines of Brown's articles, which were widely syndicated, was a great way to draw attention.[19] By March 1903 Brown was almost certainly making up quotes to attract further publicity. On March 25 he published a long dialogue about an alleged revolt among the test subjects. Some of the boarders, supposedly, refused to eat meat during Lent. Because borax was used as a preservative primarily for meat, his story suggests that they were on an all-meat diet.[20] In fact, however, they could eat a varied diet because by that time Wiley had switched to giving them the borax in capsule form.

At one point Wiley thought he might abandon the experiments because of the publicity. There were reports that people pointed to him on the street and said, "There goes the man that runs Uncle Sam's Cooking School." Others allegedly called him "Borax" to his face.[21] His boss, Secretary Wilson, ordered him to stop talking to reporters. Wiley did so for a time, but reporters came to depend upon William R. Carter, the cook for the experiment, to get anecdotes that kept the Poison Squad in the news.[22] Gradually, Wiley realized that reporters would cover the experiments no matter what he did, so he might as well get them to write what he wanted them to write. Thereafter he started taking select members of the press into his confidence.[23]

The borax experiment ended in June 1903. Wiley repeated a similar-structured experiment with salicylic acid starting in October of that same year.[24] Before the experiment began, Wiley thought borax was "no more harmful than common salt," but after the experiments he concluded that its use should be restricted to situations where it was an absolute necessity. On June 23, 1904, when Wiley submitted the bureau's final report on the borax experiment to Secretary Wilson, the recommendation was much stronger. "It appears," Wiley wrote, "that both boric acid and borax, when continuously administered in small doses for a long period or when given in large quantities over a short period, create disturbances of appetite, of digestion, and of health."[25] Altogether the Poison Squad experiments changed Wiley's mind about the dangers of a lot more than just preservatives. In this way, Wiley's change of heart about the health effects of borax had major ramifications for his career as a civil servant, turning him into a major force in the battle for the Pure Food and Drug Act.

———

"The use of preservatives in food is as old as civilization," wrote Wiley at the beginning of his report on the borax experiment.[26] The use of chemical preservatives spiked in the wake of the development of synthetic organic chemistry in Germany during the 1870s. By 1900 the Department of Agriculture reported 152 patented chemical preservatives on the market.[27] Unlike earlier methods of preservation, these substances usually did not change the taste of the product when present in small quantities. Consequently, their use could not be detected unless the food products were analyzed. This reality opened the possibility of government involvement to inform consumers about the true nature of the products they consumed.

Borax, the crystallized version of boric acid, is sometimes known as sodium borate, sodium tetraborate, or disodium tetraborate. Borax has always had many uses. Today it is used as a household cleaner, a laundry detergent, a fire retardant, an ingredient in cosmetics, and even a substitute for mercury to extract gold from gold ore. Before the late nineteenth century, people used it primarily for medicinal purposes. Doctors used borax to treat labor pains, menstruation troubles, and even diarrhea.[28] "We find [borax] the very best cockroach exterminator yet discovered," reported *Manufacturer and Builder* in 1871. (It is still the main ingredient in many ant poisons. Consuming boric acid prevents ants from processing the nutrients in food.) *Manufacturer and Builder* also reported that borax was "perfectly harmless to human beings," which explains why human beings would consider consuming it themselves, even if only as a by-product of the food preservation process.[29]

Borax is mined from lake beds, hills, and marshes in volcanic regions throughout the world. John Veatch discovered the first US borax deposits in California in 1858 in a dry lake bed. Since California's borax was often mixed with other minerals (and often mud or sand) when found in nature, borax crystals had to be extracted, crushed, and ground, and it took time to develop an industry there.[30] In 1882 William T. Coleman built two borax works near Death Valley. In 1890 he sold out to Francis Marion "Borax" Smith, who founded the Pacific Coast Borax Company, the largest firm in the United States at that time. He named the product 20 Mule Team Borax because the product was moved from the mines in Death Valley to the railroad using teams of twenty mules. Although the company first sold the product as soap, people quickly began to use it for other household cleaning purposes.[31]

Spurred by increasing demand and the discovery of new beds in San Bernardino and Ventura Counties, borax production in California increased from 24,304 pounds a year in 1864 to more than a million pounds a year in 1900. The first international borax syndicate started in 1898.[32] Increased production of borax worldwide pushed the price down significantly, from between 28 and 35 cents a pound before 1872 to between 5 and 8 cents a pound by 1905.[33] During the 1890s, American newspapers regularly offered recipes that included borax as an ingredient. This prevalence led to the beginning of a borax backlash, and while the Pacific Coast Borax Company argued for the "absolute innocence" of its product, the press regularly condemned it as "vile stuff."[34]

American meatpackers first started using the newly cheap borax as the scale of their operations expanded. Beginning in the 1860s, Chicago became the center of meatpacking in America, and the meatpacking sector became an innovator with respect to industrialization. The large packers gradually set up what came to be known as a "disassembly line," in which workers took apart particular parts of carcasses in a carefully coordinated manner. By the 1870s the packers processed more than a million hogs each year. Ice refrigeration and refrigerated railway cars, which developed gradually during the 1870s and 1880s, played an important role in expanding the city's output to include beef cattle. By 1885, 292 million pounds of meat left Chicago on just one railway line.[35] However, the supply chains had holes in their refrigeration infrastructure between the point of production and the point of sale. Furthermore, ice provided at best only intermittent refrigeration, since it always melted. It became common practice to add borax to assure that most of the product made it to market in a sellable condition. Similarly, borax played an important role when American meatpackers started exporting their products. The packers put borax in the liquid used to pickle meat to prevent the meat from rotting when shipped long distances. The use of borax also allowed packers to significantly cut the time and expense needed to salt, pickle, or smoke meat.[36]

The use of borax on internationally traded meat became an issue during the 1890s, when some public health experts both in and out of the United States began to question its safety. Germany banned American meat treated with borax shortly before the start of the Poison Squad experiments.[37] The meat industry hoped that Wiley's research would redeem the reputation of their favored preservative. The use of borax was also an issue in the debate over the Meat Inspection Act of 1906 because it could be used to hide decay. "There was never the least attention paid to what was cut up for sausage," explained Upton Sinclair in his closely researched classic muckraking novel, *The Jungle*. "There would come back from Europe old sausage that had been rejected, and was mouldy and white—it would be dosed with borax and glycerine, and dumped into the hoppers, and would be made over again for home consumption."[38] Preservation in this manner was a form of deception.

After the passage of the Pure Food and Drug Act, Wiley's alarm about the purity of the meat supply grew. He began to argue that the presence of any borax in the American food supply constituted a slippery slope that threatened the health and safety of every consumer.[39] Unwilling to specify exact limits for chemical preservatives in the food supply, Wiley eventually took the position that their use should be banned entirely unless producers could prove that they were safe for humans to consume. "The accused meat must be considered guilty until proven innocent," he explained in one of the books he wrote after leaving government service. "If it is injurious in a single case conviction must ensue."[40] In other words, the government needed to regulate the food supply to protect the most sensitive people in the population, regardless of the price benefits or convenience supplied by chemically preserved food. This position made negotiating with food producers over the regulation of preservatives impossible. Instead, this was a declaration of war.

This position required public support, and over the course of the Poison Squad experiments, Wiley learned that an easy way to gain people's support was to scare them. Here, however, Wiley had to tread a fine line. People had to be concerned enough to cede authority to the government—and specifically to the Bureau of Chemistry—to regulate the food supply. Yet no one's interests were served if the public became too scared and ceased to trust anything that they purchased rather than grew themselves. Wiley capitalized on the pure food movement to attract attention, but he wasn't using a practical definition of purity.

———

Eventually, the story of the Poison Squad became a joke, though a dark one. This combination of mirth and menace propelled the experiments into the popular culture. For example, Lew Dockstader introduced a comedic tribute to the Poison Squad into his minstrel show in October 1903. The first verse of Dockstader's song explained that

> If you ever visit the Smithsonian Institute,
> Look out that Professor Wiley doesn't make you a recruit.
> He's got a lot of fellows there that tell him how they feel—
> They take a batch of poison every time they take a meal.
> For breakfast they get cyanide of liver, coffin shaped.
> For dinner they get undertaker's pie all trimmed with crepe.
> For supper—arsenic fritters, fried in appetizing shade,
> And late at night they get a prussic acid lemonade.[41]

Wiley contributed to the mirth surrounding the Poison Squad by releasing letters from what he deemed his "crank file" in 1905. The *Washington Star* noted that Wiley had received a large number of letters from hoboes. "The fact that the food may contain a little poison," the paper noted, "hasn't deterred them from offering themselves as subjects for the experiments. What they are after is the gratuitous grub, and that grub three times a day."[42] Wiley took some reporters, especially Brown, into his confidence, feeding them exclusive facts about the experiments, as the *Washington Star*'s access to his crank file clearly demonstrated.

On July 21, 1903, shortly after the close of the borax tests, before the legitimacy of the tests had been widely been accepted by the public, Harvey Wiley spoke about the tests before the National Association of State Dairy and Food Commissioners in Saint Paul, Minnesota. "Our object has solely been to ascertain the facts," he explained, "to establish them if possible beyond cavil, to collate them in what seems a scientific and reasonable manner, and at the end to draw such conclusions as judgment, uninfluenced by prejudice, would approve."[43] Wiley later explained his position by saying, "I changed my mind as the result of my investigations here. I honestly believed that borax and boracic acid could be used without any danger or any consequence."[44] Taken together, these quotations show the impression that Wiley wanted to leave—that of a disinterested scientific observer who changed his mind after analyzing the evidence his experiment provided. However, Wiley's evaluation of his own disinterest doesn't hold up under modern scientific scrutiny.

Most notably, none of Wiley's Poison Squad experiments used a control group. Wiley told a Congressional committee, "You may ask how we knew that any disturbance produced was due to borax, and I answer because we eliminated all the variables but that one." To explain this position, he pointed to the similar life, food, and jobs of the participants in the borax experiment—but that's not how control groups work.[45] Eliminating all the variables in this experiment would have required giving some participants a placebo rather than borax and, perhaps more important, ensuring that they didn't know to which group they belonged.[46]

To be fair to Wiley, the very first experiments with control groups were being conducted right around the time that the Poison Squad tests began.[47] Whether he knew about them is impossible to establish, but it is unquestionable that Wiley did not think he needed to structure his experiment differently because he still believed that he could control for all the variables without using control groups. The *American Food Journal*, noting that these experiments were controversial in scientific circles from the moment the borax results were released, called on other scientists to duplicate the results "without brass band accompaniment" before Wiley's research became the basis for regulation.[48] Nonetheless, decades after the experiment, when control groups had become a necessary and universally accepted scientific tool, Wiley insisted that he had controlled every variable.[49]

Without a control group, there was no clear starting point for comparison. When all subjects knew they were getting borax, the incentive to complain was increased because they knew for certain that something was different about their diets. Moreover, complaining of stomach troubles meant that a subject would be temporarily released from the experiment.[50] This incentivized anyone who wanted to stop eating at the Department of Agriculture's so-called Hygienic Table to fake stomach pain. The Poison Squad members who remained got periodic vacations during which they could go back to eating normal food—meaning that the environment was not nearly as controlled as Wiley made out in his speeches.[51] Furthermore, the subjects may have gotten sick for other reasons. A borax company publicist who visited the "Hygienic Table" claimed it was far from hygienic, calling it "dark" and "gloomy," with "malodorous odors . . . everywhere," and many other visitors corroborated this assessment. Wiley's response to this criticism was to attack the publicist for looking in his icebox rather than denying the charges.[52]

Wiley's Poison Squad experiments didn't even pass muster by the standards for scientific research at that time. Wiley got the idea for the Poison Squad experiments from the German Imperial Health Board.[53] Nevertheless, the German chemist Oscar Liebreich was particularly scathing in his review of Wiley's work on borax. He concluded that the experiments

were badly planned, that the increased amount of borax could not necessarily be used to draw conclusions about how people would respond to the
preservative at lower doses, and that the long-term effects of borax might
be different in the comparatively tiny amounts that normal people regularly consumed. Commenting on the final report, he concluded that "very
strange remarks are to be found, which cannot be reconciled with the present position of natural science criticism, but which lead to the very thing
that scientific observation wishes to avoid, the admission of a subjective
opinion." This accusation of predetermined bias would become the common scientific criticism of all of Wiley's Poison Squad experiments.[54]

Anyone judging the validity of Wiley's results must also consider the conduct of the test subjects. Wiley claimed to put absolute faith in the pledges
they signed to limit their food intake to substances that had been weighed
and measured by his staff at the Department of Agriculture.[55] At least one
participant later claimed that he and other members of the Poison Squad
would sneak out of the building and go on binges downtown when Wiley
was out of Washington.[56] Test subjects may also have been unconsciously
influenced by the publicity surrounding the experiment. They had signed
a contract. They knew the purpose of the experiment and were continually
interviewed by the press. With respect to that publicity, a physiologist from
Cornell later wrote, "The young men who were the victims must have been
more than human not to have been influenced mentally by this course of
their chief."[57] Wiley's own bias also should have been a cause for concern.
Modern experiments like this would be double-blind, meaning that neither
the subjects nor the experiment's designers would know who was getting the
test substance and who was going without. Wiley had already expressed an
interest in passing a pure food law. That interest would only grow stronger
over time. He was not an unbiased observer of the results.

The way Wiley interpreted the results of the experiment was designed
to get the public to reach a particular conclusion about borax. Those results
suggested that people could ingest a few grams of borax a day before getting
sick, while also acknowledging that most people who habitually ate butter
and meat preserved with borax would consume just over half a gram a day.[58]
So while the experiment may have determined how much borax it took to

make someone sick, it did nothing to show whether a lower amount was a long-term health threat. Wiley's evidence for ill effects of borax on his subjects was not the appearance of cancer; it was stomach trouble—poor digestion, cramps, or maybe vomiting.

Wiley's intransigence on borax gave defenders of the preservative an opening. Those defenders pointed to the widespread use of the preservative with no apparent ill effects (and its widespread use also suggested its general necessity). After all, nobody in real life had gotten noticeably sick after consuming borax in the amounts found on preserved food. That alone may explain why Wiley was practically alone in the world scientific community in condemning borax at that time. Many similar experiments investigating the effects of borax on humans had completely acquitted the substance.[59] As a modern doctor looking back at the Poison Squad reports concluded, "Wiley's collated data, a hodgepodge of subjective commentary, was entirely lacking in precision."[60]

Wiley's course of action can best be explained by political concerns rather than efforts to methodically collect scientific data. He wanted to scare the public enough about chemical preservatives so they would pressure their representatives to support the passage of a strong pure food law. After the passage of that law, he wanted to scare them enough to get them to support the strict enforcement regime he favored.

Over time, the problem Wiley faced was that the damage caused by borax was not enough to achieve his desired goals. Since nobody had died from ingesting that supposed poison, Wiley argued that small amounts of borax built up over time.[61] Even the borax that was expelled, he suggested, still did damage while it was present in the body. Given that different subjects consumed different total amounts of borax over the life of his experiment, his later assertion that the cumulative effects of borax were deadly does not hold water. Yet, despite the many problems with Wiley's Poison Squad experiments, the idea behind them proved popular in scientific circles for decades, demonstrating Wiley's influence.[62]

The borax experiment got the most attention of all the Poison Squad experiments because it came first, and it became Wiley's scientific modus operandi. Over the next five years, Wiley used this same general method to test the effects of salicylic acid, sulfites, benzoic acid, and formaldehyde on similar willing volunteers. Wiley had started with borax because he thought it would be easiest to work with and he expected the effects of borax on the human system to be benign. He would go on to conclude the exact opposite. Indeed, every preservative he tested had a negative effect on human health.[63] With the exception of salicylic acid, which Wiley found less hazardous than he had expected, he eventually recommended that each of these products be banned from the American food supply, arguing that preservatives were unnecessary when manufacturers made their food well.[64]

After the passage of the Pure Food and Drug Act, Wiley quickly moved to ban borax and boric acid from the food supply, a decision supported by Secretary Wilson.[65] In 1907 Wiley insisted that the ban had improved business because customers got better meat.[66] By that time, however, the general use of borax to preserve meat was negligible. Wiley's experiments had destroyed its reputation, and local governments often banned it on that basis.[67] Small-scale producers had used borax to preserve some perishable foods, and the turn against borax forced them to use ice. Before the PFDA, the southern shrimp industry, for example, had used borax to preserve its product on the long journey to northern markets. The Bureau of Chemistry, faced with complaints from shrimpers that using ice as a preservative would destroy their industry, investigated the situation and showed shrimpers how using ice packs instead of borax would increase their costs only marginally.[68] The price of shrimp went up with the shift to ice, but so did quality. In a 1911 case brought by the Hipolite Egg Company of St. Louis, which used borax to preserve its pre-prepared eggs, the Supreme Court ruled in favor of the government and refused to strike down the Pure Food and Drug Act.[69]

The historical significance of Wiley's borax experiment lies more in its effect on Americans' attitude toward chemicals in their food than in its effect on this particular preservative. Modern research suggests that borax is not particularly dangerous when consumed in small amounts.[70] Had the first Poison Squad experiment never happened, improvements in refrigeration technology would eventually have led meatpackers to stop using the preservative. The borax tests and the subsequent Pure Food and Drug Act merely hastened the transition from borax and ice to a full mechanically refrigerated supply chain for meat. Wiley, however, pioneered a view of food safety based on whether a substance was pure or not. From the first Poison Squad experiment on, there was no in between. Substances that could do any consumer the slightest harm were deemed impure and worthy of being banned from the nation's food supply by any means necessary, even if those substances were perfectly natural. This attitude has been widely adopted ever since.

Another legacy of Wiley's borax experiment was the impact of the Poison Squad publicity on the eventual passage of the Pure Food and Drug Act. Even apparently bad publicity served to make Wiley famous. This fame increased the number of speaking invitations he received, which in turn gave him more opportunities to advocate for a pure food law.[71] Even though Wiley found nothing wrong with the meat he examined in the wake of the "embalmed beef" scandal, issues with the American meat supply continued to garner the attention of muckrakers like Upton Sinclair.[72] Sinclair is often credited with single-handedly getting the Pure Food and Drug Act and the Meat Inspection Act passed because of the fact-based sections about conditions in Chicago's Packingtown in his novel *The Jungle*. Ultimately, there were many reasons the Pure Food and Drug Act passed when it did. Upton Sinclair's book was one of them, and Harvey Wiley's efforts were another, but exactly how influential those efforts were deserves close examination.

CHAPTER SIX

PURE FOOD

I N 1904 HARVEY WILEY ADDRESSED the convention of the National Association of State Dairy and Food Departments. In his speech, he came out against substituting saccharin for sugar in canned food because it was deceptive. When the consumer "does not so demand it" and expects to get sugar instead, Wiley said, "then there is no moral right or legal right to add saccharin to food."[1] This argument, as Wiley later told the story, was enough to turn the canners dead set against his having any role in the oversight of a pure food law. At a convention in Philadelphia before the passage of the Pure Food and Drug Act (PFDA), one canner declared that he did not want Wiley to become a "dictator" with the power to control that industry. Wiley, in turn, argued that it was in the canner's best interest to support pure food because the American public demanded goods they could trust; without such assurances they would cease to buy.[2] During the years immediately following the enactment of the PFDA, canners gradually came around to Wiley's position and eventually became staunch supporters of Wiley's efforts to enforce that law.[3]

The PFDA passed Congress because Harvey Wiley and other reformers managed to bring together a disparate set of interest groups in support of that legislation. Wiley brought the canners to his side by pitting the "honest" canners who didn't use saccharin and other preservatives against the ones who did.[4] However, the canners who opposed Wiley were not necessarily opposed to pure food legislation. They were simply opposed to the kind of regulation that Wiley wanted to enact through his version of the law. When Wiley negotiated a version of the law that they found palatable, they willingly supported it. At the time it passed, Wiley understood that the PFDA was compromise legislation. Later, when he argued that the food law had been the victim of a crime, he conveniently forgot that fact.

Many historians have argued that large food manufacturers supported both Harvey Wiley and the PFDA because they sought a competitive advantage.[5] For example, manufacturers that could mass-produce food without potentially harmful preservatives could advertise the fact that their competitors' products might damage the health of the people who bought them.[6] While these incentives certainly existed, the idea that Wiley took the positions he did because of corporate influence is difficult to accept when one follows the evolution of Wiley's thinking about adulterated food. If Wiley were really influenced by corporate largesse, he would have taken a forceful stand against adulteration long before the Poison Squad experiments began. Only after the Poison Squad experiments started did Wiley become the public face of pure food. At that point, it became hard for him or anyone else to remember that he had ever played any other role.

Wiley's most tangible contribution to the passage of the Pure Food and Drug Act was the publicity generated by the Poison Squad experiments. Starting with the attention that George Rothwell Brown's articles in the *Washington Post* brought to his work, Wiley became increasingly interested in generating positive stories about the pure food movement and his role in it. Reporters were daily visitors at Wiley's offices in the Bureau of Chemistry in the years preceding and following the passage of the law, and Wiley invariably dropped everything to see them.[7] A reporter for *Scientific American*, profiling Wiley in 1911, wrote, "Dr. Wiley's greatest asset in his campaign for pure foods has been his ability to get into the papers. . . . There is not a newspaperman in Washington who does not fall back on Dr. Wiley whenever he has failed to get something to write elsewhere. It was through publicity that he finally got his message to the masses."[8] Before the Poison Squad experiments, Wiley was a follower in the pure food movement rather than a leader. After those experiments began, Wiley and his publicity machine made a much more significant contribution.

Wiley's efforts at public relations ruptured his relationship with Secretary Wilson. In a long, private 1910 letter to President William Howard Taft, Wilson complained, "Dr. Wiley gave out frequent interviews . . . that I regarded [as] unwise and new in research work. I thought that such work should be done quietly in the laboratories without calling in anyone to publish what was being done until results were reached, and so remonstrated with the Doctor regarding it, but it had no effect, and this new way of making research continued."[9] Wiley could get away with this kind of insubordination because his popularity with consumers and newspaper editors made him immune from discipline. Replying to a businessman who wanted Wiley fired, President Theodore Roosevelt wrote, "You don't understand, Sir, that Dr. Wiley has the grandest political machine in the country."[10] He built that machine using the publicity he obtained by scaring the public on behalf of both himself and his cause. As the pure food movement grew stronger, Wiley increasingly used the Poison Squad experiments as a cudgel rather than a source of scientific data.

The best example of this phenomenon was Wiley's practice of repeatedly criticizing preservatives based on test results that he hadn't yet published. This practice started with borax and continued with other experiments too. Wiley did not release the results for sulfurous acid (sulfuric acid)—a preservative best known at that time for its use on dried fruit—until 1907.[11] The sodium benzoate (benzoic acid) results were not published until 1908.[12] The results of the experiments on formaldehyde were also released in 1908.[13] In lieu of these finished reports, Wiley released partial, unprocessed data to a House committee considering the pure food bill in early 1906. For benzoic acid, he started to draw conclusions before testing had even begun. In that case, Wiley noted that every single subject got sick consuming benzoic acid at some point during the experiment.[14]

This strategy of condemning preservatives without published scientific confirmation of the evidence earned Wiley many professional critics among chemists. "We all believe in a pure food law," one chemist explained at a 1905 professional meeting in a statement that reflected the feelings of both scientists and many food processors. "But the tendency in Dr. Wiley is toward yellow journalism. We are creating a class of 'yellow chemistry.'"[15] The comparison with the journalists who sparked the Spanish-America War is not entirely apt because those newspapermen managed to create a war out of nothing. Wiley had legitimate concerns about the safety of the American food supply, but he was willing to blow those concerns up to unjustified proportions to inspire legislation and enforce the law as he saw fit. Wiley's opinions, as expressed in interviews and articles, shaped consumer food choices in ways that echo down to today. Indeed, he exercised far more influence over what Americans ate by scaring the public with his experiments than he did by helping to determine which additives were legal to use in the production of manufactured foods under the PFDA.

To be fair, Wiley never changed the results of his Poison Squad experiments between the time he conducted them and the time he released the results. What changed was his tolerance for risk. As his support for pure food legislation grew stronger, his acceptance of any level of risk disappeared. He understood that most people could consume the ordinary amounts of preservatives in food with no ill effects, yet Wiley came to believe that the government should ban any food additive that could potentially hurt anybody—including the very weakest people in society.[16]

To make that point stick, Wiley had to do everything possible to accentuate the adverse health effects that additives posed to the American public. Wiley thus came to argue that just about every additive in the food supply was poisonous. Moreover, in the battle over how to enforce the PFDA, Wiley repeatedly suggested that the government had a responsibility to make public safety its first priority. If every food additive were somehow dangerous, then the government would have to enforce the law very strictly. The substances Wiley decried eventually included not just the ones he tested during the Poison Squad experiments, whether results were published or not, but parts of the US food supply that he had never studied.

The further he got from subjects he knew well, the more likely he was to make pronouncements that appear absurd in retrospect. Before the passage of the PFDA, however, he exerted much of his influence behind the scenes.

———

Besides conducting and publicizing his experiments, Harvey Wiley pushed for passage of the pure food bill through his lobbying efforts. Much of this work involved coalition building—finding enough politicians and business interests to support the legislation without antagonizing opposing forces so much that they would raise a coalition of their own to defeat it. Wiley also organized pressure on Congress by participating in the pure food movement outside of Washington in the last years before the passage of the law. He was one of the organizers of a Pure Food Congress held at the St. Louis Exposition of 1904. Besides generating publicity, this convention was where pure food advocates decided to adopt a strategy of direct confrontation with the enemies of a pure food bill rather than adhering to their old strategy of compromise.[17]

Wiley played a particularly important role in recruiting women to lobby for a pure food bill, speaking to many women's clubs about pure food in the years preceding passage of the Pure Food and Drug Act and calling these women "enthusiastic, hard-working, persistent and effective."[18] Alice Lakey, president of the Village Improvement Association in Cranford New Jersey, invited Wiley to address her group in 1903.[19] Appalled by the conditions he described, Lakey devoted years to organizing women's groups at all levels on behalf of pure food. Like many others involved in this reform effort, Lakey used information she got from Wiley to make the case for a pure food law. Wiley was also instrumental in courting support from the Women's Christian Temperance Union, which was particularly upset about the high alcohol content of patent medicines and became an important ally in the struggle.[20]

Wiley also made frequent trips to Capitol Hill to testify before Congress on the pure food bill, and it was here, in his direct interactions with opponents of the legislation, that his wit and charm really shined. At a hearing in February 1906, Wiley took up the question of how to define whiskey. In the middle of his testimony, he called for glass tubes and other chemistry equipment to be brought into the hearing room. He told the committee that he planned to make every available kind of whiskey without using any whiskey—in other words, he would use chemicals to duplicate the natural aging process. As he produced each type, he passed out samples to the congressmen. When the results apparently left much to be desired, Wiley noted that he was not a professional and argued for the necessity of passing the pure food bill so that all consumers could enjoy the pure, aged article.[21]

Part of the reason Wiley showboated on behalf of the PFDA was its potential to greatly increase the power of his office. Many of the pure food bills that had been introduced into Congress since 1899 provided for the secretary of agriculture to set standards regarding adulterated food. They also required the secretary of agriculture to consult various professional organizations in the process of setting those standards. Wiley was deeply involved in the internecine warfare between different factions of chemists who wanted the greatest say over how the eventual law would be interpreted.[22] In 1902 Congress passed a law requiring the Department of Agriculture to draw up standards for the purity of food products like butter, sugar, and spices of all kinds. Wiley played an important role in drawing up those standards, which were published in late 1903.[23]

Wiley had pressed for the inclusion of specific standards in the pure food law that the Bureau of Chemistry could apply as cases of allegedly misbranded or adulterated food came to its attention, but he lost that fight.[24] The final bill gave the secretary of agriculture no power to set standards at all.[25] Furthermore, although the Department of Agriculture had already set standards for food purity under the appropriations act passed in 1903, Congress withdrew the agriculture secretary's authority to set even those standards in the department's appropriation bill for fiscal year 1906–1907.[26] Had Wiley been the most important force behind the passage of the law, the law would have been written to give his bureau far more power. Congress's failure to craft a law that fit Wiley's specifications was an indication of and a reaction to Wiley's failure to compromise on his conception of purity before the Pure Food and Drug Act ever passed.[27]

Unlike Wiley, who wanted the strongest law possible, the framers of the PFDA had to be mindful of constitutional issues. The act was written a year after the Supreme Court had elevated the police powers of the states and limited federal power under the Commerce Clause in *Lochner v. New York* and decades before the court expanded federal power over commerce again during the later New Deal years. It could easily have been overturned as soon as it faced a serious legal challenge on this basis. This question was itself an important issue in the debate over the legislation in the Senate.[28] In the final law, triggers for its sanctions came only when an adulterated or misbranded food or drug entered interstate commerce, or when someone who received such goods tried to deliver them over state lines.[29] A long list of banned chemicals in the legislation might have triggered closer scrutiny. The law as written first survived scrutiny from the Supreme Court in the Hipolite Egg case, which approved a ban on borax that Wiley instigated, in 1911.[30]

Had Congress opted to list banned chemicals in the legislation, the PFDA would have been much longer. As written, the law did not have nearly enough space for Congress to offer the kind of guidance required to regulate the entire food supply. However, there was another good reason to write the law in the broadest possible manner. From conception to passage, the final legislation took two decades and a diverse coalition of interests. Had the PFDA detailed exactly which substances were to be banned or regulated, it might have created more opposition and doomed the final bill. Because the Pure Food and Drug Act was so vague, its actual impact was necessarily determined by how it was administered rather than by the specific wording of the legislation.[31]

Despite the act's relative brevity, some of its language was important. The PFDA defined food adulteration, in part, as anything that had been substituted, diluted, or weakened by being packed with something other than the labeled product, anything mixed or colored to obscure damage or inferiority, and anything containing added poisonous ingredients or other substances that would adversely affect the health of the consumer. The act also defined an adulterated food as something containing "filthy, decomposed or putrid animal or vegetable substance." (Chemistry was unnecessary to enforce this part of the legislation.) The act defined goods that were "misbranded" as having labels that were "false or misleading in any particular" including labeling about where the food or drug had been "manufactured or produced."[32]

These definitions incorporate two kinds of adulteration that the act was supposed to fix: adulteration that harmed human health (whether out of malice or ignorance) and adulteration intended to deceive. Wiley came to believe that the government went easy on manufacturers that violated the law in both these ways. He was mistaken. In reality, there were many legitimate questions about which additives actually threatened human health and which practices were truly deceptive. There were also legitimate questions about how both kinds of adulteration could be mitigated. Subsequent struggles over ketchup, saccharin, baking powder, and Coca-Cola demonstrate the complexity of the policy issues involved in enforcing the PFDA. Wiley tried to assume an oversized role in enforcing the law so that he could avoid a prolonged debate over these issues.

The only part of the final text of the law that specifically mentions Wiley's Bureau of Chemistry is section 4. That section called on the Bureau of Chemistry to examine specimens of food and drugs to determine "whether such articles are adulterated or misbranded within the meaning of this Act." The law did not give the Bureau of Chemistry authority to determine the meaning of terms in the act (like "adulterated") because standards of purity did not appear in the legislation. All the bureau could do was inform the secretary of agriculture that it thought a particular good was adulterated or misbranded under the terms of the act. The secretary then notified the manufacturer and gave it a hearing. If the hearing convinced the secretary that a violation of the law had occurred, the matter was referred to the local district attorney, who would move against the goods and, by extension, their manufacturer in court.[33] Only then would those charges become public.[34] In short, Congress allowed the Bureau of Chemistry to determine what was pure and what was adulterated, but it deliberately left it up to other parties to decide what levels of adulteration or degrees of deception were acceptable.[35]

At the time of its passage, Wiley understood that the Pure Food and Drug Act was a compromise between many competing interests. The best evidence that Wiley understood Congress's intent was his public acknowledgement of this situation. Shortly after the law took effect, Wiley called on Congress to put the setting of specific standards back into the law and (more important from Wiley's perspective) to let the secretary of agriculture set them, under advisement from the Bureau of Chemistry. Such changes never took place.[36] Certainly, he would also have preferred a bill that was less ambiguous. "There are several things in the food bill that are going to take a mighty good lawyer to elucidate," he wrote the editor of the *American Grocer* shortly after the bill's passage.[37] Ultimately, the language in the bill caused him great difficulty in imposing his regulatory vision on the rest of the Department of Agriculture afterward.[38]

Despite Wiley's difficulties with the law, real improvements occurred in the safety of America's food supply. "It must be said to the credit of the great majority of manufacturers and dealers in food that they acquiesced at once in the conditions imposed by the new law and adjusted their business practices in accordance with its provisions," Wiley later remembered.[39] Adulterators complied with the law, if not for reasons of cost, then for fear of losing their case, fear of generating negative publicity, or some combination of these factors. While there is no doubt that the enforcement framework surrounding the Pure Food and Drug Act could have been more effective if the law had included specific standards, Wiley still used the broad language of the law to set de facto standards, picking and choosing to concentrate resources where adulteration was obvious, thereby changing the food supply in small steps.

The PFDA passed on June 30, 1906. It took effect on January 1, 1907. Despite its weaknesses, the law marked a sea change in the relationship between the federal government and commerce—the largest such change in American history until the New Deal of the 1930s. The Department of Agriculture had to build laboratories in Washington and at twenty-one branch locations around the country to test products confiscated by a small army of inspectors. Inspectors got desk space at the various department laboratories. Periodically they left their desks to observe conditions at factories around the country to help them decide whether a particular shipment of some product needed to be seized under the auspices of the law.[40] Until this time, the only federal employees stationed in most populated areas worked for either customhouses or the post office. Now hundreds of inspectors, their presence justified by the Constitution's Commerce Clause, were asking to take samples of commercial goods so those products could be tested for their compliance with federal law.

The new inspectors included physicians, pharmacists, a few men who were trained in chemistry, and some who had experience as local enforcement agents. None of the first inspectors had any experience in this role because their jobs had not existed before the passage of the PFDA.[41] Their training to be inspectors lasted all of one week. While their movements were ultimately controlled by Washington, inspectors had great freedom in the field to go to wherever in their territories they thought problems might arise. To gain access to factories, inspectors usually had to ask permission, which was in most cases granted. Sometimes inspectors got food samples for testing by purchasing them on the open market. Harvey Wiley, who was busy fighting for his view of how the law should be enforced, had little to do with their actions.[42]

———

While Harvey Wiley would eventually become known as the "Father of the Pure Food Law," Theodore Roosevelt had a different view of who should get credit for the passage of that legislation. "The Pure Food and Drug bill became a law purely because of the active stand I took trying to get it through Congress," the president later wrote. Looking back a few years later, the journalist Mark Sullivan took yet a different view, arguing, "The momentum of the Meat Inspection amendment carried with it the Pure Food Bill, which its enemies thought had been safely chloroformed in committee." Rather than award the credit to a single individual, Sullivan believed that a variety of factors, including Wiley's exposure of food adulteration through the Poison Squad experiments, best explained the passage of the legislation.[43]

Sullivan's reference to the "Meat Inspection amendment" refers to the Meat Inspection Act, which passed Congress on the same day as the PFDA. The fates of the two bills were so intertwined that even today they are seldom separated, even by historians. Like the PFDA, the Meat Inspection Act involved inspectors, who poured into packinghouses to inspect animals both before and after they died. That law was administered by the Department of Agriculture's Bureau of Animal Industry rather than the Bureau of Chemistry.[44] As a result, Harvey Wiley had little to do with its enforcement and seldom mentioned it during his tenure with the federal government. Wiley's relative lack of interest in this second piece of legislation highlights the degree to which his efforts on behalf of the PFDA were designed to expand his own power.

For meatpackers, Wiley's minimal role under the Meat Inspection Act was a selling point in favor of that law. An early version of the pure food bill would have given Wiley's Bureau of Chemistry jurisdiction over preservatives used on meat, but Congress instead set up an administrative structure that treated the purity of meat and the purity of the rest of food supply differently.[45] Wiley accepted this arrangement because he was always more concerned about food adulteration that his department could stop than about food safety problems in the purview of other divisions of the Department of Agriculture.[46] While it would be unfair to suggest that bureaucratic interests were Wiley's only motivation for supporting this compromise, his lack of interest in meat inspection after the passage of the bill suggests that he cared about driving chemicals out of food primarily in instances when he had the power to do so.

With the passage of the PFDA, the Bureau of Chemistry began testing a wide range of products other than meat. It then passed on information about some adulterated products for hearings and eventual prosecution, and those prosecutions suggested the parameters of the flexible concepts that the act depended upon for enforcement. In effect, new federal standards for purity developed over time as a result of prosecutorial discretion. Because Wiley's product selections proved to be, in some instances, so broad and undiscriminating, higher powers in the executive branch created two separate boards to oversee enforcement of the law. Rather than acknowledge that he was trying to assume powers that the law did not give him, Wiley incorrectly complained for the rest of his days that the law had been somehow misconstrued.

Wiley's dissatisfaction with the ultimate result shows that his lobbying efforts were of limited effectiveness.[47] No matter how important he was to the ultimate passage of the bill, he was not influential enough to get a bill passed that he liked. In a 1911 profile of Wiley published in the *World's Work*, his friend Arthur Wallace Dunn gave primary credit for passage of the law to the four Congressmen who wrote and shepherded the bill through Congress: Senators Weldon Heyburn of Idaho and Porter McCumber of North Dakota, along with Congressmen William Hepburn of Iowa and James R. Mann of Illinois. However, Dunn then wrote:

> Standing at the elbow of every one of them was Dr. Harvey W. Wiley, Chief of the Bureau of Chemistry of the Agricultural Department, who had devoted the best years of his life to improving the agricultural conditions of the country and who used his mind and time and scientific knowledge untiringly for the best interest of the Government. Every one of the four men so deeply concerned in the final enactment of the Pure Food Law acknowledges his debt to Dr. Wiley. More than that, a perusal of the hearings and debates on the bill shows that Dr. Wiley was the central figure of the pure food fight. It was he who prepared answers to attacks upon the bill: it was he who had to meet all the ingenious and subtle moves of the opposition. More than that, he had to be able to meet the assertions of the best chemists and lawyers that the opposition could employ.[48]

Around the time of the law's passage, Wiley himself credited Mann.[49] However, later efforts by Wiley and his supporters have changed the way we have looked at the history of the PFDA ever since.

The campaign to award Wiley almost sole credit for the passage of the PFDA began during the later years of his government service. It was originally a response to rumors of Wiley's retirement, which long predated his actual resignation, and continued long afterward. Wiley's own inflation of

FIGURE 6.1 Secretary of agriculture James Wilson, the longest-serving cabinet secretary in American history. Wilson supported Wiley in his early efforts on behalf of pure food but grew increasingly exasperated at Wiley's refusal to compromise on many high-profile food fights.

Courtesy Library of Congress

his role in passing the PFDA was another part of this campaign. Before and immediately after passage of the PFDA, Wiley repeatedly denied that he was the author of the law. The chemist's honorific as the "Father of the Pure Food Law" came later, as his struggle to enforce his vision of the legislation was read backward. Toward the end of his life, he would take credit for much of the law's language, claiming that he wrote all of it but two provisions.[50]

During the period of Wiley's greatest contribution to the passage of the pure food bill, he was more influential with respect to the idea of passing any law than he was in determining the exact provisions of the law that ultimately passed. In other words, Wiley was more interested in promoting Harvey Wiley than he was in getting bogged down in the exact provisions of what the pure food law might be. Strategically, this approach probably did as much to promote passage of this legislation as anything else Wiley contributed.

With the passage of the pure food law, the debate over food purity passed from the question of legislation to the nature of its enforcement. Even though Wiley recognized the law's limitations at the time of its passage, he became increasingly convinced he knew how the framers of the law meant it to be enforced. Because of his increasing intolerance to any kind of food processing, government officials from the secretary of agriculture to the president of the United States gradually moved to limit the impact of his ideas. After this opposition took shape, Wiley became much more protective of the bill he had helped get passed. At the time of its passage, Wiley never expected the enforcement of the PFDA to be punitive, in the sense that violators should be fined or imprisoned. The Department of Agriculture did not have the resources to prosecute every infraction it found to the fullest extent the law allowed, and if it had, it would have jammed the courts. The department's initial strategy therefore was to try negotiation, compromise, and even education to get companies to comply with the law.[51] The Department of Agriculture took legal action only as a last resort.[52] The debate over enforcement of the pure food law occurred because Wiley quickly decided that he wanted to expand it into a stronger law.

In reality, the contested provisions of the PFDA were never as clear-cut as Wiley would eventually make them out to be. Even something as seemingly simple as the meaning of the word "adulteration" was full of ambiguity when applied to the wide range of food products produced in the United States. Nevertheless, Harvey Wiley believed that common additives and preservatives that had no harmful effect on people who consumed them in the minute doses present in most American foods were either defrauding or slowly poisoning consumers. Because food manufacturers were often reluctant to change the way they created their products, those battles often played out in court—almost always to the detriment of Wiley's absolutist position.

CHAPTER SEVEN

WHISKEY

ON MARCH 31, 1905, Harvey Wiley spoke before the Chemists' Club of New York City. During that speech, he emphasized the deceptive element of food adulteration more than its threat to public health. "A great many adulterations are not injurious," he told his fellow chemists. "When, however, chemicals are introduced in quantities which render them impossible of detection the consumer is deceived, and I say that is a moral crime."[1] At that juncture he still harbored a greater interest in stopping deception than in preventing dangerous substances from entering the food supply. Some of the guests that evening, however, thought that even these comparatively moderate sentiments went too far.

One Wiley critic who spoke after Wiley finished was Dr. Edward Gudeman of Chicago. "When we only take one side and frighten the public it isn't right," he told the audience with Wiley still present. "The fact that not a single food chemist can point to harm being done from the use of either preservatives or colors certainly should be taken into consideration."[2] Another guest, a St. Louis lawyer named Warwick Hough, represented the National

Wholesale Liquor Dealers Association. He complained that if Wiley's definition of pure food became the universal standard, 99 percent of the whiskey
in the country would be outlawed.[3]

Wiley tried to put up a brave front during the public attacks on him. "I've
been roasted before," he told the crowd. "I'm particularly willing to be here."[4]
But in fact he was deeply upset by the reception he received that night. On
April 21 he wrote to the president of the club: "When I consider that my
address, by invitation, at the Chemists' Club, was made a means of systematic
personal abuse for the purpose of poisoning public opinion through the press
by garbled statements of what occurred, my indignation grows and grows." He
then called on the Chemists' Club to investigate how his critics got invited to
his presentation.[5]

Picking fights with manufacturers and food experts is how Wiley stayed
in the public eye after the passage of the Pure Food and Drug Act (PFDA)
and even after the Poison Squad experiments eventually ended in 1907. "Dr.
Wiley goes off half-cocked on many matters with which his acquaintance is
quite imperfect," wrote the *San Francisco Call* in 1911, "and he greatly resents
it when he is declared mistaken by higher authority."[6] This happened fairly
often, but some errors were more obvious than others.

In 1903, at the height of his celebrity over the Poison Squad experiments,
Harvey Wiley claimed that the incidence of male baldness (which he exhibited) was increasing because men were becoming more intelligent.[7] Later he
stated that within ten years men would become bald and toothless because of
their poor diets. Then he claimed that he was no longer bald (even though he
remained so). "I am growing younger every day," he told a reporter. "And I did
it myself. Any one may grow luxuriant hair by following a few simple rules.
Even the totally bald need not wholly despair."[8] Wiley repeated such claims
many times during the period when he was most in the public eye, suggesting
that he actually believed he had discovered the cure to baldness—though he
remained bald and grew more so over time.

Wiley's baldness cure reflected a personal aspect of his interest in pure
food. As the *Washington Post* explained in 1908, "He has, along lines of
advanced Agricultural Department thought, proceeded to a discovery of
the fountain of youth, and now he is growing young with astonishing rapid-

ity."[9] Eat pure, stay young, Wiley might have argued, and Exhibit A was Harvey Wiley himself. Because he was a living, breathing symbol of the benefits of eating pure food, what he ate and how he lived took on greater importance than they otherwise might have.

Wiley made his misguided assertions about baldness with the utmost confidence. What stopped his baldness, Wiley argued both in public and in private, was riding around Washington in an automobile, bareheaded.[10] "The sun got a chance at my scalp, and killed the germs which were killing my hair at the roots, and preventing it from growing. Any bald-headed man may do as I have done, and he will be cured."[11] It was also important to him that the barbers in the Cosmos Club sterilize their equipment so the baldness-inducing germs from one customer wouldn't pass to him.[12] Wiley exhibited the same confidence when pronouncing on the subject of food and drink and was more than occasionally wrong, even in his supposed area of expertise.

———

It was no coincidence that one of Wiley's critics present at the Chemists' Club of New York City dinner represented the whiskey industry. Shortly before Hough confronted Wiley in New York, Wiley had terminated a long exchange of letters with him because Hough had published that correspondence without his permission. That correspondence exhibited two entirely different perspectives on what pure food was and on whether or not whiskey fit into any potential pure food legislation.[13] The two sides of the dispute were at philosophical loggerheads. Given their two completely different definitions of whiskey, no compromise position was possible. Because the struggle between Wiley and one segment of the whiskey industry was so bitter and so public, the long argument over exactly what whiskey was took on significance beyond this particular industry.

To increase support for the pure food bill, Wiley deliberately cultivated antagonism with a large segment of the whiskey industry. For many years, Wiley aligned himself with one large minority faction of that industry against the rest of the whiskey producers as the federal government struggled to define exactly what the term "whiskey" meant for purposes of regulation. Wiley's affinity for his chosen faction in this struggle is easier to perceive than any concern for the consumers of whiskey of any kind. For his support, Wiley's friends in the whiskey industry rewarded him handsomely, sending many bottles directly to his home for his personal use.[14]

At the turn of the twentieth century, whiskey was made in two different but related ways. Each method started by distilling grain mash, traditionally barley.[15] This created a product known as high wines. Which kind of whiskey one made depended upon what one did with those high wines. Straight whiskey was (and is) a potable spirit created through aging. When the high wines were stored in charred oak barrels, they became more palatable as they aged, losing their poisonous qualities and taking on flavors from the wood. This process dates to James Crow's first experiments in Kentucky, conducted to improve whiskeys of all kinds during the 1830s. The longer the product was aged, the more it cost. Whiskey producers also had to consider the cost of storage and net loss to evaporation over time when determining where to set their prices. To connoisseurs, however, the aging process was what made great whiskey taste great.[16]

Starting in the 1870s, distillers began to duplicate the aging process by further distilling high wines into a tasteless product known as cologne spirits, then adding colors or additional flavors to simulate the smell and taste of traditional straight whiskey. This product was called rectified whiskey. The more successful rectified whiskey producers were at duplicating the aging process, the more money they stood to make by selling their product to consumers who could not distinguish between the two or who simply didn't care about the difference because they wanted to get drunk fast. At first producers needed at least some straight whiskey in their mixtures to duplicate the aging process, but by the turn of the twentieth century it became possible to produce decent rectified whiskey while forgoing straight whiskey entirely.[17] As a result of these advances, rectified whiskies became both cheap and popular. A related product, blended whiskey, did not get Wiley's approval either. This whiskey might have some straight whiskey in it, but distillers mixed it with any number of cheaper liquors—often whiskey distilled from different grains that did not require such a long and complicated aging process. These other kinds of whiskies made up about 85 percent of whiskey sales at that time.[18]

Wiley bought straight whiskey for the use of the Cosmos Club, and in his letters to straight whiskey producers he described his efforts in Congress on their behalf.[19] At one point Wiley told Congress that when he had first become a member, the Cosmos Club had carried only blended whiskey. Then he brought in a bottle of seven-year-old straight whiskey. "The first man who took a drink of it declared that it was adulterated goods," Wiley explained, "but within a week every man in the club was adding water to dilute it."[20] In 1911, the *New York Times* reported, "a prominent diplomat, on spending an evening at the club, heard Wiley speaking French and asked who he was. On being told, he exclaimed: 'I thought he was a Frenchman, but I have heard everybody near me to-night saying "Wiley's scotch," and yet you say he is an American.'"[21] Wiley's taste in whiskey won out in the end—but only in the Cosmos Club. Despite his repeated claims about the health effects and deceptiveness of rectified whiskey, Wiley was unable to destroy that industry.

Wiley's initial opposition to rectified whiskey was in line with his conception of adulterated food. To Wiley, rectified whiskey was a form of deception.[22] The traditional process of aging whiskey in barrels was natural; creating it faster was not. Therefore, cutting straight whiskey with anything else—even other whiskeys—meant that consumers would not have the pleasure of the natural article that Wiley himself preferred. Wiley insisted that most rectified whiskies were actually mixtures of pure alcohol and various additives designed to mimic the tastes and smells produced by aging.[23] Eventually he would argue that it was not the alcohol that made straight whiskey superior to all other kinds, but the various elements left over from the aging process.[24] To mimic them, often badly, with artificial chemicals was not only unethical but potentially unhealthy. He stuck to this position even when it proved unpopular with large segments of the general public.

Congress, then full of men who, like Wiley, cared deeply about the quality of their whiskey, passed the Bottled-in-Bond Act in 1897 to protect connoisseurs of quality spirits. That law set up the infrastructure to inspect and tax whiskeys that had been aged in the traditional manner for at least four years.[25] Inspected and approved whiskeys got a stamp that included the age of the product, the proof of the product, the distiller's name and location, and the date the product was bottled.[26] Here, in other words, was an early pure food measure. But whether for reasons of price or taste, the public still largely preferred the possibly impure, rectified whiskey to its traditional cousin.

Wiley did not start this fight by arguing that one kind of whiskey was more pure than another. According to Wiley, "blended and compounded whiskeys" were often sold as straight whiskeys. In a letter written shortly before the passage of the Pure Food Law, he wrote, "Should it become a law [it] would not interfere in any way with the business of the rectifier . . . except it would require his product to be so labeled as to show that it was a compound or a blend. By this labeling the intending purchaser would be fully-informed in regard to the character of the goods purchased, thus carrying out one of the basic principles of pure food legislation."[27] Unable to prove that rectified whiskeys were being mislabeled, Wiley began to argue instead that it was less healthy than straight whiskey.

In doing so, he ended up tying himself in knots. All whiskey is unhealthy, and Wiley knew it. In 1908 he told one audience "that he knew very well that all alcohol was a poison. Yet he occasionally took a sip of the distilled cereal or the juice of the grape."[28] However, to attract attention to his campaign against rectified whiskey, he had to argue that rectified whiskey was worse than the alternative—that it was somehow impure, whereas drinking straight whiskey was comparatively healthy. In this manner, his argument about whiskey mirrored his attacks on other foods or beverages that he deemed adulterated. Since no whiskey is really healthy, however, this position hurt Wiley's credibility.

Wiley's criterion for judging the relative healthfulness of whiskey depended upon his ideas about a natural but toxic substance known as fusel oil. Fusel oil was a by-product of the distilling process that was unhealthful if ingested in quantity but was later found to be useful as the base material for manufacturing all sorts of industrial chemicals. After distilling, small amounts of fusel oil remained in the whiskey, however, and contributed to its body and flavor. Before the passage of the PFDA, Wiley argued that for any whiskey to be fit for human consumption, fusel oil had to be largely eliminated. However, in the immediate run-up to the passage of the PFDA, Wiley changed his mind and argued that fusel oil was actually harmless. He tried to explain this inconsistency by claiming that the science on this subject had changed.[29] It hadn't.

What had changed was Wiley's willingness to argue that some chemicals associated with food processing were not just deceptive, but dangerous. At one point during the debate over whiskey, he claimed, "I said I believed the general effect of alcohol on mankind was wholly bad; that it was bad even in small quantities; that if distilled beverages, such as whisky, brandy and rum, had any good effects, they were due to the fact that the aromatic and fragrant substances therein stimulated the digestive secretions and thus overcame, to a certain extent, the bad effect of the alcohol which they contained."[30] In other words, Wiley came to believe that fusel oil was acceptable because he came to look at distillation itself as a natural process. This attitude did not make sense when looking at the chemicals in whiskey in isolation (like fusel oil, which could be toxic), but it matched Wiley's inclination to favor less-processed products (straight whiskey).

Conveniently, Wiley's war against rectified whiskey complemented the politics surrounding the passage of the pure food law. In the early 1890s, pure food reformers attacked the producers of rectified and blended whiskeys as a "Whiskey Trust." Congressional hearings at that time revealed that many of the ingredients used to make rectified whiskey—like propyl alcohol—were themselves poisonous.[31] Wiley first entered the public record with respect to whiskey when he testified before this investigation. Asked whether rectified whiskey was less healthful than the straight product, he answered in the negative. His objection to rectified whiskey came on the grounds of deception.[32] A decade later, in the debate over the PFDA, Wiley took up these attacks on the Whiskey Trust because they proved to be good politics.[33]

While not calling for a ban on rectified whiskey, he made a public case that rectified whiskey was not a real spirit and should instead be labeled "imitation whiskey."[34] Rectified whiskey producers protested, fearing that no one would buy their product if it were so labeled. Like so many of Wiley's enemies, the rectified whiskey makers were not against pure food legislation.[35]

Wiley could have accepted moderate regulation based on the existing status of the trade, perhaps strengthening the Bottled-in-Bond Act, for example, to improve the quality of labeling. Such a solution could have been written into the pure food law itself or implemented in the evolving regulatory standards under which it was administered. Instead, he wanted to benefit from the perception that the hated "Whiskey Trust" opposed pure food legislation.[36] Once the PFDA took effect, Wiley arranged for the seizure of many shipments of rectified whiskey of variable quality, including more than fifty barrels in a week.[37] As a consequence, distillers of rectified whiskey, believing themselves to be in a life or death struggle, became Wiley's bitterest enemies. Indeed, if Wiley had held all the power to determine their fate, the rectified whiskey industry would probably have died.

While there were fierce fights within the Roosevelt and Taft administrations over how to regulate various foods and drinks, none were quite as fierce as the struggle over whiskey, thanks to Harvey Wiley. Because of their political power and the fact that they began lobbying long before the pure food bill passed Congress, rectified whiskey distillers managed to bypass the normal process for defining purity under the PFDA and went straight to Wiley's superiors for judgment. For Wiley, the entire enforcement mechanism of the Pure Food and Drug Act would live or die based on the government's decision about whiskey.[38] Because of the strong and constant opposition of these distillers, this issue assumed an importance in Wiley's work far greater than the significance of whiskey in the overall fight for pure food. Wiley's reputation among scientists never fully recovered.

———◆———

As long as Wiley treated whiskey as an important test of the act, so did the federal government. But the government never spoke with one mind on the answer to the question "What is whiskey?" until Harvey Wiley forced President Taft's hand. Up to that point the federal government had reversed itself repeatedly over a period of a few years. With the passage of the PFDA, rectifiers flooded the federal government to ask how the law's regulatory apparatus would handle the labeling of whiskey. On December 1, 1906, weeks before he set up the bodies that would eventually enforce the new law, agriculture secretary James Wilson declared, "The Department is of the opinion that the mixtures presented cannot legally be labeled either 'blended whiskies' or 'blended whisky.'"[39] The reasoning in this opinion, labeled Food Inspection Decision No. 45, was based on Wiley's idea of rectified and blended whiskeys as deceiving and reflects his influence in the department at that time.

Unfortunately for Wiley's position, Wilson changed his mind in February 1907, shortly after the pure food law took effect.[40] In response, on February 23, 1908, Harvey Wiley went to the White House to discuss whiskey with President Theodore Roosevelt. His goal was to get Roosevelt to reverse Wilson's new position on what exactly whiskey was. He brought with him a variety of chemicals, along with samples of whiskey, rye, scotch, and other alcoholic beverages. He then repeated the demonstration he had performed for Congress before the passage of the pure food law, creating whiskey out of nothing but pure alcohol and chemicals. He must have gotten better at it: when he handed Roosevelt samples of the whiskey he had created and the straight whiskey he had brought with him, Roosevelt had trouble distinguishing between the two. Wiley's demonstration lasted about two hours, and Roosevelt interrupted him with questions only once or twice. At the end, the president told him, "Dr. Wiley, I have heard nothing but whiskey for the past three months, but this is the first time anyone has given me any idea as to what it is."[41] As a result of the meeting, Roosevelt asked Attorney General Charles J. Bonaparte to decide the issue once and for all. Bonaparte upheld the Bureau of Chemistry's position, Roosevelt signed onto the decision, and Wiley was happy.

Whiskey rectifiers were not. They sued to get the whiskey decision overturned. Various cases got nowhere. Because they were convinced that nobody would buy a product labeled "imitation whiskey," they also adopted other means to change the regulations. Eventually, political pressure during the Roosevelt administration led to the appointment of a special Whiskey Commission.[42] They commission decided in favor of the whiskey rectifiers, but Bonaparte would not back down.[43] Neither would Wiley, who leaked word of the internal dispute to a group called the People's Lobby so they too could pressure Roosevelt in the opposite direction. When Wiley wrote to the governor of Alabama in support of an effort to ban rectified whiskey there, his action was reported in the press. While Wilson had no particular interest in the whiskey question, he was deeply disturbed by Wiley's acts of insubordination.[44]

As a result of these competing pressures, the struggle bled into the Taft administration. Soon after Taft took office, whiskey rectifiers petitioned for a hearing and got one. Taft's solicitor general, Lloyd Bowers, took testimony for five solid weeks. Harvey Wiley personally coached many of the witnesses in support of his definition of whiskey, and Bowers was largely convinced. He argued that rectified whiskey did not deserve to be called "whiskey" because consumers did not understand exactly what spirits they were buying. Many observers thought this decision went against Wiley, but because Wiley's case against blended whiskey was based on the evils of consumer deception, he saw it as a victory.[45]

Those rectifiers unhappy with Bowers's decision petitioned President Taft to review the ruling, and this final word on the issue favored the makers of rectified whiskey. Taft decided that the term "whiskey" included any liquor made from grain alcohol, regardless of its final composition. Based on Taft's finding, three cabinet secretaries issued a food inspection decision that required blended whiskeys to be labeled as blends but did not ban them. Whiskeys that were mixed with non-grain-based alcohols had to be labeled "compound" whiskeys.[46] This decision was a complete rejection of Wiley's view that labeling anything other than straight whiskey as "whiskey" constituted deception. Taft's definition of whiskey holds to this day.

One line from Taft's statement reveals much about why Wiley's reputation suffered so as a result of this particular struggle. Right after noting his disagreement with Attorney General Bowers, Taft turns to history for the context of his reasoning. "Whiskey for more than one hundred years has been the most general and comprehensive term applied to liquor distilled from grain," he wrote. "Therefore it is a perversion of the Pure Food Act to attempt now to limit the meaning of the term 'whiskey' to that which modern manufacture and taste have made the most desirable variety."[47] Of all the struggles in which Wiley engaged, his opposition to blended and rectified whiskeys would have led to the greatest disruption if it had succeeded. However, the logic behind his opposition—whether misbranding or ill effects on health—made no sense to anyone but Harvey Wiley and the producers of straight whiskey.

Wiley repeatedly made the somewhat bizarre claim that the aging process for straight whiskey was "natural" even though it involved the manipulation of different grains and sugars in procedures developed and controlled through human intervention.[48] As a chemist, Wiley obviously understood this but was either unwilling or unable to voice it. Viewed in the context of all of Wiley's food fights, it seems likely was what he objected to was the speeding up of the aging process in the name of mass production because of its effect on the taste of the final product. In other words, his individual preference influenced his definition of whiskey. By couching his position in scientific terms that were easy to refute, Wiley left ample ground for his enemies to attack him. Even food producers who had nothing to do with whiskey distilling could cite Wiley's actions with respect to rectified whiskey as a reason he could not be trusted to oversee regulation of their little corner of the food supply. Attacking rectified whiskey may have been good politics before the passage of the Pure Food and Drug Act, but continuing those attacks afterward made no sense.

———

After President Taft settled the dispute over whiskey and Wiley left government service in 1912, Wiley found new reasons to favor one kind of whiskey over another. These new positions ran even further afield from his expertise in food chemistry. In a *Good Housekeeping* column published in November 1913 entitled "The Food Law and 'Nigger Gin,'" Wiley resorted to race-baiting to make his point. Wiley wrote: "A short time ago, a negro in the town of Americus, Georgia, having imbibed some so-called 'rectified whiskey,' became involved in a quarrel as a result of his intoxication. In the melee which ensued the chief of police and a negro were fatally wounded." The perpetrator, Wiley explained, was later lynched. The point of the story was that rectified whiskey got people drunker faster than straight whiskey.[49] In 1915 Wiley made the argument that rectified whiskey was for poor people. "The man at hard labor evidently wants nothing but alcohol," he wrote, "and why should he pay four or five dollars a gallon for it in the form of old, mellow whiskey when he can get a larger amount of intoxication out of the cheaper, fabricated, artificially-flavored substitutes?"[50] This was one of the very few times Wiley wrote about the taste of food rather than its chemical components.

Thwarted by President Taft in his campaign against rectified whiskey, Wiley began a new struggle against rectified medicinal whiskey that lasted long after he left the government. An encyclopedic book called the *Pharmacopeia of the United States* listed all effective drugs and their ideal doses. It had been created decades earlier to guide doctors in determining treatment for their patients. Congress included the *Pharmacopeia* in the Pure Food and Drug Act as the standard to which to compare drugs to determine whether they were adulterated.[51] Wiley played a major role in revising the *Pharmacopeia* in 1910 and chaired the convention that revised it in 1920. At that time he argued, "The physician is the leading offender in the illegal sale of liquor. The pharmacist is merely doing his duty when he fills prescriptions for whisky and brandy. If the writing of such prescriptions is abused, the medical profession must accept part of the criticism and blame." Wiley got whiskey and brandy removed from the 1910 edition and kept it off in 1920. Wiley took issue with those physicians who continued to prescribe alcohol regardless of the *Pharmacopeia* recommendation, but changing these recommendations was the best he could do at that time.[52]

These sentiments toward medicinal whiskey reflected Wiley's change in attitude toward alcohol in general. In the May 1916 issue of *Good Housekeeping*, despite his earlier public admission that he was a drinker, Harvey Wiley came out in favor of Prohibition. While he had expressed some sympathy for the position before, the first time he publicly supported making all alcohol illegal came two years before the passage of the Eighteenth Amendment and marked the end of his attempts to differentiate one type of whiskey from another. Since all alcohol was poison, Wiley now wanted the government to ban it. Confronting the argument that Prohibition would hinder individual liberty, Wiley responded, "The principle of personal liberty cannot be so extended as to cover actions which injure society. . . . If one insists on eating poisoned food and giving it to his family, he threatens

the existence of the state."[53] Freed from the constraints of government service, Wiley turned against his one-time allies in the straight whiskey trade
because he had chosen to follow his position on food purity to its natural end. In old age, he would no longer tolerate anyone's risking their own
health by consuming alcohol, presumably including his own.

The passage of the Eighteenth Amendment and the Volstead Act, Wiley
noted, rendered President Taft's decision about whiskey moot.[54] Although
Wiley did not live to see Prohibition lifted, he did see the beginning of a
change in America's drinking habits. "From the point of view of public health,
Prohibition has been a wonder worker," wrote Wiley in a letter to the editor
of the *Manufacturers Record* in 1922. His justification for this position was
the increased difficulty of obtaining medicinal whiskey and other nostrums
that consisted mostly of alcohol.[55] (Products like Duffy's Pure Malt Whiskey
were very nearly straight alcohol with added flavor or were cut with water.)[56]
Wiley understood that because these remedies were now harder to obtain,
people were more likely to see a physician and get real medicine instead.

Wiley's long educational campaign against medicinal whiskey taught
physicians, and by extension the public, that there was no difference
between whiskeys—at least when it came to their medicinal value. Just as
the struggle over the Pure Food and Drug Act affected spurious drugs of
all kinds, Wiley's struggle to define whiskey devastated the reputation of
medicinal whiskey. When Prohibition came, it encouraged Americans to
drink because they wanted to, not because they thought it might cure them
of anything in particular.

Medicinal whiskey was something of a joke while the Eighteenth Amendment was in force. It quickly became one of the easier ways to get access to
alcohol in those states that allowed such whiskey to be sold. At the beginning
of Prohibition, many of the old-line distillers had closed, and entrepreneurs
had bought up the remainders to produce medicinal whiskey. Of course, most
people who got prescriptions during Prohibition weren't actually consuming
whiskey for medical reasons.[57] After Prohibition, when there was no longer
any reason to pretend, medicinal whiskey producers became the bulwark of
the revived recreational whiskey industry.[58] So although Wiley's attacks did
not change the definition of whiskey, they did help transform how whiskey

got marketed. This was not the result Wiley had intended for his campaign against blended whiskey, but it probably did enormous good for the health of the American people by getting them to forgo the notion that alcohol was effective medicine.

In the long run, however, Wiley's views on what whiskey was have had no effect on what kind of whiskey Americans preferred. In 2014 blended Scotch whiskey made up 80 percent of all sales in the American market.[59] Rye and bourbon are recognized as distinct types of whiskey, but not as a result of Wiley's efforts. Moreover, distillers have begun experimenting in earnest with nontraditional grains like oats, triticale, quinoa, and millet as part of the proprietary formulas for their particular products.[60] While these experiments are legal under current definitions of the various kinds of grain alcohol, there is no question that Harvey Wiley, a strict traditionalist in these matters, would have called them adulterations. Accepting Wiley's definition of pure whiskey would have prevented innovation, as was the case with many of the food fights in which he engaged.

CHAPTER EIGHT

ENFORCEMENT

THE DEVELOPMENT OF SYNTHETIC FLAVORS during the late nineteenth century has gotten little attention from historians. Pioneered by small chemical companies in the United States and elsewhere mostly as additives, the main purpose of these flavors was to make processed foods more palatable—in some cases even more palatable than the natural foods that would have been available to working-class consumers. For example, the development of penny candies would have been impossible without these flavors because they made it viable for machines to fuse increasingly inexpensive sugar and flavor together into a standardized, marketable product.[1]

The debate over the use of artificial flavors highlighted the issues underlying debates over the purity of foods. Chemists recognized pure substances as being chemically homogeneous, but consumers sometimes imbued the term "pure" with other values whether the substance in question was chemically pure or not. Focused on deception, Wiley thought artificial flavors had no place in the American food supply since they adversely affected the quality—in other words, the purity—of the food.[2] In the debate over the Pure

Food and Drug Act (PFDA), Wiley advocated for outlawing artificial flavors. This attempt, though unsuccessful, illustrates both Wiley's goals and his philosophical differences with much of his opposition.

As part of his general dislike of food processing, which he deemed unnatural, Wiley opposed the kinds of shortcuts and substitutions necessary for the mass production of food and drinks of all kinds. At first, his opposition to artificial flavors, as with so many other foods, was based on producers' ability to deceive consumers. Gradually, Wiley came to depend on an argument that additives—even natural additives—were unsafe, whether he had tested those ingredients in Poison Squad–style experiments or not. Most other scientists, barring reliable scientific testing that suggested otherwise, saw these same controversial ingredients as acceptable whether or not they appeared where nature intended.

When Wiley was working to establish a standard for flavoring extract, he required that vanilla flavoring contain at least a small amount of vanilla. Chemist Alois von Isakovics had been working on a synthetic vanilla flavor for ten years when he wrote to Wiley in 1905 to argue that artificial vanilla was superior in both flavor and price. "Our product has now been marketed for years and has been used by some of the largest consumers in the country," von Isakovics bragged. "Yet you step in as a chemist and desire to kill my interests with one stroke. . . . Why should you as a chemist try to hold back advance in the science instead of encouraging it to your best ability[?]"[3] Vanilla was (and is) extremely expensive in its natural form. Without artificial vanilla, products like vanilla ice cream would be inaccessible to the vast majority of consumers.[4] For most people other than Wiley, making that flavor available to everyone was progress.

Wiley took a similar uncompromising stand against artificial colors. In 1905 he publicly described them as deceptive because the "idea of adding an artificial color to food [was] to cause a food product to imitate a natural product of higher quality." He was particularly opposed to the coloring of butter, not recognizing that dairy producers had an interest in making an irregular natural product look consistent. Yet deception was not the mandated criterion for determining whether food dyes were legal. Even though Wiley would have banned them all for misleading consumers, the Pure

Food and Drug Act charged Wiley's Bureau of Chemistry with determining which dyes were hazardous to consumers' health and which were not.[5]

What kinds of food ingredients societies accept depends upon factors like the availability of resources, the overall cost of food, and, perhaps most important, on how much risk consumers are willing to take. Wiley's growing unwillingness to accept any risk associated with additives in the food supply led him to take an extreme position. In 1909, replying to a correspondent who had sent him a clipping from a local paper, Wiley explained, "I thoroughly believe . . . in the position I have taken, and I have an abiding conviction that it will be sustained in the end and chemicals of every kind excluded from foods."[6] It didn't matter if that ingredient, like caffeine or benzoic acid, appeared naturally in other contexts. If it was added to foods where it did not appear originally, Wiley considered its presence to be an adulteration. Von Isakovics, in contrast, laid out the case that chemicals in the form of natural flavors could make food better tasting.[7]

As manufactured foods became increasingly removed from their original contexts, Wiley grew convinced that they were dangerous, whether the science he conducted backed up that conclusion or not. To reinforce his new set of beliefs, he wanted to leave the impression that he had always been against preservatives even though his opposition to chemical additives was late blooming, dating approximately from the start of his Poison Squad experiments. Besides the publicity he received, he had another motivation for his stronger opposition to additives like sodium benzoate and caffeine: to move the administrative structure designed to enforce the Pure Food and Drug Act to do what he thought of as their jobs. To try to get these kinds of additives banned, he had to fight not only food manufacturers but also other government officials who had more tolerance for risk than he did.

As a result of this difference of opinion, both food manufacturers and their allies in the Roosevelt and Taft administrations (including both presidents) worked to limit Wiley's power to enforce the law. To them, the PFDA had to allow the continued innovation and mass production of foods unless a particular additive was proven to be noxious. While the health costs of using most untested chemical preservatives were unproven and far removed (since they wouldn't be experienced by anyone until years later), the benefits of mass production to consumers on limited budgets were immediately apparent. Wiley, however, treated even hypothetical ill effects of every chemical as disastrous. But as long as food regulation remained subject to the political process, Wiley's enemies made sure that most of these chemicals were deemed acceptable. In response, Wiley protested vigorously.

———

Two boards appointed by Wiley's bosses, neither one specified in the language of PFDA, were the vehicle by which Wiley lost this argument. Both bodies got in the way of Wiley's conception of how the law should be implemented. While Wiley was undoubtedly offended on a personal level by the appointment of these boards, his real problem with them stemmed from his desire to be the sole arbiter of what was and was not impure because he believed that would have been best for American consumers. Unfortunately for Wiley, food producers were constituents of the federal government too, and the politicians quickly divided the power to determine exactly what pure food was. Over time, Wiley himself came to believe, incorrectly, that his legacy had been effectively destroyed by these bureaucratic impediments to the law's proper administration.

Secretary Wilson created the Board of Food and Drug Inspection in April 1907.[8] While this new body was no doubt designed to check the chemist's power, Wilson nonetheless named Wiley chairman of the board. It met twice a week in his office and for separate hearings with manufacturers of potentially adulterated food products as necessary. Its final decisions for prosecution were passed on to the secretary of agriculture. When the secretary agreed with those decisions, they were referred back to the solicitor of the Department of Agriculture, who served on the same board and who passed that information on to the appropriate US attorney for prosecution.[9] Even though in many cases the board agreed unanimously on whether to prosecute, Wiley eventually became upset that he did not have full control over how the government enforced the law.

The composition of the Board of Food and Drug Inspection reflected the Roosevelt administration's interest in balancing the interests of both consumers and manufacturers. This balancing act produced tensions by design. "I am fully aware that the Board of Food Inspection has no control over the work of the Bureau of Chemistry as you state in your memo," wrote one of his fellow board members, the chemist Frederick Dunlap, to Wiley in 1909. "It might, however, with like truthfulness and with as much point might be stated that the Bureau of Chemistry has no control over the actions of the Board of Food and Drug Inspection."[10] Roosevelt and Wilson didn't want Wiley to have total control over how the government enforced the PFDA. As a result, Wiley became frustrated every time the other members of the board outvoted him on any question on which he had tried to sway them otherwise. Infighting on the board seldom appears in the group's transcripts and reports of hearings, in part because all members often agreed on the proper course of action. Nevertheless, many of the board's internal memos reflect sharp philosophical divisions.

Dunlap had been a research chemist at the University of Michigan until Secretary Wilson persuaded President Roosevelt to recruit him so that someone in the Department of Agriculture besides Wiley could advise Roosevelt on matters involving chemistry. Wilson did not want Dunlap to participate in the normal work of the Bureau of Chemistry, only to advise him and serve as Wiley's administrative replacement during the chemist's many absences.[11] Wilson also hoped that a second chemist who could review decisions would speed up the work of the bureau.[12] In response to Dunlap's appointment, Wiley shunned him. Dunlap and one secretary were assigned a small space far away from the rest of the bureau staff, who were generally loyal to Wiley.[13]

Wiley ostracized Dunlap because the two chemists held diametrically opposed ideas about what the Pure Food and Drug Act was supposed to do. Whereas Wiley wanted to use the law to remove chemicals from food, Dunlap, referring to a debate over the use of alum in baking powder, argued, "This decision does not forbid the use of a product for the mere reason that it is a chemical, but for the reason that the chemical may be injurious to health."[14] Even if the risks of a particular substance were minimal, Wiley demanded that government protect even the weakest consumers. It didn't matter whether the struggle was between the consumer and the government or the consumer and a particular food manufacturer. Wiley always sided with the consumer, never recognizing that consumer sentiment was often divided over pure food issues.

Wiley's refusal to recognize any competing interest besides that of consumers played out in his absolutist stance against admitting any quantity of a suspect substance into the food supply. "The argument of [admitting] small quantities has absolutely no ethical, logical or legal foundation and is most dangerous," Wiley wrote in 1911. "The result of admitting the justice of this argument and acting thereon would validate under the high authority of the law the use of small quantities of dangerous and threatening substances and thus entrench the practice of adulteration firmly under the protection of the law."[15] Any breaching of the dam would potentially inundate the American consumer with impure foods of all kinds. In contrast, Wiley's bureaucratic enemies looked at their jobs as a balancing act between competing interests. Unsurprisingly, food manufacturers opposed to Wiley's perspective started calling for his ouster from the Department of Agriculture.

The department's solicitor, George McCabe, was the other member of the three-man Board of Food and Drug Inspection with whom Wiley sometimes fought. McCabe had begun working at the Department of Agriculture as a law clerk in the fiscal office and was both aggressive and ambitious.[16] Early on, McCabe took charge by doing much of the work of the board, deciding what questions actually came before the group. McCabe, not Wiley, also took responsibility for issuing its decisions. The Agricultural Appropriation Act of 1910 then placed "supervision and direction" of all legal work at the Department of Agriculture under his purview. Ultimately, McCabe used this phrase to bring every administrative mechanism for enforcing the Pure Food and Drug Act under his control.[17] This situation explains the frequent rumors that Wiley would resign during these years.

As with Dunlap, Wiley had philosophical differences with McCabe about how to enforce the PFDA. Whereas McCabe was worried about whether the Department of Agriculture could win in court if a case went that far, Wiley was primarily concerned with making what he saw as objective decisions about whether a product was adulterated.[18] When a member of Wiley's staff pointed out to him that an action he proposed was not authorized by law, the chemist exclaimed, "We must read it into the law!" a former staffer later remembered. Heated arguments between Wiley and McCabe continued for years over a wide variety of foods.[19]

The differences on the Board of Food and Drug Inspection played out most often with respect to precisely how the inspectors appointed under the PFDA did their jobs on a daily basis. It quickly became the practice of the Board of Food and Drug Inspection to determine the rules under which suspect goods could be seized. Wiley generally favored a much stricter system of oversight than did the other two members of the board. In 1909, for example, Wiley wrote to the secretary of agriculture encouraging the seizure of a shipment of canned tomatoes that traveled from Maryland to Philadelphia because the actual weight was less than the weight listed on the label. In the case of a first offense, like this one, Wiley believed that seizure of the goods was required to encourage future compliance with the law. McCabe and Dunlap thought otherwise. Together they let off first offenders in short weight situations with a warning.[20] Eventually, as a result, consumers were sold countless short-weighted packages of goods of all kinds.

Wiley's hard feelings over his many battles with the rest of the board grew worse over time. He came to consider the mere existence of the Board of Food and Drug Inspection—not just its method of operation—to be illegal under the PFDA because he believed, erroneously, that the PFDA had vested the entire power of enforcement in the Bureau of Chemistry. "The result of the appointment of a board of Food and Drug Inspection was that the functions of the Bureau as defined by the law were entirely paralyzed," wrote Wiley in *The History of a Crime against the Food Law*.[21] But the story that Wiley told himself and his readers near the end of his life did not reflect the usual day-to-day reality of how the Board of Food and Drug Inspection enforced the PFDA.

———

The turmoil on the Board of Food and Drug Inspection did not grind enforcement of the PFDA to a halt. Wiley's disagreements with Dunlap and McCabe mostly involved cases that became prolonged scientific struggles, like those involving sodium benzoate or caffeine. On many questions over how to implement the PFDA, there was no debate at all because all three board members agreed that the law should be put into action to protect consumers. For example, misbranding and other easy-to-interpret violations of the law were common topics for consideration before the board, and the votes were overwhelmingly unanimous against the food manufacturers whose products were the subject of these cases.

Such actions led to significant improvement in the quality of the US food supply. As Wiley himself summarized the effectiveness of enforcement under the law up to 1909, "Judgements which have been obtained under the [pure food] law include shortages of weight in canned goods, coffee misbranded as to origin, 'maple syrup' made of cane sugar syrup flavored with an extract made from the wood of the maple in the factory, spring water supposed to be especially pure, but in reality dangerously contaminated, eggs in a putrid condition broken into a tub and frozen into a solid mass, presumably for use in bakeries, and also 'cold storage eggs' masquerading as perfectly fresh."[22] Agreement on these kinds of questions came easily since the accuracy of the labels could be easily determined by chemistry or, in some cases, the naked eye.

Other companies settled with the Department of Agriculture even before the law had to be invoked. One example of this was the case against Grape-Nuts, the breakfast cereal invented just a few years earlier by C. W. Post. Grape-Nuts ran afoul of the Pure Food and Drug Act because the box said it was sweetened by grape sugar when it was, in fact, sweetened by dextrose.[23] Post's firm, then called the Postum Cereal Company, changed the label on the box even before that hearing began, thereby avoiding prosecution.[24] Many other smaller companies who found themselves in similar positions took similar actions.

Although adulteration of milk did not attract the same amount of public attention as disputes over chemical additives, it is an excellent example of a different form of improvement brought about by the law. Poor milk quality had been a problem for Americans since the industry had begun industrializing in the early to mid-nineteenth century. When farms became too distant or unable to produce enough milk for urban populations, cows moved

into the cities. With the move, the quality of their feed dropped significantly, and, as a result, the quality of their milk did too. Even high-quality
milk was visibly filthy as it was conveyed in open pails in the years preceding
the invention of the milk bottle in 1883.[25] Adulterated milk was a problem
that technology alone could not solve. Sometimes the adulteration was simply done with water. "A water shortage would put the milkman out of business," quipped one wag. This practice was particularly dangerous because
urban water supplies in this era carried deadly diseases. Other additives,
like chalk, improved the color of the product.[26] The Bureau of Chemistry
had investigated milk during the 1880s and 1890s and found that the situation had not improved since the mid-1800s. One sample they examined had
worms floating in it.[27]

One of the later Poison Squad experiments focused on a new problem
with the nation's milk supply: the addition of formaldehyde to keep it from
spoiling. The tiniest amount of formaldehyde could keep milk fresh for
forty-eight hours, long enough to get it far away from its point of production, where the conditions under which it was produced would be unknown
to the consumer.[28] This additive gave the product a slightly sweet taste that
masked the taste of spoilage. To make matters worse, name-brand preservatives like "Freezine" and "Preservaline" had formaldehyde as an active
ingredient.[29] Local milk producers would likely have used these products
without knowing exactly what they were adding to their milk. Producers
could also use formaldehyde to conceal dirt, a significant problem in the
filthy urban dairy operations of that era.[30]

After Wiley's experiments with formaldehyde, the Bureau of Chemistry
condemned the additive in a report issued in 1908, writing that its use in
food was "never justifiable." The bureau noted its particular ill effects upon
children, who made up a large portion of regular milk drinkers. In the conclusion of the study, Wiley noted that it "tends to derange metabolism" and
can "disturb the normal functions" of digestion.[31] Formaldehyde was so obviously toxic that no other segment in the government fought for its continued use, including the Board of Food and Drug Inspection.[32] Since there was
no pro-formaldehyde lobby to thwart the unanimous will of the Department of Agriculture, the government invoked the PFDA to outlaw its use.

The case of milk demonstrates how the Pure Food and Drug Act dramatically boosted the quality of what Americans ate in the first years of the law, not in spite of the Board of Food and Drug Inspection but because of it. Before the passage of the law, milk may have been the most-often adulterated product in the United States. Even apart from the successful effort to keep formaldehyde out of food, the passage of the pure food law did much to improve the quality of America's milk supply. Secretary Wilson, writing in the *Department of Agriculture Yearbook* for 1909, described a series of "milk crusades" conducted against adulteration and unsanitary conditions in dairies. The Bureau of Chemistry discovered, for example, that many small dairies put excess ice in their milk, ostensibly for cooling, but sold the result as pure milk once it melted. The bureau worked with municipal governments to stop the practice.[33]

Of all the judgments against food companies made under the auspices of the Pure Food and Drug Act in its first five years, milk was the food most often found lacking.[34] Wiley believed that if they attacked all such problems in one place, then other local milk producers would fall in line. Wiley's badgering cross-examination of the head of a Cincinnati dairy in 1909 typifies his use of the Board of Food and Drug Inspection to inspire change, whether or not the hearing led to a legal prosecution. At that time, he explained why helping improve the milk in one city along the state border with Kentucky would be so important. "If we can control the milk that goes from state to state," he declared, "we will be doing a great help to state authorities." Dunlap, the only other member of the board present at this hearing, helped Wiley in this cross-examination rather than hindered him.[35]

At the end of 1911, Wiley claimed publicly that the Department of Agriculture had won 90 percent of the cases it had brought that year.[36] That figure includes complaints relating to adulteration, deception, and filth. With respect to adulteration, the question was never whether or not something had been added, but whether that additive was harmful to the people who consumed it. Wiley, as we have seen, managed to ban borax under the auspices of the Pure Food and Drug Act. Ultimately, as we will see, he won an adulteration case against the Coca-Cola Company. While Wiley lost other struggles over how the Pure Food and Drug Act should be carried out,

he almost always had at least some effect on how particular foods were manufactured, marketed, or consumed—in the short run and down to today.

———

The Board of Food and Drug Inspection was the Roosevelt administration's initial response to criticism from industry that Wiley was acting like
a food dictator. When food manufacturers grew concerned that this board
was not enough to stop Wiley's extraordinarily strict interpretation of the
Pure Food and Drug Act from taking hold, they pressed for the creation
of another board. The Referee Board of Consulting Scientific Experts (or
Remsen Board, after its chair, Professor Ira Remsen, then the president of
the Johns Hopkins University) was the administration's next response. Secretary Wilson appointed this body in February 1908 after calls from food
manufacturers to get disinterested scientific experts to review the Board of
Food and Drug Inspection's most controversial decisions. Besides Remsen,
its members included Russell Chittenden of Yale University, C. A. Herter
of Columbia University, John Long of Northwestern University, and A. E.
Taylor of the University of California, Berkeley.[37]

The Remsen Board examined topics on a case-by-case basis. Remsen
performed no chemistry himself on the board's behalf but only took on
administrative leadership of the body.[38] This board was brought in to resolve
particularly important but divisive questions on whether certain additives or
substances were harmful to health through targeted scientific research. To
test the effects of substances on people, it commissioned Poison Squad–style
experiments at the home institutions of its members. During its existence, the
board only studied five substances: (1) sodium benzoate (a preservative upon
which Wiley had earlier conducted his own experiments), (2) sulfur dioxide
(the residue of the process that California fruit growers used when drying their
product), (3) copper sulfate (a food coloring to make green vegetables greener),
(4) saccharin (an artificial sweetener derived from sodium benzoate), and
(5) aluminum compounds (alum, an additive to baking powder and pickles).[39]

The controversies over three of these substances will be considered later,
but for now it is worth noting that only in one case—sodium benzoate—did

FIGURE 8.1 Ira Remsen, professor of chemistry and president of the Johns Hopkins University, 1901. Remsen followed a different set of rules than Wiley did when it came to talking to the media about his work, and as a result he got substantially worse press on pure food issues.

Courtesy Library of Congress

the Remsen Board contradict Wiley's position on the substance's healthfulness (even though it did agree with other parts of his reasoning). In all other cases they either hedged on Wiley's conclusion (as with alum) or failed to release a report on the subject because their own scientists did not agree (as with sulfur dioxide and dried fruit). Yet in his autobiography, Wiley insisted that the only subject he and the Remsen Board agreed upon was copper sulfate—a revealing reaction to having his decisions questioned.[40]

To Wiley, the mere existence of the Remsen Board was a personal slight. With this new board, as with the Board of Food and Drug Inspection, Wiley was generally apoplectic about having his work reviewed and took it personally when anyone questioned his judgments. At a gathering of the Society of Chemical Industry in late 1908, a member of the Remsen Board objected publicly and vociferously to Wiley's interpretation of the health risks associated with sulfur dioxide. "These remarks from Dr. Smith greatly affected Dr. Wiley," wrote a reporter on the scene. "It appeared to be an unexpected and staggering blow that Dr. Smith disagreed with him on a vital point, and from that time on he seemed to grow nervous and disheartened, to realize that his was a losing cause and that he was steadily losing ground, his pet ideas and theories crumbling before his eyes."[41]

This episode shows why the Remsen Board frustrated Wiley no matter what decisions it made. Asked about the purpose of the Remsen Board while testifying in a southern Illinois courtroom during the Hipolite egg case, Wiley responded, "I think it was created for the purpose of overruling my decisions."[42] In those cases where the Remsen Board agreed with Wiley, he was angry that the board had wasted taxpayer money duplicating his work. Nothing could undo his belief that the Pure Food and Drug Act had been effectively destroyed when the power to control its enforcement slipped away from him. Later, Wiley would fault the Remsen Board for adopting his experimental methods without giving him proper credit—a professional slight he took very seriously.[43]

Here Wiley had a valid point. Without Wiley, the Remsen Board would never have existed. However, Wiley also suffered from professional jealousy. On the surface, the Remsen Board's work resembled Wiley's, but unlike Wiley's experiments, the experiments sponsored by the Remsen Board had control groups.[44] Not only had the board improved upon his experimental methods (or at least the experimental design that made him famous), but many of the scientists that performed experiments at the Remsen Board's request referred to their subjects in their letters back to Remsen as "squads."[45] It is easy to see that a man with Wiley's ego would bitterly resent the lack of recognition.

Despite this rivalry, the Remsen Board's research actually cemented one of Wiley's most important legacies. When duplicated by the Remsen Board, Wiley's human subject research established the principle that it was the federal government's responsibility to determine whether food additives were safe for human consumption. It seems eminently possible that without Harvey Wiley, officials at the Department of Agriculture in that laissez-faire era would have assumed that humans could safely consume substances like borax or sodium benzoate precisely because they were natural. Wiley loudly and repeatedly insisted that this was not necessarily true. The Remsen Board, in its efforts to test his conclusions, indirectly assumed the premise upon which Wiley based the objections that would become his life's work. Without Harvey Wiley then, it is possible that the Food and Drug Administration would not be sponsoring food safety experiments now.

Where Wiley and the Remsen Board differed most was in their approaches to the press. Wiley spoke about his Poison Squad research long before he published any results—in effect preparing the public for his conclusions—whereas Remsen took the traditional approach of waiting for the results of experiments before saying anything about them. Asked to comment upon the Remsen Board's sodium benzoate research by a *New York Times* reporter in 1909, Remsen responded, "It does not seem wise, or indeed proper, for members of our Committee to discuss the matter publicly."[46] Wiley's willingness to talk about the health effects of any food additive, whether he had conducted research on it or not, broke this silence for the American public and prepared them in advance to resist any information that contradicted Wiley's views. All the Remsen Board studies took years to complete.

In the case of sodium benzoate, Wiley released his report about its dangers without the permission of Secretary Wilson, while the secretary was visiting California. That move generated publicity favorable to Wiley and unfavorable to sodium benzoate, as Wiley argued that the harms of sodium benzoate had been conclusively established. He launched plans to try to pass legislation banning sodium benzoate at the state level regardless of the Remsen Board's conclusions and gathered chemists from the private sector to support his position on sodium benzoate before the Remsen Board's scientists had completed their research.[47]

Wiley's ongoing campaign against the Remsen Board guaranteed that it got uniformly terrible press.[48] Privately, Remsen blamed Wiley for these attacks. Presented with one of these articles at the time of its publication, Remsen noted in a letter to a fellow board member, "I should say without hesitation that it was written by Wiley.... It is extraordinary to what lengths some people will go to accomplish their ends."[49] He privately expressed support for President Taft's firing Wiley years before anyone in the Department of Agriculture actually moved to do so but never made these sentiments public.[50]

To Wiley, the requirement to test certain substances more than once showed that his superiors cared more about industry than about consumers. As he declared in a private hearing of the Board of Food and Drug Inspection with the Cincinnati dairy, "I want to make this law so effective that nobody is going to disobey it, and I for one, mean to do what is right and administer this law without fear or favor. If the purpose of this law is to punish the little fellows and let the big ones go free, then I'll get out of it today."[51] To Wiley's bureaucratic enemies, this stance was entirely impractical.

Unlike Wiley, Ira Remsen understood the actual constituency of his board. It wasn't industry. It wasn't the public. It was the Roosevelt and Taft administrations. They wanted additional research conducted on substances before they were banned not to undermine Wiley's position, but to put the focus of the debate on the additives themselves rather than the personalities involved in testing them. The more science they could point to in support of the Department of Agriculture's decisions, the fewer protests they would hear from either industry or the public. Wiley, in contrast, refused to acknowledge that businesses had any legitimate interest in using substances that might prove unhealthy to even a fraction of the general public. This dynamic played itself out repeatedly in some of the most hotly contested, Wiley-inspired food fights of this era.

CHAPTER NINE

SACCHARIN

AND

KETCHUP

WILEY STARTED THE FOURTH OF SEVEN Poison Squad experiments in April 1904—this time on sodium benzoate, the salt of benzoic acid.[1] Discovered in the sixteenth century, benzoic acid is a plant hormone that appears naturally in many foods, including berries, cinnamon, and even meat, and confers immunity against a broad range of pathogens. It was not until 1875 that the German biochemist Ernst Leopold Salkowski discovered its effectiveness as a food preservative.[2] Sodium benzoate inhibits fermentation, organic decomposition, and microbial growth in foods while having no effect on the foods' taste or texture. By 1880 it was in widespread use, and the first methods to detect this colorless, flavorless substance appeared in print.

As a preservative, benzoic acid gradually replaced salicylic acid (which Wiley also investigated) because it was cheaper to produce. Whereas borax worked best for meat and dairy products, food manufacturers used sodium

THE WILEY BOY SEEMS TO BE IN
GOOD COMPANY

FIGURE 9.1 A cartoon depicting Wiley's efforts to promote pure food in direct opposition to the additive benzoate of soda, which he saw as immoral. It has since gained wide acceptance in the American diet.

Charles Lewis Bartholomew, "The Wiley boy seems to be in good company," 1912. Courtesy Library of Congress.

benzoate to preserve fruits and vegetables, especially in canned goods, as well as wine and beer.[3] Perhaps its best-known use was in tomato ketchup. Although more-respected brands like Heinz did not use benzoic acid at the time, lesser-quality ones did.[4]

The new Poison Squad experiment resembled the borax experiment, with some differences. This time there was great resistance inside the government to Wiley's publishing his findings. Officials demanded that a delay be imposed for Wiley to run follow-up experiments and communicate with food producers about this chemical.[5] Eventually, sodium benzoate became the first food additive to ignite a major controversy between Harvey Wiley and the Remsen Board. Whereas the Remsen Board thought that sodium benzoate was problematic only in very large doses, both Wiley and the Board of Food and Drug Inspection thought it should be banned entirely in products like ketchup, where it did not appear naturally.

From the standpoint of purity, this argument made no sense. After all, if sodium benzoate was a sign of impurity in one context (such as ketchup), how could it be fine in another (such as berries)? It took some time for Wiley to reach this position. In 1904, long before he had completed his experimental write-up, Wiley announced publicly that his experiments had persuaded him that sodium benzoate was harmful, yet two years later he suggested that it was safe for anyone who wanted to keep it in a salt shaker at their table and use it if they were so inclined.[6] When he finally released his report in 1908, Wiley argued that "its effects are always injurious or tend to injury."[7] This was enough to get the Board of Food and Drug Inspection and Agriculture Secretary Wilson to agree that sodium benzoate should be banned.[8]

The pro–sodium benzoate lobby pushed back on this decision, arguing against Wiley's conclusions because benzoic acid occurs naturally in many food products.[9] It didn't take a science background to wonder why something could be hazardous in one context and not hazardous where it appeared naturally. Led by Congressman James Sherman of New York, who owned a canning facility, food manufacturers of all kinds lobbied Preident Roosevelt to overturn the Department of Agriculture's decision.[10] As a consequence, the Remsen Board sponsored its own "Poison Squad" experiments on sodium benzoate. Wiley attacked those experiments, indirectly, before they even began; he had come out entirely against the substance and did not want his position undercut by some of the leading practitioners in his field.

In its report on the experiments, the Remsen Board dealt Wiley the ultimate insult by completely ignoring his earlier work. While most scientific papers at least mention earlier conclusions, in the report on Russell Chittenden's Remsen Board experiments, Wiley did not even merit a mention.[11] Chittenden concluded that low levels of sodium benzoate had no deleterious effects on the subjects.[12] With the report in hand, Secretary Wilson reversed Wiley's findings of the previous year and again permitted the use of benzoic acid as a preservative.[13]

Upon final publication of Wiley's results, other chemists attacked him as the only chemist who had examined benzoic acid that found the substance harmful. The most serious of these attacks came from K. B. Lehman in a German journal that was eventually translated and published in the journal *Science*. "In my honest opinion," Lehman wrote, "Wiley's publication is lacking in every proof, every objective proof, of the harmfulness of benzoic acid, and from the voluminous metabolism investigations which Wiley has so pitilessly used against benzoic acid exactly the opposite conclusion may be drawn."[14] It seems likely that the sodium benzoate controversy hurt Wiley's scientific reputation more than it did that of the Remsen Board.

The dispute did, however, reduce morale inside the Department of Agriculture. In 1910 two companies challenged an Indiana law banning sodium benzoate. Members of the Remsen Board all testified in Indiana on behalf of the plaintiffs. As a show of support for the Remsen Board, President Taft turned down a direct request to send Wiley to Indiana to testify on the opposite side.[15] In response, Wiley testified on behalf of the State of Indiana in a special session in Washington, DC, even though he had been explicitly forbidden to do so by Solicitor McCabe.[16] Through his actions, he encouraged the employees of the Bureau of Chemistry to be more loyal to him than to the administration they supposedly served.[17]

Publicly, Wiley's disloyalty did not take the form of a direct attack on the Remsen Board's findings on sodium benzoate. However, he refused to sign the Board of Food and Drug Inspection's opinion on the subject.

Privately, he continued to express his opposition to the Remsen Board's conclusion.[18] He picked apart the structure of the Remsen Board's experiments in private and got some of his friends to do so in public.[19] Officially, he did not claim that sodium benzoate was dangerous, but he argued that the preservative should be banned because it could be used to cover up inferiority in food products.[20] A member of the Remsen Board responded by noting—as the sodium benzoate–using ketchup makers had previously done—that an odorless and colorless preservative couldn't really cover up anything.[21]

Wiley would engage in other food fights over the rest of his career, but this was the last of the serious disagreements in which he had direct expertise. As a result, his complaints about the introduction of sodium benzoate into the food supply were stronger and more frequent than his complaints about other additives. They were not, however, any more scientifically accurate. Modern research has tended to support the accuracy of the Remsen Board's experiments over Wiley's for many of the same reasons that the boric acid experiments have been criticized, such as the lack of a control group.[22] Wiley took the question of sodium benzoate so seriously because of the principle involved. He believed he had to hold the line against all preservatives; if any preservatives got through the regulatory hurdles, the entire edifice of the Pure Food and Drug Act would collapse.[23]

———

Benzoic acid is the root of the well-known sugar substitute saccharin. Both come from the same coal-tar derivative, and are therefore chemically similar.[24] Saccharin had been discovered in 1879, by Constantin Fahlberg, a chemist at Johns Hopkins University working under Ira Remsen (when Remsen was still a practicing chemist). Fahlberg was working on benzoic acid compounds when he touched the result to his lips and discovered it was sweet.[25] In 1901 John Queeny established the first factory to produce saccharin in the United States. That company would eventually be known as Monsanto, the modern chemical giant of today.[26]

In its early days, manufacturers constituted the entire market for saccharin. Many used it as a substitute for sugar without listing it on the label, especially in canned vegetables like sweet corn. It was far cheaper than sugar. Made in a laboratory rather than grown, saccharin also had the advantage of being available year-round on a market that was far less volatile than that for cane sugar, which could be grown only in tropical or subtropical areas. The same sugar tariffs that created a market for Wiley's beet sugar also increased a market for saccharin. Yet most consumers didn't realize that it had become part of their diets in the years preceding the passage of the Pure Food and Drug Act (PFDA). In fact, most consumers likely didn't know what saccharin was.[27]

Following his normal line of attack, Wiley argued that saccharin was both deceptive and unhealthful. "I have strongly advised all manufacturers who have written me on the subject not to use saccharine in their goods," wrote Wiley in a letter to the editor of the *American Grocer* in 1904. "Aside from any effect it may have upon the digestion, I consider it a fraud, since the sweet taste it imparts is attributed by the consumer to sugar."[28] Even if manufacturers had labeled saccharin on their cans, Wiley would have considered it dishonest because it allowed packers to cover the inferiority of the corn they canned by sweetening it themselves.[29] Wiley never conducted an experiment on saccharin, but he often cited other work that found it to be harmful and noted that it was banned in other countries.[30]

Unfortunately for Wiley, his position on saccharin ran afoul of the dietary practices of the president of the United States. As he told the story two decades later, in early 1908 he had convinced President Theodore Roosevelt that benzoic acid was harmful and should not be added to canned goods. Then a canning executive in the room brought up saccharin. Roosevelt questioned Wiley: "You tell me that saccharin is injurious to health?" I said, "Yes, Mr. President, I do tell you that." He replied, "Dr. Rixey gives it to me every day." I answered, "Mr. President, he probably thinks you may be threatened with diabetes." To this he retorted, "Anybody who says saccharin is injurious to health is an idiot." The day after the meeting, Roosevelt ordered the creation of the Remsen Board.[31]

When Wiley moved to ban saccharin, the Remsen Board reviewed his decision. As with sodium benzoate, the board commissioned Poison Squad–style experiments, this time at Columbia University. The board arrived at a surprisingly intermediate position given that its chairman had run the lab where saccharin was invented. Board members concluded that saccharin would not hurt people who added less than three grams a day to their food and would cause only "stomach disturbances" at higher amounts. Most important, they found that adding saccharin to processed foods was a substitution and therefore constituted a "reduction in its quality."[32] Three cabinet members—the secretaries of treasury, agriculture, and commerce—approved the Remsen Board's decision to ban saccharin from food products in the United States, including the District of Columbia, effective July 1, 1911.[33]

But the regulation didn't go into effect. President Taft recognized that there was a big difference between Wiley's conclusion (that saccharin should be banned outright) and the Remsen Board's (that it was safe at levels below three grams per day). He therefore asked for a supplemental report from the Remsen Board. Saccharin manufacturers lobbied the board's members to allow greater use of their product and won. In early 1912 the Remsen Board issued two reports. The first acknowledged that saccharin could be used to lower the quality of foods, but it hedged on the significance of its daily limits for individual consumption. Because saccharin was so sweet, the board concluded, no one would want to consume more than three grams per day. The second report opened up over-the-counter sales for people, like diabetics, who might want saccharin because their doctor prescribed it. These regulations went into effect on April 1, 1912.[34]

When the Remsen Board failed to ban saccharin outright, Wiley attacked its decisions as illegal since the pure food law, as written, contained no mechanism for checking the decisions of the Bureau of Chemistry.[35] Wiley never acknowledged that the Remsen Board decisions helped in the battle against adulteration, even if they fell short of what he wanted. At the turn of the twentieth century, it was common practice for manufacturers, particularly of canned goods, to substitute saccharin for at least some sugar in sweet products to decrease their costs.[36] The Remsen Board found this an obvious violation of the PFDA. Labeling saccharin as a substitute for sugar remained legal. Using saccharin to deceive consumers was not.[37] Wiley, however, was never satisfied with partial victories. Because he could not remove saccharin from the food supply entirely, he considered this struggle a defeat.

By 1922 Wiley was complaining publicly about America's "almost endless riot of saccharine consumption."[38] But even Wiley was never terribly concerned with saccharin per se; he was worried about what it represented. To Wiley, the continued availability of saccharin to consumers in any form constituted a gross violation of the intent of the pure food law because of how the Remsen Board and the Board of Food and Drug Inspection had usurped the authority of the Bureau of Chemistry.[39] During the years following World War I, long after Wiley had resigned his position, Wiley's successors at the Bureau of Chemistry repeatedly took Monsanto, the manufacturer of saccharin, to court to enforce the order that came from Remsen Board's findings. Unable to ban the substance outright, the government managed to force food manufacturers to label any food that contained saccharin, which proved effective at limiting the product's use.[40]

———

Wiley had better luck getting sodium benzoate out of ketchup manufacturing than he did banning saccharin. Although the Remsen Board eventually overruled his judgment on this additive, the Board of Food and Drug Inspection (under a motion made by George McCabe) specifically asked him to examine these issue of preservatives in ketchup.[41] Benzoic acid (or sodium benzoate) was once a common preservative for ketchup. Ketchup, of course, was (and is) a common condiment, one of people's many options for making food taste better. Originating in Asia, ketchup began as a fermented fish sauce without tomatoes. English sailors carried it throughout the empire, including to colonists in America. Ketchup was initially homemade, and people made many varieties besides the now-standard tomato version.[42]

Mass-produced commercial tomato ketchups arrived with mass-produced industrial foods during the late nineteenth century, starting as a by-product of tomato canning. Making ketchup was a good way to use surplus tomatoes during the early fall tomato season. Sugar, spices, and vinegar added to the pulp of leftover tomato trimmings both hid the poor quality of the surplus tomatoes and helped make the taste of tomatoes available out of season. By the turn of the twentieth century, ketchup resembled the modern product we know today. The deep red condiment came in bottles.[43] Ketchup makers generally used artificial preservatives, either salicylic acid or, starting shortly before 1900, sodium benzoate. The flavor of different brands of ketchup varied widely, but in general adding vinegar was a way to obscure the taste of inferior tomatoes. And adding sugar was a way to counteract the taste of the vinegar.[44]

The H. J. Heinz Company of Pittsburgh, Pennsylvania, was a latecomer to the ketchup business. Although the product had been manufactured in the United States since at least the 1850s, Heinz started producing it only in the early 1870s. In the 1890s Heinz sold four different grades of ketchup, each at a different level of quality, but around the turn of the twentieth century Heinz began to consolidate around one type, its highest-quality ketchup.[45] In 1904, as part of this effort, Heinz gradually shifted away from using sodium benzoate. This shift meant using higher-quality tomatoes, and the result was a better-tasting, benzoate-free product. When the PFDA passed in June 1906, the company made all of its ketchup without added preservatives. The company highlighted its benzoate-free ketchup in advertisements for years afterward to attract health-conscious customers and to indirectly discredit its lower-quality competition.[46]

For Heinz, going preservative-free was both a case of corporate benevolence and a smart business decision. H. J. Heinz was a deeply religious man who associated the purity of the food he produced with religious purity.[47] But what was Wiley's role in the elimination of sodium benzoate from Heinz ketchup?[48] As the company wrote Wiley in 1908, "Long before we became acquainted with you, and before we knew of your attitude toward preservatives, we looked upon them as being undesirable in food products, even though there might be no positive proof as to their injuriousness." In fact, the company had started its anti-preservative efforts all the way back in 1896, when it began to take salicylic acid out of its products.[49] Better ingredients and fewer preservatives were key to making a higher-quality ketchup that was easier to market. Both the high-quality tomatoes and the lack of preservatives became important elements in Heinz's advertising.[50]

Wiley, who was close to Heinz officials, took what he had learned from Heinz and brought that knowledge to the company's competitors. In 1907

Wiley sent Arvin W. Bitting, an inspector from the Bureau of Chemistry, to the Loudon Packing Company of Terre Haute, Indiana, to help the company formulate a recipe for ketchup that did not require chemical preservatives. The process took time, but Bitting, with the help of his wife, Katherine, eventually succeeded.[51] Notably, Bitting published his findings as Bulletin 119 from the Bureau of Chemistry.[52] Now everyone who wanted to make better-quality ketchup chose to do so. However, explaining how to make ketchup without preservatives obviously undercut whatever competitive advantage Heinz had had.

Many of Heinz's competitors made use of the work that Wiley commissioned from the Bittings. "In season and out of season," wrote Charles Loudon of the Loudon Packing Company, "I consistently opposed Dr. Wiley's views on the preservative question, until I was convinced of the results of my own experiments and by the favor which my non-preservative goods were received by the trade, that I was right in packing them. It was not a case of catering to Dr. Wiley at all, but simply a cold-blooded business proposition."[53] Such experiments showed that if manufacturers used high-quality tomatoes in their ketchup, it could keep well without preservatives. Heinz's experiments confirmed this.[54] Those tomatoes had to be handled in a sanitary manner, and the final product had to be sterilized.[55] The new method also required adding enough vinegar to essentially pickle them.[56] If a producer cut the ketchup with other substances, even water, it became necessary to add preservatives to prevent fermentation.[57]

The reason preservative-free ketchup tasted better had everything to do with the tomatoes. Many ketchup manufacturers used what was known as trimming stock for their ketchup. While some of those tomatoes might have been acceptable, they also might have included moldy, broken, rotten, or unripe fruits. It didn't help that tomato season lasted only two months a year, from mid-August to mid-October. In the days before cold storage or refrigerated transport, making ketchup during any other part of the year required using marginal tomatoes. Manufacturers who preserved tomato pulp to meet the needs for year-round ketchup making inevitably used inferior fruits or fruits that had already aged significantly before they were ever made into ketchup.[58]

Thanks to the low cost of inferior tomatoes, any fly-by-night operation could sell that product as ketchup, and the use of preservatives helped low-quality ketchup manufacturers maintain less than hygienic conditions. If the ketchup did not appear spoiled, there was no obvious sign that it carried harmful germs since the benzoic acid would have prevented mold from breaking out.[59] Poor-quality ketchup makers obscured other potentially visible problems, such as inferior tomatoes, by using artificial colors.[60] Wiley's efforts against preservatives meant that makers had to use superior tomatoes, resulting in a better-tasting, vinegar-free ketchup without artificial colors. Thanks to Wiley, ketchup went from being a thin, watery product often made from bad tomatoes to being a thick product that tastes more like the fruit from which it is made.[61]

Invariably, ketchup manufacturers passed on the increased cost of making a better product to consumers. Heinz could make preservative-free ketchup starting in 1905, but they couldn't make it cheaper than they had before. Heinz's preservative-free ketchup generally cost more than twice as much as most of the kinds made with sodium benzoate.[62] This price gap did not bother Wiley. He believed consumers would choose to pay the difference to get better ketchup.[63] To Wiley, at least, healthier, better-tasting ketchup was worth this kind of sacrifice.

Even though the Remsen Board approved sodium benzoate in 1909, ketchup makers had largely eliminated it from their product lines by 1915.[64] Some other food processors followed Heinz's lead and used fewer preservatives in their products. Over time, other processed foods have shifted to include sodium benzoate, but it remains rare in ketchup.[65] Wiley didn't need to get anything banned to influence the way Americans ate. He just used the bully pulpit he had developed through his office, drawing on his skill at influencing media of all kinds. For years, the only vocal force in Washington warning about the effect of sodium benzoate was Harvey Wiley. He had set the Department of Agriculture's agenda by choosing to test goods preserved with sodium benzoate. The rest of the Department of Agriculture's bureaucracy responded negatively, but they had to respond.

Today, sodium benzoate is present in many beverages, margarines, jellies, jams, fruit juices, and prepared salads. It is contained in many drugs and even used as a rust inhibitor for iron.[66] It remains controversial in some circles thanks to studies that link it to attention deficit hyperactivity disorder, asthma, and eczema.[67] The Center for Science in the Public Interest, a large American consumer watchdog group, notes that sodium benzoate and benzoic acid are safe for most people, although a few particularly sensitive individuals may have an allergic reaction if they consume it.[68] In short, Harvey Wiley lost his battle against sodium benzoate, and rightfully so, because the risks from consuming it are very small.

CHAPTER TEN

DRUGS

ON AUGUST 10, 1910, the Board of Food and Drug Inspection held a hearing about a product called Dr. Bull's Celebrated Cough Syrup, produced by the A. C. Meyer Company. The Bureau of Chemistry had found that the syrup violated the Pure Food and Drug Act (PFDA) on a number of grounds: the product was not, in fact, the same syrup that had been invented by Dr. John W. Bull in Baltimore during the 1850s; Dr. Bull was not a practicing physician; and, contrary to the claim on the label, two million bottles of the syrup had not been sold. At the hearing, Harvey Wiley had nice things to say about the A. C. Meyer Company, but he was highly suspicious of this particular medicine.[1]

The most heated part of the hearing involved the company's claim that Dr. Bull's Celebrated Cough Syrup cured croup. The label read, "Mothers can always depend upon it. For croup and whooping cough it is invaluable." Wiley contended that this statement might cost the lives of thousands of children. As he explained at the hearing, "The mother may depend on this until the child is beyond the scope of medical aid. I consider that not only a misleading statement, but almost a criminal statement." To counter Wiley's concern, the lawyer for A. C. Meyer pointed to thousands of testimonials about the effectiveness of the product. When Wiley asked for pledges from doctors that the cough syrup cured croup, the lawyer could not provide any.[2] The company never changed its advertising.[3] Despite this setback, Wiley managed to use the powers given to the Department of Agriculture under the PFDA to change the way that many drugs besides this one were made and marketed in the United States.

Although Wiley had gone to medical school, he did not consider himself a doctor. Nonetheless, he knew enough about medicine to defer to doctors on whether particular proprietary medicines—also called patent medicines, since some of the formulas were protected by patents—were effective.[4] "Those who are legitimately engaged in the practice of [medicine and pharmacy] are required to take a long course in preparatory trying, and secure a license after examination before State and Municipal Boards in medicine and pharmacy," Wiley observed in 1907. "On the other hand, the quack doctor or the proprietor of a fake remedy may practice medicine through the public Press, and dispense drugs in the same manner, through the mails . . . without any medical or pharmaceutical training whatever."[5] Wiley trusted doctors and pharmacists—not private companies of questionable morality—to make decisions in the best interests of their patients.

Whereas reputable drug companies sold their products through medical professionals, patent medicine makers sold their products directly to customers. Without doctors to judge whether their products were effective, patent medicine producers could make money whether their medicines—sometimes laced with cocaine or drowning in alcohol—helped people or not. In 1900 the country's two most important medical journals began a campaign to educate physicians about the dangers that patent medicines posed to their patients. This was the beginning of a groundswell of support for legislation guaranteeing the purity of drugs.[6] Wiley joined that groundswell long before the passage of the PFDA.

America had a longer history of regulating drugs than regulating food. As far back as 1848, the Drug Import Act barred the import of adulterated drugs into the country. Yet at the turn of the twentieth century adulterated drugs remained a significant problem, especially among domestic products.

While adulteration occurred in the kinds of quack medicines that were a special target of the PFDA, even many "legitimate" producers adulterated their medicines as a matter of course.[7]

Recognizing the extent of this problem, Harvey Wiley worked with the American Pharmaceutical Association (APA) to establish a drug laboratory within the Bureau of Chemistry in 1902. At a time when there were no national standards on how drugs should be assayed, this was a huge leap toward pure drugs since it promoted uniform methods of chemical analysis.[8] Wiley hired the chair of the scientific section of the APA, Lyman Kebler, to run the laboratory. Kebler was probably the most qualified person in the country for the job. As Wiley had done with food, Kebler had established all the standard methods for determining the ingredients in drugs over a long research career at the University of Michigan and the drug company Smith, Kline and French.[9] Kebler released the Bureau of Chemistry's first report on impure drugs in 1904.[10]

The Bureau of Chemistry produced research to persuade people of the problems with quack medicines at a time when it was uncertain whether drugs would even be included in any pure food legislation. While Kebler conducted research, Wiley became the public face of the cause of pure drugs. This collaboration made sense given that many drugs were also consumed as food or beverages during this period. (Medicinal whiskey is just one example.) In the years before 1906 Wiley gave multiple speeches devoted entirely to impure drugs. Wiley had been concerned about the adverse effects of untested drugs since childhood, when he had seen the effects of one particular antimalarial nostrum on his neighbors in Indiana. At the Bureau of Chemistry, he had collected pamphlets full of outrageous, unproven claims for such products. Now he was putting his personal prestige into the anti-nostrum campaign to strengthen the PFDA.[11] His efforts to strengthen the law with respect to drugs helped the campaign against adulterated foods because many drugs were foods at this time and because any efforts to strengthen the law increased the power of the Department of Agriculture in general.

The exposure of adulterated drugs, rather than adulterated foods, had a great deal to do with getting the PFDA passed. A major upswing in reporting on the problem of patent medicines and nostrums beginning in fall 1905 convinced Congress to include drugs in the final version of the law. The journalist Samuel Hopkins Adams labeled this industry "The Great American Fraud" in a series of articles published in *Collier's* magazine starting in October 1905. Adams made his attack on the patent medicine industry on several fronts. One issue was that they were mostly alcohol. This fact drew the attention of Prohibitionists, who supported pure food legislation. Pairing the regulation of drugs and food led them to support broad legislation and was an important reason the bill eventually passed.

Another problem Adams highlighted was that patent medicines were often fraudulent and therefore dangerous. One of Adams's articles centered on Liquozone, which was 99 percent water mixed with a little bit of sulfuric acid. The problem with Liquozone was not just that somebody was making money misrepresenting what this compound could do; it was that people who believed that this useless compound could treat their diseases would not go to a doctor for treatment and could die as a result. A different class of nostrums was laced with addictive drugs like cocaine. Once hooked, even the smartest people would have trouble kicking their new habit.

The last class of drugs Adams highlighted were the fake cures. These substances shared characteristics with some of the other classes—some contained habit-forming drugs or alcohol—but the claims behind them were designed solely to attract the dollars of the desperate. Fake cancer cures were particularly popular. Many were full of substances that were downright dangerous—like chloroform, opium, or hashish—and that might well hasten the deaths of the sick people who consumed them.[12]

The final version of the PFDA was weaker for drugs than it was for foods. It authorized the Department of Agriculture to use the legal system to pursue food manufacturers guilty of infractions of any kind whenever possible. There was no exception for transparency; any attempt to introduce harmful ingredients into food or to lower quality violated the law by definition.

This approach attracted attention from the press, and Wiley cultivated that attention. But Congress decided that drug makers could not be prosecuted if they listed their "standard of strength, quality, or purity" on the container, even if those standards were different from what medical professionals favored as being most effective. This made it harder to prosecute any drug company, patent medicine or not, that followed these rules.[13]

———◆———

Because the PFDA treated impure food and impure drugs differently, Wiley pursued the two problems differently. This hasn't stopped Wiley critics—from the early days of the Pure Food and Drug Act to historians writing about his activities much later—from arguing that Wiley did not really care about enforcing the PFDA against drug companies big or small. They noted that of the first 1,000 cases considered by the Bureau of Chemistry under the law, only 135 concerned drugs. Those firms that were prosecuted tended to be small-scale producers rather than the largest companies responsible for most of the patent medicine problem in America.[14] This critique of Wiley is unfair. The Pure Food and Drug Act did much to improve the quality of drugs in America well beyond the relatively few prosecutions suggested by the Bureau of Chemistry. Because many drug companies complied with the law before their cases reached the prosecution stage, there was a much smaller field of drug companies to prosecute. Although it may have appeared that the Bureau of Chemistry did comparatively little to combat nostrums, the mere threat of legal action was often enough to change how drug companies made or marketed their products.

Many manufacturers went directly to the government to make sure that their labels described the content of their medicines in ways that complied with the law. "I should like to know if it will be necessary for me to state on a label the name of the products from which I prepare my proprietary medicine," wrote one producer to the Department of Agriculture shortly after the passage of the PFDA. "If I do this, it will prohibit me from manufacturing and selling a remedy which is a secret of my own; and anyone buying it could, from the label, tell which ingredients were used in its preparation, and make his own supply of this medicine."[15] He had no choice, however, if he wanted to comply with the law. Indeed, many drug manufacturers listed the strength of their products, as well as their ingredients, on their bottles or boxes.[16] Just as the law prevented customers from being deceived by adulterated foods, it prevented the buyers of these medicines from being deceived by drug makers who might sell them substances they did not want to consume.

Other drug manufacturers changed the claims that they made for their products in their advertising or on their labels. When the law passed, Dr. Duke Munyon of Munyon's Remedy Company went to the Department of Agriculture to learn as much as he could about how it would affect his business. As a result, he changed the name of his individual products (and his company) from "Cure" to "Remedy." To avoid legal action, he also softened the claims he made on his packaging. When the Department of Agriculture finally prosecuted him, he agreed to soften those claims even more to avoid legal sanction.[17]

Furthermore, Wiley was not soft on those drug manufacturers who did go before the Board of Food and Drug Inspection. The first case to go to trial under the Pure Food and Drug Act was against a patent medicine that Wiley and his colleagues had determined to be mislabeled on multiple grounds: Cuforhedake Brane-Fude. Despite its ridiculous name, this headache remedy was manufactured by a trained pharmacist named Robert N. Harper. It contained some acetanilide, which might have done something for people whose heads hurt, but it also contained a substantial amount of alcohol. In one of his magazine articles, Samuel Hopkins Adams had suggested (correctly it turns out) that acetanilide had poisonous side effects and blamed the deaths of twenty-two people on this substance.[18]

The case against Cuforhedake Brane-Fude proceeded as the Pure Food and Drug Act mandated, with a seizure of a shipment of the product followed by a hearing. After that, rather than just engage in a civil action against the product, Wiley wanted to proceed with a criminal prosecution against Harper. At the trial in 1908, the case against Harper proved rather slapdash, but he was nonetheless convicted. President Roosevelt called in the prosecutor for a meeting and suggested he press for jail time. The judge disagreed, noting that Harper had both reformulated the product to make it less dangerous and relabeled it to better reflect its actual effects. Wiley was upset that Harper didn't get jail time, and Harper continued to sell his modified product.[19]

The Board of Food and Drug Inspection took up the question of acetanilide in 1908. They ruled unanimously that Monsanto had to label it as such (rather than as acetophenetidin, a derivative of acetanilide) to avoid deceiving customers since acetanilide was much less expensive than the alternative. Like so many food companies that had tangled with Wiley, Monsanto responded by questioning his expertise and his judgment: "Dr. Wiley does not claim to be a chemical authority, yet he seems to be powerful enough to maintain his idea against the opinions expressed by the leading chemical authorities of the United States. Why cannot the question be referred to the authorized Board of Consulting Scientific experts [the Remsen Board]? It would not take them five minutes to pass on the question and we would be satisfied with the results."[20] Yet Wiley's judgment stood, despite the apparatus set up to review his decisions; the Remsen Board never heard a case on any drug.

In light of Wiley's later claim that the Board of Food and Drug Inspection constantly disagreed with him, it is worth noting that Frederick Dunlap was in lockstep with Wiley on the labeling of acetanilide.[21] Later Wiley commissioned Lyman Kebler to examine the health effects of acetanilide and two related drugs. The Bureau of Chemistry released a scathing report on the three drugs in 1909, but acetanilide remained legal until 1983, when the Food and Drug Administration banned it for causing kidney damage and blood disorders.[22]

When Wiley took action against particular drugs, he concentrated his efforts against those with the most dangerous ingredients or making the most outrageous claims. In 1909 the Board of Food and Drug Inspection reported on its unanimously supported seizure of forty-one boxes of "Muco-Solvent," a drug that the manufacturer claimed could cure "croup, whooping cough, diphtheria, all throat troubles and catarrhal disorders." It was mostly just alcohol and glycerin, a simple sweetener. Nobody came to claim the seized goods, undoubtedly because they knew they could not prove the claims it made.[23] For the fiscal year 1910–11, the Bureau of Chemistry reported that its Washington drug inspection laboratory examined

752 domestic drug samples and found that 231 samples were adulterated, misbranded, or both. Including imported drugs, the laboratory referred 275 cases to the Board of Food and Drug Inspection that year.[24] If, for whatever reason, Wiley had been limiting the cases the Board of Food and Drug Inspection could refer for prosecution, that situation had significantly improved by the end of Wiley's career in government service.

———

Efforts by Dunlap and George McCabe to embarrass Wiley because of the way he handled adulterated drug cases began in early 1910. In January of that year, McCabe had a special agent pick up patent medicines that made outrageous and misleading claims in local Washington, DC, drug stores, then wrote Wiley asking why such substances were still available. In the letter he noted the drug cases pursued had been few in number and mostly of a trivial nature—small manufacturers that misled people rather than the large manufacturers selling patent medicines that actively harmed consumers. McCabe also alleged that there had been a tacit deal between the bureau and the drug industry to hold off on prosecutions.[25] As a member of the Board of Food and Drug Inspection, McCabe couldn't bring prosecutions himself; the Bureau of Chemistry had to bring a case forward for the board's consideration. Even then, it was possible for affected companies to negotiate a settlement (like a reformulation) before their case ever reached the board.

This dispute between the members of the Board of Food and Drug Inspection lasted for months. Wiley's initial response centered on inadequate funds for enforcement of the act. "The present force [of inspectors] available for handling products of this type is absolutely inadequate," Wiley wrote. Rather than acknowledge an arrangement with drug manufacturers, Wiley blamed the secretary of agriculture for the austerity that he credited with producing this result.[26] This argument obviously did nothing to endear him to his boss, but it proved difficult to fire someone with such a strong public constituency, even if his actions did not always serve the public's best interests.

McCabe countered Wiley's claims of inadequate funding by noting the varieties of such drugs on the market and explaining why inspectors were not always necessary to enforce the provisions of the act. He wrote to Wiley:

> Day after day I consider cases reported by the Bureau of Chemistry for prosecution where, at the most, there has only been a technical violation of the law, where no question of public health is involved, and where all that is necessary in bringing about a compliance with the law is a simple letter to the person responsible for the shipment. It is so obvious that if part of the work must be neglected because of insufficient appropriations, it should be the cases where there is no menace to public health.[27]

Frederick Dunlap, supporting McCabe in this struggle with Wiley, argued that money wasn't lacking but had simply been expended regulating foods rather than drugs. As a result, Dunlap argued, the board was guilty of "criminal negligence" if it didn't do more to prosecute the makers of patent medicines and nostrums.[28] In his autobiography, Wiley claimed that it was impossible to bring cases against these producers because of the oversight boards placed above him in the Department of Agriculture bureaucracy.[29] McCabe and Dunlap's contemporaneous writings prove otherwise.

Wiley gave McCabe other excuses as well. He wrote that performing chemical analysis on drugs was incredibly laborious "because it is necessary to look for many substances before we are certain as to its composition." He complained about the sheer number of patent medicines available and the futility of trying to shut down every one of the companies that made them.[30] McCabe contradicted Wiley's high estimate and countered that at the very least the board could shut down the worst offenders.[31] While the entire board generally agreed that the drugs that came before the board deserved to be seized and taken out of circulation, McCabe and Dunlap would have preferred that more cases came before the Board of Food and Drug Inspection in the first place. This was a debate over tactics rather than a debate over goals.

In the course of their debate over the enforcement of the PFDA against drug makers, McCabe borrowed one of Wiley's own tactics and shifted the focus of their debate to the most vulnerable members of society who might consume these fraudulent medicines. "Is there any class of individuals who demands the attention to be afforded by the food and drugs act more than helpless children, who are given remedies of this character, administered to them by confiding Mothers with full belief in the false claims that the remedies will put an end to children's suffering and affect a speedy cure of their ills?" McCabe asked rhetorically. "Mothers relying upon these false statements, use the remedies and fail to consult a physician, and I have no doubt that the light has departed from many homes because of the use of these remedies, such use being induced through the misrepresentations above referred to."[32] McCabe probably made this point because he was accustomed to Wiley's making such arguments against his own position in similar cases involving foods.

It is hard to imagine why Wiley did not respond more quickly and forcefully to McCabe's criticism. Distracted by his struggle over food on multiple fronts and wedded to a more subtle response in the area of drugs and nostrums, perhaps he simply didn't want to engage his bureaucratic enemies on turf that required complicated explanations. Regardless, in April 1911 Wiley finally began a "crusade" against nostrums and patent medicines.[33] As part of that crusade, he created a blacklist of twenty-four nostrums that he told people not to buy, focusing primarily on headache powders, which he considered bad for people with weak hearts.[34] He also proposed the passage of a law to keep nostrums and patent medicines from being sent through the mail.[35] This was public relations on Wiley's part. He had been opposed to nostrums since well before the passage of the PFDA, but McCabe's efforts made him feel the need to do more, and more important, he wanted those efforts to be visible to the public. However, his quieter efforts to reform which drugs Americans could purchase may have had a greater long-term effect.

―――――

Harvey Wiley actively pursued the best strategy against ineffective drugs offered to him by the text of the PFDA. For drugs, in contrast to foods, the

Pure Food and Drug Act recognized a particular set of standards for judging purity. Two books, the *United States Pharmacopeia* and the *National Formulary*, appear in the text of the act as sources for the definitions of drugs and the standards by which drugs could be judged (although if a drug stated on its label that its formula differed from the standard, it could not be seized under the terms of the act).[36] The *United States Pharmacopeia* was by far the larger of the two volumes and the one to which Wiley devoted the vast majority of his attention.

Wiley trusted doctors to prescribe the best cures available to their patients—but only those who sought out accurate information about the drugs they prescribed. "I have little faith in a physician who would prescribe a remedy of which he knew nothing except perhaps in having observed its pharmacological effects," Wiley wrote in 1920. "We go to great trouble and expense in preparing national formularies and pharmacopeias and new and non-official remedies, the exact composition of which is made known to every physician who cares to consider the matter."[37] Over a period of fifteen years, Wiley used the *Pharmacopeia* as a way to encourage doctors to steer their patients away from nostrums that could do them harm.

The *United States Pharmacopeia* had been around since 1820. During and between the revisions of 1910 and 1920, Wiley worked continually to improve this list of all substances recognized as effective so that doctors would know what to prescribe their patients. (This included an effort to delegitimize the use of rectified whiskey as medicine.) Although reputable doctors had followed its recommendations before the passage of the pure food law, that law essentially codified its contents.[38] Every ten years a group of doctors and pharmacists met to determine which medicines were most effective and thus deserved to be included in the volume. By the turn of the twentieth century, the convention to assemble the *Pharmacopeia* had become a highly structured effort to assemble all the best drugs on the market whose effectiveness had been demonstrated by modern scientific studies.[39]

The *Pharmacopeia*, argued Wiley, "is of the highest value, and, in so far as it goes, a satisfactory tribunal to which may be referred all questions concerning the strength and purity of drugs described therein."[40] Wiley made that argument years before the PFDA passed Congress. It was no wonder then that he was reluctant to let the Board of Food and Drug Inspection decide upon the purity of drugs when doctors and pharmacists would eventually be able to do the same thing. Wiley's primary strategy with respect to drug purity was to revise the *Pharmacopeia* to remove drugs with no therapeutic value from the volume, thereby discouraging doctors from prescribing them and limiting their use.[41] This approach enabled doctors to prescribe those drugs that had been scientifically tested in the right amounts. Obvious frauds, like Dr. Bull's Celebrated Cough Syrup or Cuforhedake Brane-Fude, could meet Wiley's wrath directly.

As head of the Bureau of Chemistry, Wiley expended enormous amounts of thought, time, energy, and department resources to the decennial revision of the *Pharmacopeia* in 1910. To Wiley, his work on the *Pharmacopeia* revision was no different from his fight against the food adulterators. "I feel very keenly about these matters because now for a quarter of a century I have seen how the canker of commercialism eats into the ethical body," he explained to the man who ran the convention that year. "Instead of interests growing less active they are growing more active and are gaining more and more control over the governing bodies as they lose caste among the people. I am astounded every day to meet these hydra-headed monsters at every turn."[42] These efforts began a long effort to undercut the potential market for patent medicines of all kinds by undermining their legitimacy.

To strengthen the *Pharmacopeia* as a tool against drug adulteration, Wiley served as president of the United States Pharmacopeia Convention in 1920 as part of its regular schedule to revise the book to reflect current thinking.[43] He also served as an ex officio member of the Committee on Revision during the ten years between the 1910 and 1920 meetings. It was through Wiley's efforts at the 1920 convention that the group removed alcohol from the volume entirely, an important step toward effectively ending the medicinal whiskey industry after Prohibition.[44] That same year, the convention agreed to let proprietary medicines with known ingredients and proven effectiveness into the *Pharmacopeia* for the first time.[45] This signaled to doctors that medicines that were not included should not be prescribed. Like his less-publicized efforts to influence the production of foods like ketchup, his work in this area promoted better products and helped those improved products survive by spreading the knowledge needed to manufacture them.

Along these same lines, Wiley served on the American Medical Association's Council on Pharmacy and Chemistry, a consulting body of physicians and pharmacists created in advance of the passage of the PFDA in 1905. Drug companies submitted evidence that their products worked to this group so that they could publish it and reach members of the medical profession who would prescribe these products. By promoting the testing of medicines through rational scientific experiments so that physicians would know what worked, they could slowly drive drugs that did not work from the market. At the same time, the council's efforts toward publicity and physician education supported the more reputable progressive drug companies.[46]

The importance of Wiley's long, subtle campaign against patent medicines grew, even as the legal environment made it harder to prosecute drug producers the way food adulterators were being prosecuted. In *United States v. Johnson* (1911), the Supreme Court ruled that the Pure Food and Drug Act did not apply to false statements about the curative powers of nostrums or patent medicines, only the ingredients that made up the products.[47] The ruling meant that US attorneys could act against obviously ridiculous products only if the government could prove fraudulent intent. Congress followed up the next year by passing the Sherley Amendment to the Pure Food and Drug Act, banning from drug labels "any statement . . . regarding the curative or therapeutic effect . . . which is false and fraudulent." However, this amended law forced the government to make the difficult case that perpetrators had committed fraud. Furthermore, this particular fix did not extend to advertising, which could go on making fantastical claims.[48]

Despite their different treatment under the PFDA, in the early twentieth century foods and drugs were not separated by the same bright line as they are today. Coca-Cola had begun its life a few decades earlier not as a soft drink, but as a nerve tonic. Ergot, the source of the first drug manufactured in the United States, came from a mold that grew on rye bread.[49] And doctors regularly prescribed whiskey as medicine. As Wiley himself explained to a whiskey manufacturer during a hearing of the Board of Food and Drug

Inspection, "That while a manufacturer claimed for his whiskey that it had certain medicinal properties and that claim would bring it within the class of drugs, it would not at the same time remove it from the class of foods. Physicians prescribe olive oil, but that does not remove it from its position as a food."[50] To Wiley, it was necessary to treat such products as foods first.

The fact that Wiley pursued different strategies does not mean he thought of impure food and impure drugs differently. In the September 1914 issue of *Good Housekeeping*, Wiley cowrote an article demonstrating his concern about impure drugs even after he left government service. "Money spent on patent medicines would do more to produce health if spent for whole-wheat, milk, eggs and fruit, or even to provide a pleasant outing in the open air," he and Anne Lewis Pierce explained. "These things we know will help."[51] While working at the Bureau of Chemistry, he did everything the law allowed to take the most dangerous drugs off the market. Although he worked to educate and protect the general public from all kinds of potential dangers, for Wiley, drugs that were merely ineffective and taken occasionally did not pose the same dangers as the poisonous substances added to the foods people ate every day. His work in drugs and his work in foodstuffs were two sides of the same coin: consumers had a right to be protected from impure products so they could make choices that would help them live longer and healthier lives.

CHAPTER ELEVEN

BLEACHED FLOUR

AND

BAKING POWDER

KARL MARX TRACED THE ADULTERATION of bread to the early 1700s, when individual millers entered capitalist competition. In fact, the practice long predated that time and continued well into Harvey Wiley's era.[1] Marx, citing a source on adulteration in Great Britain from 1855, noted that cheap bread there was adulterated with "alum, soap, pearl ashes, chalk, Derbyshire stone dust, and such like agreeable and nourishing and wholesome ingredients." While this kind of adulteration hurt the nutrient value of the bread which the poor bought, it did not poison them.[2] The American food reformer Sylvester Graham often denounced mid-nineteenth century bakers for adulterating their flour with harmful substances.[3] Following Graham, Harvey Wiley shifted the focus of his case against the adulteration of bread from deception to health. Adulteration of products like flour, Wiley gradually came to argue, was not just deceptive, but dangerous.

In 1898, well before the passage of the Pure Food and Drug Act, the adulteration of flour was a serious enough problem that Congress passed one of its first pure food laws, disguised as a revenue-raising measure. Like so many food producers in industrialized settings, far from consumers, many millers were tempted to mix cheaper cereals with their wheat flour to cut costs and increase profits. The Mixed Flour Law, as it was known, charged manufacturers of mixed flour for an inspection regimen for their product while also requiring them to declare all ingredients on the labels of their bags. By forcing up the price of mixed flour, this act essentially put an end to that product as a trade good in legitimate commerce.[4]

Bleached flours, however, came relatively late to America. The most popular form of bleaching was known as the Alsop process, invented by the British scientist J. N. Alsop and patented in America in 1904. The first flours created by this process did not enter the American market until 1907.[5] Millers cited consumer demand for whiter flour as the reason they used this process. Wiley argued that millers developed bleaching methods like the Alsop process so that they could sell cheaper wheat at a higher price.[6] Since people were willing to pay more for white flour even if it tasted the same as the alternatives, these positions were not mutually exclusive.

In the course of litigation over the effect of bleached flour, a chemistry professor from South Dakota State University described the Alsop process. "The process is electrical," he explained:

> And the apparatus consists essentially of a cubical box, usually with glass sides, and inside of this box are two terminals of an electric current, and the upper one of these terminals is attached to a crank shaft that is alternately raised and lowered. . . . When drawn apart by the crank motion there ensues a flaming discharge of electricity. This discharge, at a very high temperature, causes the free nitrogen of the atmosphere

to combine with the free oxygen of the atmosphere, producing various oxides of nitrogen, the most important one of
which is nitrogen peroxide.[7]

As he grew more focused on the health effects of adulteration, Wiley's concern with the process centered on this residue of nitrogen peroxide left in the
flour after bleaching.[8] As he told a meeting of millers in September 1907, "It
has never appeared quite plain to me that a harmful substance can be used
in minute quantities without danger."[9] Here in a nutshell was Wiley's absolutist view about purity. Pure food was food containing absolutely nothing
that could harm somebody, even in tiny amounts that weren't necessarily
harmful. The principle of purity trumped every other consideration, especially something so petty as the color of flour.

Even though Wiley had not yet come out against bleached flour, the reaction to his speech from industry representatives was swift and severe. The
Northwestern Miller quickly called his tentative ideas about bleaching "quite
absurd and irrelevant." It excoriated him for his previous statements about
preferring black bread in the European style to any bread that had a significant market in the United States.[10] A few months later, the same publication
recommended that makers of "legitimate food products" band together to
"restrain Dr. Wiley from his uncalled for vicious attacks." By then, he had
told a crowd at a New York gathering, "I look forward to the time . . . when
white flour is no longer used for bread."[11] For an industry that had a popular
product it could now make cheaply, these were fighting words.

To get to the bottom of whether the residues in bleached flour were harmful, Wiley authorized two separate studies of the Alsop process at Bureau
of Chemistry branch laboratories in the Midwest.[12] However, when Wiley
drafted a food inspection opinion on bleached flour that prohibited the
Alsop process, the two chemists who conducted those studies opposed his
conclusion.[13] After all, the amount of residue involved was miniscule. For
example, one case, decided in 1910, involved 350 sacks of flour seized in Louisiana; it found 1.3 parts per million of nitrogen peroxide residue.[14]

The question of the health effects of bleached flour went before the
Board of Food and Drug Inspection in a public hearing held in November

1908. Seventy-five millers and allied interest group members attended. Wiley emphasized the health threat posed by the residues.[15] For Wiley, anything that was potentially poisonous should be banned from the food supply even before scientists drew their conclusions. In this case, Wiley's boss, secretary of agriculture James Wilson, agreed with him. Wilson, who sat in on this hearing, issued a food inspection decision strongly condemning bleached flour and requiring it to be removed from commerce within six months of the decision. Merely listing the ingredients on the label, Wilson concluded, could not bring bleached flour into compliance with the Pure Food and Drug Act (PFDA), suggesting that he agreed with Wiley about its deleterious effects on people's health.[16]

Some millers agreed to stop using the Alsop process for bleaching immediately after the Board of Food and Drug Inspection ruled against it. Others sent hundreds of letters to Secretary Wilson and their congressmen to get the bleached flour decision sent to the Remsen Board, an idea that Secretary Wilson opposed.[17] Like the vast majority of food purity enforcement decisions, the bleached flour decision never went to the Remsen Board. The issue was resolved by the United States Supreme Court after Wiley left office, with great impact on the future of pure food.

———

Long before the battle over bleached flour ran its course, Wiley had opened up a new front in his campaign for pure bread. The first commercial baking powders appeared in the United States during the 1840s. These powders (like all powders since) had three components: a baking soda base, an acid agent, and a filler or starch to protect against moisture.[18] When water was added, the mixture produced carbon dioxide, causing bread or cake to rise.

Before baking powder came along, women had to make yeast themselves (and it was invariably women who did the baking, and indeed all forms of cooking, in the early nineteenth century). That task alone took hours, and yeast was difficult to keep in hot weather. It could take from twelve to twenty-four hours to bake bread this way, and the cook had to have considerable skill to make bread at all. Women had to bake in large batches, raising the issue of how to keep bread fresh. People consumed a lot of stale bread.[19] The object of baking powder was to make baking easier; chemical leavening agents worked more reliably than yeast and resulted in breads and cakes that took less time to make. Chemical leavening through baking powder was a convenient way to cut labor in the home; equally important, it simplified the baking process enough to make the mass production of breads and cakes possible for the first time.

Baking powder was one of the first food products to be made in factories. One of the earliest large producers was known as Rumford Chemical Works, a name that suggests both what went into the product and the scale at which it was produced. A major competitor, Royal, was at one point known as the Royal Chemical Company.[20] Between 1870 and 1909, the number of baking powder factories in America rose from 30 to 144 and the number of people employed jumped from 235 to 3,531, giving some idea of the scale of this industry.[21]

To differentiate themselves, the largest baking powder companies depended on advertising, much of it disparaging the safety of their competitors' products. One advertisement claimed that the competitor's product was "made from old bones covered in vitriol."[22] How could the consumer know which baking powder company to trust? Food factories were mysterious places where unknown ingredients turned into useful household products. Still, it was far easier to trust the manufacturer of a product as convenient as baking powder than it was to go back to baking bread with yeast.

Then, as now, there were three kinds of baking powder. Each is distinguished by its acid agent. One such agent is cream of tartar or tartrate, a by-product of wine making. Royal Baking Powder, which used cream of tartar as its acid agent, faced more than 500 competitors that manufactured their baking powders with alum, another name for aluminum salts.[23] A third kind of baking powder—with the smallest segment of the market—was phosphate baking powder, which used calcium phosphate as its acid agent.[24] Cream of tartar was much more expensive than alum, but alum improved the color and appearance of bread. Since bread made from inferior wheat and baking powder with alum would look better than it should, the use of alum in baking powder was considered by some to be a deceptive adulteration.[25]

By the late nineteenth century alum had also developed a reputation for leaving a toxic residue in bread. In point of fact, it did leave a residue, but the question of whether or not that residue hurt people who consumed even tiny amounts of it was the subject of debate. Various baking powder companies used advertising, lobbying, and even house-to-house canvassing to persuade consumers to buy their kind of baking powder rather than the other kind. Much of this fusillade of propaganda was directed against baking powders that contained alum.[26] Still, the market share for alum baking powders gradually grew, and sometime during the 1880s it became the most popular kind of baking powder in America. It helped that the competition just among cream of tartar baking powders—which, being more expensive, all aimed for upscale consumers—proved particularly fierce in its own right.[27]

Besides its struggle against other cream of tartar baking powders, Royal Baking Powder was at the forefront of slandering the alum baking powders, whose increased market share threatened its profitable existence. Royal pioneered the use of the idea of pure food to gain commercial advantage. Its advertising tagline was "Absolutely Pure," a dig at the safety of its numerous rivals. The firm lobbied for state laws to outlaw alum powders on safety grounds. It created phony organizations that released questionable scientific studies about the comparative health effects of different baking powders.[28] From 1899 to 1905 the company's lobbyists managed to get the Missouri state legislature to outlaw the sale of alum baking powder altogether.[29]

———

The Division of Chemistry first investigated adulteration in baking powder in 1889. In that report, Wiley's colleague, Arthur Crampton, refused to endorse the notion that alum in baking powder was harmful.[30] By that time, plenty of scientists had studied whether baking powder with alum had ill effects on people's health. Crampton's attitude toward that controversy speaks volumes about the limited mission of Wiley's office at that moment. The Division of Chemistry was interested in detecting adulteration, not studying its health effects.[31] While the Royal Baking Powder Company might have appreciated the division's decision to not weigh in on the safety of alum, Wiley was unwilling to align his office with any particular kind of baking powder.

The best place to see Wiley's early views on baking powder is in his congressional testimony around the turn of the century. Wiley was a frequent witness in congressional hearings spurred both by the already active baking powder wars and by the gradual strengthening of efforts to pass a pure food law. In these hearings, Wiley struggled to support the cause of pure food legislation without becoming embroiled in the science of how baking powder of any kind affected the human system. "Alum is an irritant," he testified in 1899. "It is poison to the extent of being an irritant, but to not such a great extent as many irritants." Even though Wiley believed that alum irritated some people's stomachs, he also recognized that many people could ingest it with no problem. His solution was to mark the presence of the irritant on the label so that people could make up their own minds.[32]

Gradually, as his support for pure food legislation grew more active, Wiley began to criticize cream of tartar baking powders.[33] Nonetheless, for some time afterward Wiley stuck to the position that all baking powders were a problem. In 1901 Wiley told Congress's Industrial Commission on Agriculture that all baking powder was injurious because all unnecessary ingestion of minerals was injurious. However, he refused to call for taking alum baking powder off the market because he did "not intend to be the judge of another man's diet." Instead he merely advocated for all ingredients in baking powder to be listed on the label.[34] Surprisingly, in light of his later position on alum, when Wiley was confronted by alum baking powder interests during early debates over the pure food bill, he offered to sit down with them and find language that was mutually satisfactory.[35]

Despite all the study of baking powder, Wiley remained ambivalent about it until he had a reason to choose sides. As late as 1902 he refused to condemn any kind of baking powder.[36] In his 1908 annual report, the Army's director of health in the Philippines mentioned that Wiley had told him that the alum in baking powders "had no marked effect" on health except it "has a tendency to produce constipation."[37] When Wiley made these assessments, alum baking powder was already a huge public health issue.

His tendency to stay out of the debate—perhaps because he recognized that he knew little about it—is noteworthy.

Because alum was not a preservative, Wiley did not consider testing its effects on human subjects in Poison Squad–style experiments. He claimed that the vast majority of people who had tested its safety already considered alum a poison. Later Wiley said that he wanted to use the Pure Food and Drug Act to force alum out of the food supply at the first opportunity, but he did not express that view publicly.[38] In the first edition of his 1907 book *Foods and Their Adulteration*, Wiley concluded, "It would be better, evidently, if more people used more yeast bread and less baking powder rolls." Wiley acknowledged the utility and convenience of baking powder but did not go beyond warning about chemical leavening agents in general (which would have included alum), stating, "It is too early yet to formulate definite principles either of inclusion or exclusion of these products."[39]

Such reticence eventually disappeared. When Harvey Wiley finally took a side in the baking powder dispute, he favored cream of tartar over alum. In late 1908 he condemned alum before the Board of Food and Drug Inspection, stating that "the literature [was] very plain and full of evidence bearing on the [harmfulness of alum]."[40] In the heat of bureaucratic battle, a substance about which Wiley had been ambivalent had become impure.

The Board of Food and Drug Inspection did not address the healthfulness of alum until July 1909. The deeply divided board referred the question to the secretary of agriculture with a recommendation that "feeding experiments" be conducted to test its safety, and the secretary referred alum to the Remsen Board.[41] The Remsen Board farmed out three Poison Squad–style experiments, to Yale University, the University of Pennsylvania, and Northwestern University. The results did not come back until 1914, long after Wiley had left government service. Noting the similar results of the three experiments, the board unanimously concluded that alum baking powders were no worse than any other baking powder but that consumers should probably cut back on using them anyway.[42] This solution pleased nobody.

Wiley turned harshly against alum only at the end of his government career, when he was fighting with the Remsen Board over additives of all kinds. Anticipating the board's decision on alum, he turned against it as a way of criticizing the Remsen Board's judgment in general. In a memo written in the course of preparing his autobiography, Wiley noted that the decision "damn[ed] alum with faint praise" and that "the only logical conclusion is that the Remsen Board found all baking powders unwholesome."[43] Yet this is exactly the position Wiley had taken in his book *Foods and Their Adulteration*. At this point, Wiley was so set upon attacking the Remsen Board that he had either forgotten his previous position or thrown any effort at consistency out the window.

The controversy over alum in baking powder illustrates an important point about Wiley's philosophy of food purity. According to Wiley, "The law does not require that evidence shall be of a character to show that in a particular case the food will produce a deleterious effect. . . . A substance added to food products which 'may' prove injurious to health is the language of the statute and not 'which is injurious to health.'"[44] In other words, the possibility that an additive would cause harm was enough to justify banning it. Wiley's interpretation of the pure food law allowed no tolerance for any risk whatsoever. The long-term viability of this position disappeared when the Supreme Court gave its final ruling in the bleached flour case two years later. Nonetheless, Wiley's attempts to persuade the government to ban various substances—including alum baking powder—had important effects upon the American diet.

———◆———

The effects of the campaign against alum, which began before Wiley took up the cause, grew much more apparent once he entered the struggle. "Baking powder was never used," wrote the author Richard Wright of his grandmother's house, remembering his pre–World War I childhood, "it was alleged to contain a chemical harmful to the body."[45] This was obviously alum. Exactly why Wright's grandmother refused to buy alum baking powder is impossible to pinpoint, but his time at his grandmother's house occurred at the height of Wiley's anti-alum campaign. While there had been anti-alum allegations long before Wiley became involved in the dispute, they had appeared in advertisements designed to get consumers to buy cream of tartar baking powder instead. This particular African American woman, unable to afford baking powder without that dangerous chemical, forwent baking powder entirely. As a result, Wright could eat biscuits only when at home.

Wiley exercised most of his power over baking powder manufacturing from his position at *Good Housekeeping* after his government service ended. That's when he was most fiercely opposed to alum, had the biggest pulpit, and was less distracted by other serious food fights. Writing shortly after the Remsen Board's decision on alum, Wiley concluded, "Any aluminum compound, I don't care what it is, nor in what quantity it is used, if mixed or packed with a food, not only reduces the quality or strength of said food in proportion to the amount used, but it also injuriously affects it by adding a substance which not only is not a food but has well-defined deleterious properties."[46] His relatively new bias against alum baking powder expressed itself most clearly in the magazine's product ratings. The Good Housekeeping Institute gave every alum baking powder it tested a D rating, for disapproved.[47] Wiley's disapproval mattered.

In 1920, spurred on by alum baking powder manufacturers, the Federal Trade Commission (FTC) filed a case against the Royal Baking Powder Company for unfair trade practices. The complaint was based on Royal's disparagement of its alum-using competitors in its advertising. Royal, the FTC stated, had claimed that its competitors' products were poisonous and that other powders were "made from ground-up aluminum cooking utensils."[48] Since the government had held that all kinds of baking powder were equally safe—or unsafe (the Remsen Board decided that they all had the same basic effect on people's systems)—the FTC wanted Royal to stop committing "defamation and disparagement of its competitor's products." The company countered that the presence of alum was a fact and that consumers had a right to know what was in the products they bought.[49]

The case proceeded in fits and starts. At one point it ended temporarily when Royal agreed to stop disparaging its competition in its advertisements, but it resumed shortly thereafter when Royal suspended the truce. At another point Royal countersued the FTC. In April 1926 the complaint against Royal Baking Powder was dismissed. The grounds of that decision were very narrow: the FTC agreed that Royal Baking Powder was allowed to point out the presence of alum in its competition, but the commission explicitly stated that it was not making a judgment about whether alum was safe.[50]

In 1924, as part of the case, Wiley testified for the defense, offering a stark revision of his previous views on alum. He argued that alum ingested in any way was not soluble in the stomach and instead entered the bloodstream, where its adverse effects were felt. He cited new research along these lines but spent most of his testimony recounting his old Poison Squad experiments and arguing that they were an adequate analogy for what happens when people consume alum in baking soda residue. He said nothing about the problems with the rigor of those experiments, which by then formed the basis of his scientific reputation.[51]

In his testimony Wiley tried to wipe out his history of agnosticism over alum. He claimed to have an early prejudice against alum on the grounds that his mother refused to use it because it was "unwholesome" and "not good for the children."[52] Writing in the late 1920s, shortly after the dismissal of the FTC complaint, he accused the Remsen Board of carving out an exception for alum under the food law rather than working to determine whether alum was actually harmful.[53] Conveniently, he forgot about the Remsen Board's own experiments designed to answer that question. Those experiments had had scientific problems (particularly since they followed Wiley's own Poison Squad format), but Wiley was counting on people in the late 1920s to forget that history so that he could complain that the PFDA had become essentially inoperative.

Despite years of advertising from Royal implying that alum was poisonous, alum baking powder remained a popular option at the turn of the twentieth century. Testifying before Congress in 1911, though, not long after Wiley came out against alum, agriculture secretary James Wilson reported that he had talked to many bakers who told him that nobody used alum baking powder anymore.[54] That changed during the Depression, when consumers turned back to alum baking powder because it was so much cheaper than the alternatives. In 1935 the top three alum baking powders controlled 61 percent of the baking powder market.[55] "There are several kinds of baking powder," explained the magazine *Hygeia* in 1940, "which are all satisfactory when properly used."[56] All the earlier warnings—about baking powder in general and alum baking powder in particular—had been forgotten.

The history of baking powder, both before and after Harvey Wiley's role, shows the wide range of factors that have influenced the ingredients used in it. Sometimes, as in the early days of the industry, consumers have been most interested in convenience. Wiley then played a role by magnifying fears about safety. During the Depression, most consumers' primary concern was price. Today concerns about baking powder are less influenced by fear of particular ingredients than by a general interest in foods that are "natural," even if the meaning of that term is not particularly well defined.

Harvey Wiley's lasting influence was not so much on the ingredients of baking powder, but on the creation of a general suspicion of artificial ingredients of all kinds. His enormous body of written work has been resurrected for a new age by anti-modernist organizations concerned about the nutritional implications of the ingredients he fought to keep out of the food supply in the early the twentieth century.[57] Their efforts require that safety be privileged over other factors such as convenience and price. This was Wiley's position in controversies over food additives of all kinds. However, since Wiley frequently exaggerated the health risks associated with many of these additives, his example may not be the best model to follow. Just look at his long running-campaign against Coca-Cola.

CHAPTER TWELVE

COCA-COLA

IN THE YEARS FOLLOWING THE PASSAGE of the Pure Food and Drug Act (PFDA), when Harvey Wiley was deeply engaged in the battle to determine exactly how that law would be enforced, his typical day began at eight in the morning. First, he spent about an hour studying reports or any publications from the Bureau of Chemistry that would go out under his name. Between nine and ten he gave dictation in his usual rapid-fire delivery for all the letters that would go out under his name that day. Around ten began a series of conferences. Often there were food producers protesting some particular labeling requirement. He nearly always conferred with the department's chief food inspector, his assistants, and the visiting press. The secretary of agriculture often called him in for consultation.[1]

At three, Wiley often took a train to New York City, where he might deliver an address at a trade association banquet at 8 p.m. Then he would take a midnight train back to Washington.[2] When this schedule didn't hold, it was usually because Wiley was traveling farther afield in a mixture of business and pleasure. "Dr. Wiley's headquarters are supposed to be in Washington," explained a 1910 profile of the chemist. "As a matter of fact he

FIGURE 12.1 A portrait of Wiley at work, c. 1910. Wiley had essentially stopped working on chemistry at this point in his career, so this photo was almost certainly staged.

Courtesy Library of Congress

Dear Harve my heart is wholly thine
Please take me for Thy valentine

FIGURE 12.2 A Valentine's Day portrait of Wiley drawn by one of his many girlfriends. It is impossible to identify the artist as the drawing has become separated from the letters that accompanied it. Held out of the donation of Wiley's papers to the Library of Congress, those letters and this drawing all ended up in the papers of Wiley's wife.

Anna Kelton Wiley Papers, Box 309. Courtesy Library of Congress.

is usually almost anywhere else. His duties summon him now to Chicago, then to Seattle, then again to Boston or New Orleans. He is ubiquitous."[3] Even Wiley's frequent summers in Europe were working vacations, designed to acquaint him with the many developments in chemistry and medicine going on outside of the United States. One messenger, accustomed to seeing Wiley's personal assistant, Fred Linton, in Wiley's office rather than the famous chemist himself, asked at one point upon seeing Wiley, "Who's that fat man who works for Mr. Linton?"[4]

Wiley readily admitted how hard he worked. "I do a great deal more work now than I did [fifteen years ago]," he explained to the Yale economist Irving Fisher in a 1905 letter, "but I do not think I worked up to my full limit as I am compelled to do now."[5] In 1909 Wiley noted that he worked between sixteen and eighteen hours each day.[6] Wiley brought many of his obligations upon himself as part of his dual quests for attention and money. He wrote magazine articles and scholarly treatises, he tended to his personal investments, and he found time for plenty of socializing at his beloved Cosmos Club. Indeed, one can't help but wonder how he managed to practice any chemistry at all. "In the last few years, I have had my assistants, many of them much more competent to make the investigations than I am, to make investigations," he explained to a Congressional Committee in 1911. "The Chief of the Bureau, with the usual human limitations, cannot know very much about very many subjects."[7] Most of his time went toward fulfilling the executive duties associated with his office.[8]

Another casualty of Wiley's intense schedule during this period was his home life. Had he been married, time with his spouse would certainly have taken time away from his extensive work and travel schedule.[9] Nonetheless, Wiley did maintain relationships with multiple girlfriends. More than anyone, these women saw the effects of Wiley's brutal schedule on his health and happiness, and their concerns are clear in their surviving letters. "Take care of yourself and stop keeping such late hours. . . . Do as I am doing and lead the simple life," wrote Caroline Niernsee in April 1908.[10] "Have you taken your rest yet?" asked another longtime girlfriend named Blanche Thayer in the first weeks following the passage of the Pure Food and Drug Act. The two had first met when she lived in Boston, but by 1906 Thayer lived in New York City, and Wiley visited her periodically over many years.[11] When they were not together, she berated him for not writing enough.

Despite his many varied pursuits, Harvey Wiley found time to reconnect with his former personal assistant, Anna Campbell Kelton, who was supporting her widowed mother and six siblings in their Washington, DC, home.[12] In the years after she had left his office, Wiley had sent her periodic reminders of his interest and affection, including little presents from his worldwide travels.[13] They met again by chance on a streetcar outside the Cosmos Club in October 1909, and he asked to call on her formally. In the spring of 1910, Kelton, a law student and an established suffragette, invited him to address a club meeting in the spring of 1910. They announced the engagement that December.[14]

Before the wedding, Wiley and his future mother-in-law fought about money. "Nan, you have worked hard all these years for pay," Wiley joked at a New Year's Eve Party on the last day of 1910, "now you will continue to work hard for nothing!" Josephine Kelton, who had struggled to support her large family since her husband had died close to penniless in 1893, took offense.[15] In a series of letters to Wiley before the wedding, she argued that Wiley should give his wife a regular allowance so that she wouldn't have to beg him for money. She also assured her future son-in-law (who was only three years younger than she was) that he would never have to financially support his wife's family.[16]

Harvey Wiley wed Anna Kelton in February 1911, and by all accounts their union was a happy one. They had a "pure food wedding," with no adulterated food of any kind served at the reception. Their honeymoon destination, Chattanooga, Tennessee, may have seemed dull at first glance, but Wiley took her there because he was unable to separate business from his personal life. Chattanooga was the site of a prosecution in support of banning Coca-Cola under the Pure Food and Drug Act as an adulterated and misbranded good. At Wiley's urging, federal agents had in 1909 seized forty barrels and twenty kegs of Coca-Cola syrup in East Ridge, Tennessee, as soon as it crossed the state line from Georgia and thus represented interstate commerce. The Division of Chemistry claimed that it was adulterated

with a harmful ingredient: caffeine.[17] The trial would receive national attention, which, in contrast to the Poison Squad experiments, would greatly
damage Wiley's reputation.

———

The use of coffee and other caffeinated substances goes back to the earliest
days of human history. Caffeine itself, however, was not isolated from these
substances until the German chemist Friedlieb Ferdinand Runge did so at
the behest of Johann Wolfgang von Goethe in 1819.[18] Although industrial
caffeine derived in part from the cola nut, in Wiley's era most of it came from
processing tea sweepings. It could also be synthesized from uric acid derived
from guano deposits left by birds in South America. During Wiley's time
caffeine was a common product in the colas sold at soda fountains.[19] Wiley
probably went after Coca-Cola directly because it was then, as now, the
industry leader. The popular association between Coca-Cola and cocaine,
which still exists to a limited degree because of the product's name, also
contributed to that decision.

Wiley first publicly expressed enmity against caffeine in Congressional testimony in 1902, claiming that free caffeine—the kind industrially
extracted from cola nuts or synthetically manufactured—was like strychnine or morphine. His argument here ran parallel to his case against patent
medicines, upon which he began to focus at about the same time. "A short
time ago I received a very pathetic letter from a person who had acquired the
cocaine habit by the use of a remedy for catarrh," Wiley wrote in 1903. "It
was not until the habit was thoroughly established that the victim was made
acquainted with the nature of it."[20] By 1906 Wiley had begun to repeatedly
argue publicly that caffeine was dangerously habit forming.[21] By 1909 the
Bureau of Chemistry had investigated many "medicated soft drinks," Wiley
reported, "and many of them have been found to contain cocaine or caffeine
and coal-tar coloring." Others were no different from patent medicines.[22]
Caffeine is, in fact, toxic in gigantic amounts—amounts far, far greater than
anybody would consume drinking Coca-Cola, coffee, or tea.

When Wiley condemned a product, he did not necessarily stop consuming it. Wiley the whiskey drinker was also a regular coffee drinker. How could Wiley drink coffee, which had far more caffeine than Coca-Cola, yet prosecute the Coca-Cola Company under the PFDA? It is useful to compare the struggle with Coca-Cola to another topic Wiley pursued around this same time. In 1904, at the peak of his fame from the Poison Squad experiments, Wiley began to test the healthfulness of food kept in cold storage. He suspected that all foods would deteriorate when kept in cold storage.[23] His plan was to conduct tests on how long this would take. Wiley leased two cold storage vaults on behalf of the Department of Agriculture, but rather than conduct a Poison Squad–style experiment, he kept a "jury" of department officers who conducted blind taste tests of the cold storage food (after it had been kept in cold storage for various periods ranging from a month to a year) and fresh food.[24]

Wiley's initial results were mixed. Sometimes it was easy to tell which food had been kept in cold storage. Sometimes it wasn't. The cold storage industry was in its infancy when Wiley tested the results of this technology. Nobody really understood how cold to keep most goods in cold storage or for how long.[25] Wiley did not release the final report of his experiments until 1910, by which time his attitude toward cold storage had considerably softened. At that point, he called cold storage "a legitimate exercise . . . when it is practiced for the purpose of bringing a fresh article to market in the best possible condition."[26] By 1912 Wiley's worries about the dangers of cold storage had completely disappeared.[27] Some of Wiley's change of opinion on cold storage can be attributed to technological improvement, which was occurring during precisely these years. Wiley's studies of the cold storage industry allayed his longstanding fears of deception—that goods that weren't fresh would be passed off as fresh. As the technology improved, he recognized the advantages of using cold storage to increase supply by preventing spoilage and therefore to decrease prices.[28]

The distinction between Wiley's eventual acceptance of cold storage and his condemnation of added caffeine was between natural and unnatural. Once cold storage technology could keep perishable food well enough to maintain its natural state for an extended period of time, Wiley saw it as a blessing. Wiley noted that cold storage might increase food prices in some instances, but he came to believe that the convenience of increased availability justified the practice.[29] By the end of his tenure in government, Wiley's remaining objections to cold storage had more to do with the products before they were put into cold storage than with the practice that kept them fresh.[30]

In other words, as long as the food itself hadn't changed significantly over time, Wiley did not consider selling it to be deceptive or unhealthy. Wiley felt the same way about canning, calling it in 1906 "the most important, economically, of the whole list of unobjectionable methods of preserving goods . . . preserv[ing] natural flavor better than any other method."[31] Canning wasn't processing. It was flavor preservation. Cold storage wasn't processing. It was food preservation. Decay was a natural process, but manufacturers who fought that natural process with natural methods did not attract Wiley's ire.

Soda makers, in contrast, used caffeine, a natural product, in unnatural ways. As with sodium benzoate, Wiley illogically distinguished the effects of caffeine that appeared naturally in foods from the effects of caffeine added by manufacturers like Coca-Cola. If Coca-Cola was forced to remove caffeine on health grounds, his opponents' argument went, then the government would have to ban coffee. Wiley's response was that tea and coffee in their natural states provided a buzz to those consumers who craved it, and they knew what they were getting. Coke, on the other hand, was an unnatural substance, created in the laboratory. By his logic, all caffeinated soft drinks were by definition impure (and therefore unsafe). That made Wiley a threat to the very existence of Coca-Cola.

As long as nobody placed extra caffeine in coffee or tea, Wiley was fine with it. Wiley's fear was that Coca-Cola was enticing customers—especially children—to become hooked on their product. This view aligned with his longstanding fears of deception; in this case the deception was failure to disclose the product's addictive qualities. He vacillated between comparing caffeine to strychnine (a poison) and morphine (a drug), but, given that humans had safely ingested caffeine for centuries through coffee and tea, he gravitated over time toward comparing it with morphine.

A 1912 letter to the editor of the *Journal of the American Medical Association* is an example of the labored way Wiley struggled with this contradiction. "I think I could prove that thousands of men carry concealed weapons who never committed murder," he wrote, "but that would be no justification for carrying concealed weapons. We may assume, for the sake of argument, that people may drink moderate quantities of tea and coffee without harm, but that does not justify the placing of caffein in a beverage taken almost always on an empty stomach, a condition which favors its more vigorous action."[32] The key word for understanding Wiley's thinking is "placing," as opposed to using substances in a product that contained caffeine naturally.

———

In early 1907 Wiley announced his desire to take on what the newspapers called "soda fountain dope."[33] Wiley's interest in Coca-Cola stemmed from his concern over "temperance drinks"—popular substitutes for alcohol served at soda fountains, which were coming into their heyday. Wiley gave other soft drink makers a pass because they didn't use ingredients he deemed potentially unhealthy. He objected to added caffeine rather than added sugar because he was far more concerned about caffeine addiction than he was about tooth decay.[34]

Coca-Cola signed its first bottling contract in 1894, a few years before Wiley targeted the soda for extinction, and grew rapidly during the first decade of the twentieth century.[35] Writing in *Ladies' Home Journal* in April 1907, Wiley argued that "temperance drinks, especially those of the soda fountain, are often modified by the expert in charge in such a way as not to improve their wholesomeness." He singled out "the designing manufacturer [who] may introduce some secret habit-forming drug into such drinks, in order that they may be used in greater and greater quantities." Even though Coca-Cola had removed the cocaine from its formula by this time, his writing strongly suggests that Wiley had Coca-Cola in mind.[36]

In June 1907, the US Army temporarily banned Coca-Cola from its bases, not because of caffeine but because it contained trace amounts of alcohol. The company, in the hopes of getting the Army to remove its ban, asked Wiley to analyze its product. As part of this investigation, Wiley sent a Bureau of Chemistry official south to investigate the bottling process. He discovered the soda was popular with children—and that it was bottled in unsanitary conditions. When Wiley argued before the Board of Food and Drug Inspection that these unsanitary conditions merited taking action against Coca-Cola as an adulterated product, McCabe and Dunlap rejected his argument.[37] Because the rest of the Department of Agriculture apparatus resisted Wiley's arguments, Wilson did nothing. But when a Georgia newspaper reporter visited the Division of Chemistry and threatened to go public with Wiley's research on the drink, Secretary Wilson changed his mind.[38]

After the 1909 seizure of Coca-Cola in Tennessee, the local US attorney charged the company with violating the PFDA on the grounds of both health risk and deception. First, it charged that the added caffeine was a "deleterious ingredient" that was "injurious to health." Furthermore, the product was misbranded, because the caffeine came from tea sweepings rather than the cola nut and because the cola flavor came from exhausted coca leaves instead of the cola nut.[39] The trial began in federal court in Chattanooga in the spring of 1911 and lasted about a month.

Fearing that Chattanooga was not the best place for the government to make its stand against the soft drink maker, Wiley employed spies to watch the jurors with the idea of turning up evidence that could be used to impugn their integrity in court. This proved to be money wasted. Nevertheless, it seems likely that the jury didn't understand much of the highly technical testimony, some of which had to be translated from the original German. All of the testimony received enormous national attention, even if newspapermen didn't always understand the complicated arguments and evidence. "EIGHT COCA-COLAS CONTAIN ENOUGH CAFFEINE TO KILL," read one particularly misguided headline.[40]

There was great anticipation that Wiley himself would take the stand in support of the charges. Because of his tendency to change his mind on food issues (usually by further sharpening his warnings about particular additives), government lawyers became increasingly unwilling to put Wiley on the witness stand in cases about particular additives.[41] In this instance, he ultimately demurred, citing the fact that "he could not qualify as a physiologist, a chemist, a toxicologist, a topological chemist, a pharmacologist or a doctor of medicine, to the satisfaction of himself or the government." His enemies had a field day with this admission, arguing that he was not qualified for any of the duties that came with his government position. He had, however, served as an expert witness for a sodium benzoate case in Indiana, so his admission likely meant that he was willing to serve as a courtroom expert only for cases involving substances upon which he had conducted experiments.[42]

The key moment of the trial was the testimony of the Barnard College psychologist Harry Hollingsworth. Coca-Cola had hired Hollingsworth to study the secondary effects of caffeine, and he quickly delivered three experiments in just forty days so that he could be done in time for the trial. Those experiments remain models for such examinations today. Like the Poison Squad experiments, this was human subject research, but unlike Wiley, Hollingsworth conducted double-blind experiments: neither the experimenter nor the subjects knew whether they had received caffeine or not. Hollingsworth found caffeine to be a moderate stimulant with no secondary effects on mental or motor skills.[43] His findings also challenged Wiley's assertion that Coca-Cola produced depression or fatigue.[44]

The trial lasted about a week after Hollingsworth testified, until Coca-Cola moved for a summary dismissal, arguing that the caffeine in Coke was not an added ingredient but part of the formula itself. The judge in the case agreed, and the jury delivered a directed verdict in favor of the Coca-Cola Company. "The caffeine contained in the article Coca-Cola is one of its regular, habitual and essential constituents," wrote judge and future US Supreme Court justice Edward Sanford, "and that without its presence, that is, if it were de-caffeinized, so to speak, the product would lack one of its essential elements and fail to produce upon the consumer a characteristic, if not the most characteristic effect which is obtained by its use."[45] As in the resolution of the whiskey controversy, the judge argued that things that do not go together in nature sometimes become the "natural" state of things and should be protected.

The publicity from this suit hurt Wiley's image. "The Coca-Cola people, as well as the government," argued the *Chattanooga Times*, "have been put to an enormous expense in testing a question which, it would seem, should never have been entertained."[46] Even though Wiley did not testify, his enemies at the *American Food Journal* took him on directly. "Under Dr. Wiley's theory," it editorialized, the sixty million pounds of caffeine consumed by Americans in coffee and tea were "perfectly wholesome and non-injurious, but the mere bagatelle in Coca-Cola was not only poisonous and deleterious, but there as an added ingredient. Might we not ask how long this irresponsible faddist and political doctor be allowed to continue his autocratic interference with legitimate industries?"[47]

Wiley was unapologetic. He blamed the loss on a technicality rather than the merits of the case.[48] In truth, Sanford was agnostic about the health effects of caffeine in his decision. His ruling made the same point about caffeine that Wiley's critics did: since much more caffeine occurred naturally in substances like coffee and those couldn't be taken off the market under the Pure Food and Drug Act, it was irrelevant whether caffeine was harmful or not; people would continue to get it anyway. In fact, Sanford thought that to take the caffeine out of Coca-Cola, when people expected caffeine in a product with that distinctive trademark, would have been deceptive.[49] In other words, this decision was not based on a legal technicality—it was based on a concern about deception, which had once been Wiley's paramount concern about food.

Instead of weighing different concerns in appropriate degrees, Wiley continued to trumpet the adverse health effects of caffeine, inflating the danger well beyond the actual risk that consumers faced. "Caffeine," Wiley explained while still working at the Bureau of Chemistry, "which is being used so generally by many unscrupulous soft drink dispensers, should be driven from the market by law."[50] Asked about the Coca-Cola trial in Congressional testimony in 1912, shortly after he resigned his office, Wiley argued that caffeine was comparable to strychnine because the effects of both built up over time.[51] His testimony ignored the obvious differences: one of these substances is acutely poisonous and the other is not; one appears naturally in beverages that many consumers drink every day such as coffee or tea and the other does not.

Freed from the political concerns of government officialdom, Wiley wrote a May 1912 letter to the *Journal of the American Medical Association* that took his case against caffeine to an extraordinary extreme. He repeated an earlier statement calling caffeine a "lethal poison in not very large doses." He named Coca-Cola "a constant threat to the health, not only of children, but of grown persons in this county. It is a business which has no moral right to exist. It exists today because eminent scientific men have given it the help of their assistance."[52] To what degree these sentiments reflected his real views or stemmed from his bitterness at losing the case in Chattanooga is difficult to tell. What is obvious is that Wiley never understood that most Americans were more than willing to drink Coca-Cola regularly, despite potential health risks, whether they were addicted to the product or not. That remains true today.

After losing in Chattanooga, the government appealed that decision to the federal circuit court of appeals in Cincinnati. The decision that came down in June 1914 affirmed the lower court's ruling. The judges cited the lack of difference between the caffeine in Coca-Cola and that in coffee or tea as the key to their decision. If the larger amounts of caffeine in coffee or tea weren't "poisonous" or "deleterious" under the law, how could the government force Coca-Cola to take the caffeine out of its product?[53] The court ruled that Coca-Cola's use of caffeine over many years had made it an integral part of the product, and since there was less caffeine in that beverage than in many other available drinks, Congress could not have intended that the Pure Food and Drug Act be enforced against Coca-Cola and not those other drinks.[54] This was a general rule that could apply just as well to the creosote that shows up in minute quantities in smoked ham as it did to the tiny amount of caffeine in Coca-Cola. In other words, natural substances don't suddenly become dangerous poisons just because they are added to foods in which they don't appear already.

But the United States Supreme Court disagreed. In the May 1916 case *United States v. Forty Barrels and Twenty Kegs of Coca-Cola,* the justices overturned both earlier decisions. The new decision, written by Justice Charles Evans Hughes, ruled that caffeine should be considered an added ingredient because doing otherwise would open up a huge loophole in the Pure Food and Drug Act. Manufacturers could include harmful substances in their products just because those substances were already part of their existing ingredients. The decision also contradicted the notion that Coca-Cola had a legitimate claim under the act because of its distinctive name. The court sent the case back to Chattanooga for retrial on the question of whether or not caffeine was "deleterious."[55] Though Wiley, having left government service, was no longer in a position to continue prosecuting the Coca-Cola Company, his position had won in court.

Fearing further prosecution even without Wiley, the Coca-Cola Company settled out of court with the government on November 12, 1917.[56] In exchange for a plea of no contest, Coca-Cola dropped its caffeine levels by half and increased the amount of coca leaf (without the cocaine) and kola nut that went into the syrup.[57] Coca-Cola also changed its marketing in response to the government's action. During the trial, Wiley had pushed the prosecution to stress the negative effects of caffeine upon children. This was the defense's weak point: they denied that children drank Coca-Cola even though young children appeared in many of the company's own advertisements. After the trial, the company stopped marketing to children under twelve, a policy that remained in effect until 1986. Perhaps more important, the company almost entirely stopped marketing their product as a pick-me-up. They now preferred that people drink the soda for its fresh taste instead.[58]

Not surprisingly, Wiley considered his position on caffeine vindicated by Justice Hughes's decision, but he was unhappy with how the case eventually turned out. Although the government had won a great legal victory in the Supreme Court, Wiley thought it did too little to capitalize on that success. Moreover, the *Forty Barrels of Coca-Cola* decision applied only to the Coca-Cola Company, not to the other soda manufacturers who made use of caffeine, and caffeine thus continued to pose a threat to the Pure Food and Drug Act. Even though Coca-Cola had a new formula, the Supreme Court had interpreted the pure food law to cover any caffeine, so there was nothing stopping the government from seizing forty more barrels of Coca-Cola and fighting the same battle again—this time with Supreme Court precedent squarely on its side.[59]

Inevitably, if he were alive today, Wiley would blame the Wilson administration's failure to act on its victory for the growth of Coca-Cola into a worldwide behemoth. In *The History of a Crime against the Food Law,* he attributed ten years of the company's success to the government's decision to settle with Coca-Cola rather than drive it out of business.[60] A more interesting question is what Wiley would have thought about the success of Diet Coke. He objected to saccharin primarily because of its health effects rather than its deceptive nature. New substitutes for saccharin are certainly not natural, but they are clearly labeled. Millions of people around the world consume a drink that is designed to mimic the taste of a product that Wiley already thought to be unnatural. Would he have considered that an improvement over the Coca-Cola he decried? Would he be more worried about the growth of American sugar consumption or caffeine consumption?

Wiley brooked no compromise with Coca-Cola because he thought its product was a scourge. "The evidence at Chattanooga showed hundreds of addicts to Coca-Cola," Wiley wrote in 1925, "and this devastating beverage is now moving rapidly northward."[61] On the one hand, in retrospect such sentiments seem laughable. What would Wiley have thought of the rise of Starbucks? Many of its drinks contain more caffeine and just as much sugar as the now-iconic Coca-Cola, yet people do not drop dead in the streets as a result. On the other hand, in many ways the world would indeed be better off if Coca-Cola were not as readily available as it is. Still, Wiley's case helped make Coca-Cola a more pure, less caffeinated drink than it would otherwise have been.

Wiley refused to admit that the government had actually won the case; such an admission went against his longstanding notion that a "crime against the food law" had occurred. Instead, he perceived a significant improvement—that is, a reduction in the amount of caffeine contained in Coca-Cola—as a loss for the cause of pure food. By the end of his life, unwilling to even acknowledge other interpretations of the law, Wiley was unable to see his own influence upon what Americans ate and drank every day. Wiley's impact on the nation's food supply remains his primary historical legacy. It is significant for the sheer number of foods he changed for the better—whether Coca-Cola, ketchup, or unnecessary (even if not unhealthful) preservatives like borax. Sadly, Wiley judged his entire career a failure because its impact did not meet his initial, unrealistic goals.

CHAPTER THIRTEEN

RESIGNATION

NEAR THE END OF HIS TIME IN WASHINGTON, rumors began circulating that Harvey Wiley had become rich while working in public service, probably by scandalous means. In 1912 Wiley's archenemies, the editors of the *American Food Journal*, suggested that he was worth $300,000. He did, in fact, have a "fine home" in Loudon County, Virginia, which he had bought in 1909, an orchard in the Blue Ridge Mountains, and an interest in another farm in Montgomery County, Maryland.[1] His patents and his related work for the Marsden Company starting the late 1890s had helped him make money. In addition, he held a part-time position at Columbian University, which became George Washington University in 1904, for which he was paid $40 per student per year.[2] The *American Food Journal* pointed to payments he had received from his friends at the Arbuckle Coffee Company.[3] Wiley had also helped establish the New York Sugar Trade Laboratory to settle disputes over the quality of the product in that industry. John Arbuckle may have paid him $10,000 for that effort.[4]

Wiley likely obtained whatever assets he had legally. Most notably, the many investments in stocks and real estate that he had been making since the early 1890s were potentially very lucrative. Had the public known about his investments in food manufacturing companies that operated in areas that Wiley was in charge of regulating he might have gotten into serious trouble. In 1902, for example, shortly before Wiley began testing salicylic acid as part of a Poison Squad experiment, he bought an interest in a New Jersey salicylic plant.[5] When Wiley compiled the data from that experiment in 1906, he approved of its use.[6] In every other experiment of this kind, results from the Poison Squad tests strengthened his position against the preservative in question, raising a question about whether his approval of salicylic acid was more than a coincidence.

Throughout his campaign for the pure food law, Wiley's critics attacked him for the magazine articles he wrote about research he did using government equipment on government time.[7] Wiley took payment for those articles and accepted what was, in effect, free advertising for his views on various pure food–related disputes. The articles were part of a vast public relations campaign that promoted both his cause and his image. In this way he used resources provided to him by the federal government to become both rich and famous.

Imagine these critics' reactions had they known that Wiley conducted private chemical tests on food after hours on government equipment for his own gain.[8] He often referred to the companies that sent him samples to test as "my clients."[9] In 1902, for example, a New York "client" wrote Wiley, "I have managed to gather together a small assortment of our . . . high grade goods . . . and I am shipping the same to your home address as per your suggestion. . . . I want to again repeat that this is a purely personal matter, and that I am asking your opinion purely personally, and I will not, under any circumstances, show your letter or repeat what you have said or use it any way, shape, or form."[10] Wiley's clients clearly understood that they were buying influence with their gifts to Wiley, not advertising.

Despite such practices, Wiley assiduously cultivated a reputation for frugality and integrity. "I have never tried to make money," he told one magazine journalist writing a profile of him in 1911. "Nor have I spent much money.

No man of my age has spent as little money on himself." [11] In many cases he didn't have to spend money on himself because of all the gifts he received from food companies, including some whose markets he was attempting to regulate. These gifts, which included wine, whiskey, pineapple, and oysters, complemented his luxurious lifestyle. [12] Wiley's actual diet challenged his image as a dispassionate food scientist who seldom discussed how the foods he regulated actually tasted. [13]

Wiley's acceptance of even small gifts could have threatened his government employment. Starting in 1905, the Department of Agriculture had been rocked by a series of scandals, all involving money and personal gain by government officials. That year, Edwin Holmes, a statistician, had been discovered leaking advance information on cotton futures to speculators and sharing in those gains. Shortly thereafter, the press had accused the chief of the department's weather bureau of growing rich off his government expense account. Later, the New York Herald revealed that the chief of the Bureau of Animal Industry held an interest in the printing company that printed up meat inspection labels. He resigned. [14]

Wiley may have thought his popularity with the public would immunize him if the truth about the gifts he received had been revealed. Nevertheless, his correspondence suggests that he was nervous about these relationships coming to light. He didn't want to test his popularity by having his secrets exposed. Indeed, despite the risks he took, Wiley was scrupulous about protecting his public image, which was so important to his cause. Perhaps the easiest way for Wiley to earn more would have been to endorse products for money. Many firms slapped his words (both real and imagined) on advertisements for their food products during Wiley's tenure in government, but he always sent letters asking them to stop. He never let his name be used in ads and even turned down offers of compensation. [15] Wiley was not corrupt in the sense that he did his job only for the money; however, he did behave as if making money were the natural result of doing his job.

Had Wiley ever been directly confronted about his moneymaking activities, he probably would have blamed his behavior on his employer. "The pay in the Department of Agriculture is ridiculously small," wrote Wiley in a letter to the Department of the Treasury looking for extra money for some things he had done on its behalf. Wiley had earned $2,500 a year for his first seventeen years in the Department of Agriculture, $3,000 for the year after that, and $3,500 for the two years preceding that 1903 complaint.[16] Asked about his salary while testifying before the Congressional committee that determined the Department of Agriculture's budget in 1907, Wiley responded, "I am a bachelor and I do not need the mony, but I believe that the office ought to be recognized with the dignity of a salary commensurate with the importance of the work." If they raised his salary to $5,000 he offered to donate the difference to "two worthy colleges" instead of keeping it for himself.[17]

Actually, Wiley did need the money—or at least wanted it badly to support his expensive lifestyle. When considering another job in government service in 1904, he wrote, "I am not all mercenary but realize that advancing years render it necessary that I should look somewhat more closely than in my youth to the matter of salary."[18] When he resigned from the Department of Agriculture in 1912, Wiley was making $5,000 a year.[19] Despite his many protestations about his ability to do more for the cause of pure food outside of government than inside it, Harvey Wiley left government service, at least in part, for the money.

———

One of the consequences of Wiley's frequent side work was its negative effect on the office he ran. Harvey Wiley was a terrible administrator. He was popular with his employees at the Bureau of Chemistry, but even they recognized his shortcomings in this regard. "There is little to be said of Wiley as a boss, because he never was a boss, in the sense which the term is commonly used," remembered one of the secretaries there after Wiley's death. "He gave responsibilities, not orders, to his subordinates, and all worked together with one object in view, the boss working harder, longer hours and to better purpose than any of the others. When he was around, he was not much of a leader." She credited his "marvelous" personality with holding his staff together, but that tactic worked for only so long.[20]

FIGURE 18.1 Wiley with a tray of food on a scale, between 1910 and 1930. This portrait suggests efforts to remind the public of his work on the Poison Squad experiments at a time when that work was starting to fade from public memory.

Courtesy Library of Congress

As his division grew from 5 to 350 people between 1883 and 1908, his management skills increasingly became a liability.[21] Yet he had stopped doing actual chemistry. Without chemistry, administering his office was his only responsibility in Washington. By the turn of the twentieth century, Wiley was spending most summers in Europe and much of the rest of the year on the road. He wasn't around to run his own office.

One way to judge Wiley's abilities as an administrator is to examine the Bureau of Chemistry's expenses. Before the passage of the Pure Food and Drug Act (PFDA), Wiley estimated that his bureau would require an additional $150,000 to $200,000 to perform all the new duties assigned to it under that legislation. In fact, however, he required additional appropriations of one million dollars more than that over the next two years alone.[22] Wiley's public reputation as a champion of consumers insulated him from any pressure to lower the costs of operating his department just as it insulated him from the food manufacturers who wanted him fired from the Bureau of Chemistry. As long as the public believed that he was the embodiment of the spirit behind the PFDA, then there was no gift he could take or no expense he could inflate that would lead to his unwilling ouster from government.

This last point becomes very clear in the reaction to the largest public scandal of Wiley's long government career. On July 12, 1911, news broke in the *New York Times* that the Committee of Personnel at the Department of Agriculture had accused Wiley of conspiring with the head of its Division on Drugs, Lyman Kebler, to pay Henry H. Rusby, a pharmacologist at Columbia University, an illegally high salary to serve as an expert witness at the Coca-Cola trial. They recommended that Wiley be "permitted to resign," and the attorney general of the United States agreed. The charges against Wiley were brought by his associates on the Board of Food and Drug Inspection, Frederick Dunlap and George McCabe.[23]

Asked about his defense against the charges against him, Wiley responded, "We need no defense. I am planning an attack."[24] Nevertheless, Wiley's response to the report was essentially to plead administrative incompetence. He claimed he knew nothing whatsoever of the agreement.[25] The investigation of these charges demonstrated that Wiley was not included in the correspondence that led to the agreement. Besides, employment arrangements were simply not something in which he showed any interest. Nevertheless, Rusby's contract was in Wiley's realm of responsibility.

Congressional hearings were conducted by what came to be known as the Moss Committee (after its chairman, Congressman Ralph W. Moss from Wiley's home state of Indiana). The hearings began before President Taft made his decision whether to keep Wiley in his position, but the committee released its report months afterward. Unsurprisingly, when the committee eventually released its report, it cleared Wiley of this conspiracy charge. It found that Wiley's enemies within the department had altered the letter that had formed the basis of an alleged conspiracy to hire Rusby at an illegal salary. Not only had Wiley never seen the letter in question, the letter itself had never even been sent. With Wiley's innocence easily determined, the committee took extensive testimony showing just how marginalized Wiley had become in the enforcement of the pure food law.[26]

For his part, Wiley used his testimony before a committee that was nominally investigating him to detail for a public audience all the difficulties he had with both the Board of Food and Drug Inspection and the Remsen Board. He questioned the integrity and reputation of both boards' members, using the decisions that had gone against him as the basis of his judgment. He offered statistics showing the public for the first time just how often he had been overruled at various steps in the enforcement process, saying that two-thirds of the cases he had brought before the Board of Food and Drug Inspection had been overruled by the other members. By Wiley's count, 6,000 cases in total had not reached the courts, thereby wasting $162 per case of the government's money—this was what it cost for the Bureau of Chemistry to inspect the food that had been brought before it.[27]

Wiley knew that assessment was misleading. Just because a case didn't make it to court didn't necessarily mean that adulteration continued. It could mean that the accused adulterators changed their practices to avoid prosecution. Nevertheless, the press coverage of Wiley's testimony suggests that he effectively made his case before both Congress and the public. "Dr. Wiley was so much affected that he had difficulty controlling his voice," explained a reporter from the *Washington Times* who was in the hearing room. "When he told about the long years of his fight to get national pure food legislation, of the bitter opposition to which he was subjected, of final success—and then of the practical nullification of the law by administrative actions which took away all his powers while leaving him in the same nominal position, his voice broke, he could not be heard, and it looked once or twice he would find it difficult to proceed."[28] Love him or hate him, from a reporter's point of view, Wiley always offered great copy.

Before congressional investigation of the matter had even finished, President William Howard Taft refused to fire Wiley from his position at the Bureau of Chemistry. In a letter to Secretary Wilson, Taft declared that Wiley "was justified in all that he did" with respect to employing Dr. Rusby, who was also allowed to keep his job with the Department of Agriculture.[29] Taft understood that he could not let Wiley go—no matter how much he may have wished to—because of Wiley's substantial support among the general public.[30] The extent of that support among both the press and the public became obvious to all when Congress began its hearings on the charges against him.

Presidents Roosevelt and Taft had kept Wiley around as long as they did because his popularity rubbed off to some degree on them. As long as Wiley ran the Division of Chemistry, it seemed as if the government cared about the cause of pure food, even if obscure committees like the Remsen Board ultimately undercut Wiley's radical positions. In effect, during his time at the Bureau of Chemistry, Wiley developed his own constituency. It included a large segment of the public, a segment of the press, and even some food manufacturers who wanted to produce pure food at a profit. When Wiley left for *Good Housekeeping*, he managed to bring much of that constituency with him.

———

Wiley issued his formal resignation from the Bureau of Chemistry on March 15, 1912, shortly after the Moss Committee vindicated him in the Rusby affair. Wiley, in his resignation letter, explained his decision to resign by pointing out the differences between himself and his superiors in the Department of Agriculture over how the Pure Food and Drug Act should be enforced. Six years after the law's passage, Wiley wrote that he realized that its "fundamental principles" had been "paralyzed or discredited." Wiley's letter also repeated his now old complaint about the bureau's authority being usurped. "One by one," he recalled, "I found that the activities pertaining to the Bureau of Chemistry were restricted and various forms of manipulated food products were withdrawn from its consideration and either referred to other bodies not contemplated by law or directly relieved from further control."[31]

Privately, Wiley specifically cited his enemies in the bureaucracy as the reason he left his longtime position. In a conversation with Secretary Wilson, he mentioned Dunlap in particular. "Dr. Wiley used plain words," the *New York Times* reported, "in which the characterization of 'sneak,' 'liar' and 'thief' found place."[32] His resignation letter also included a section about who were conspiring against him. "After the President of the United States and a Committee of Congress completely exonerated me from any wrongdoing, I naturally expected that those who made these false charges against me would no longer be continued in a position which would make a repetition of such actions possible." Instead, Wiley wrote, "I was still left to come into daily contact with the men who secretly plotted my destruction."[33] The idea of escaping this toxic work environment must have seemed appealing.

But Harvey Wiley left many friends in the Department of Agriculture too. "When the official day came to an end hundreds of the clerks and employes in other departments than Dr. Wiley's filed through his office to shake hands with him and say good-bye," the *New York Times* informed its readers on the day after his resignation took effect. "The scene was an affecting one. A few had been with him for the nearly thirty years he has been at the head of the bureau. Many had been under him for a quarter of a century. All respected and loved him, and they showed their feelings plainly in words and act. Many were choked with tears and could not speak, and went away crying like children."[34] The staff at the Bureau of Chemistry gave him a silver case. The inscription read, "To Harvey W. Wiley, whose leadership has been an inspiration to all who have had the privilege of knowing personally, day by day, the breadth and depth of his well-stored mind, his unshakable integrity, and his splendid poise and never failing geniality, under any and all conditions,—from the Bureau of Chemistry, U.S. Dept. of Agriculture, 1883–1912."[35] Presumably, those responsible for the Rusby investigation did not contribute to the purchase of this extravagant retirement gift.

Yet Wiley did not really retire from working when he left the Department of Agriculture. Though at the time of his resignation Wiley gave only a hint about what he would do next, he had already secured a path to making substantially more money than he had in government service. By the time he left the Department of Agriculture, he had been negotiating an arrangement with *Good Housekeeping* for months. He had agreed on terms with the American Home Magazine Company, the publisher of *Good Housekeeping*, by early November of the previous year. For the first three years his salary would be $10,000 a year—twice as much as he earned working for the federal government. Moreover, *Good Housekeeping* gave him explicit permission to continue writing for other magazines (as long as they had the right of first refusal) and to work on the Chautauqua lecture circuit.[36] As a result, his total earnings would dwarf what he had made while in government service.

Although *Good Housekeeping* wanted Wiley to appear in its pages for the first time in the March 1912 issue, Wiley refused to start until the Moss Committee returned its report on the Rusby issue that same month. Leaving before then "would be an act almost of treason which I do not feel I could perform," he wrote during the negotiation over the final terms of his new employment.[37] He correctly understood that the House would discuss not just Rusby, but the entire set-up of pure food decisions, including the Remsen Board's ability to overturn the Bureau of Chemistry's findings. By staying until the Moss Committee concluded its work, Wiley could be assured of leaving on high note rather than have it appear that the Rusby charges had driven him out of government service.

The announcement of Wiley's new role at *Good Housekeeping* came about a month after his resignation, generating more headlines, though it received less publicity than the charges against Wiley or his resignation. The *New York Times* claimed it had gotten a letter from Wiley to a "friend in the city" in which he explained his new career. "I have had a great number of offers to go into commercial life," the letter read, "and I may say most favorable ones from a financial point of view. These offers, as a rule, have been legitimate from high-grade organizations, and have been of a character which anyone might accept with honor and profit. None of them, however, have been in the exact line of the propaganda that I am trying to preach."[38] That "line of propaganda" was, of course, the cause of pure food.

Ironically, stressing the financial sacrifice he was making by continuing his work on pure food gave Wiley his best chance of minimizing that financial sacrifice. Maintaining his reputation as a fighter was essential for attracting readers to *Good Housekeeping*, as well as for booking speeches about pure food on the Chautauqua circuit. Furthermore, working outside of government for the first time in thirty years freed him from whatever ethical constraints he was subject to at the Department of Agriculture. Indeed, Wiley continued to receive small gifts from food producers during his first few years at *Good Housekeeping*.[39]

Outside of government, Wiley was also free from pressure to compromise. "My own views are very well known," he wrote in that letter to a friend published by the *Times*, "perhaps they are what would be classed as radical; but they are based upon the one plank of my simple platform, namely, that all doubtful questions in the food and drug discussion should be resolved in favor of the consumer. . . . What is best for him, what bests conserves his interest and his health, what is best for his pocketbook, and for his labor, are to me the controlling factors, in reaching conclusions."[40] Declarations like this suggest that Wiley intended his letter to reach an audience much broader than just one New York City friend.

This entire episode, from the release of the Rusby-related charges to the release of the news that he would be joining *Good Housekeeping*, demonstrate how skilled Wiley had become at manipulating the press. Whereas his prose had once been limited to technical papers and correspondence, by the end of his government tenure Wiley wrote and released long letters intended as press releases. He used these letters, like his speeches, to identify himself with the cause of pure food, and he had no trouble admitting that the goal of his "line of propaganda" was to persuade people to join his cause. If you supported pure food, you had to support Wiley.

Wiley continued to argue his side of the dispute over enforcement of the PFDA even after he left government, but the same cannot be said of his enemies inside the Board of Food and Drug Inspection. At the end of the Taft administration, James Wilson retired, the longest-serving cabinet secretary in American history. Solicitor McCabe resigned from the Board of Food and Drug Inspection after the end of the Moss Committee hearings in 1911.[41] In early 1913 he left government service to practice law in Portland, Oregon. "It was said by officials that Dr. Wiley and Mr. McCabe had agreed on some of the most controverted questions arising under the Pure Food law far more thoroughly than the public had supposed," the *New York Times* reported at the time of McCabe's resignation.[42] Frederick Dunlap left the Bureau of Chemistry to work for a Chicago chemical company in September 1912.[43]

Wilson's successor as secretary of agriculture abolished the Board of Food and Drug Inspection in early 1914.[44] In late 1915 the members of the Remsen Board all handed in their resignations because they had nothing left to investigate,[45] and that board was never reassembled. Without Harvey Wiley, there was no need for these organizations to check his excesses. And Wiley, seeking to improve his reputation and take credit for the passage of the Pure Food and Drug Act, would spend the rest of his life arguing that the formation of these boards was a "crime against the food law," both in the pages of *Good Housekeeping* and elsewhere.

━━━◆━━━

Long before the end of his life, Harvey Wiley began to question the durability of what he considered his most important legacy. He thought the Pure Food and Drug Act was being taken for granted and that his contributions to the act were being undermined by poor administration. To strike back at his enemies, Wiley began to downplay the contributions of the law in its entirety. Had they only listened to me, his argument went, the quality of our food supply would be substantially better. Though his challengers had merely resisted Wiley's efforts to use the law to ban chemicals of all kinds from the food supply, Wiley sought to relitigate that prolonged debate, arguing that the spirit of the entire law had been betrayed.

In 1929 he self-published the book *The History of a Crime against the Food Law*.[46] Wiley was a prolific author who did not need to self-publish to find an audience, but this work was unlike anything he had ever written. Rather than a scientific tract or a nutrition guide for a general audience, this book settled old scores. In between a hodgepodge of transcripts of past Congressional testimony and old newspaper clippings, Wiley's commentary explained how he saw the fight surrounding the passage and implementation of the Pure Food and Drug Act of 1906. Wiley blamed a cabal of officials at the Department of Agriculture for thwarting his efforts to enforce the PFDA as Congress had intended.

In the book, Wiley claimed the way the law had been implemented was both illegal and a fundamental violation of the original intent of the law's framers. To make this case, he singled out the work of the Board of Food and Drug Inspection and the Remsen Board, which his administrative superiors had created to help decide whether foods were pure. According to Wiley, through their influence upon these bodies, special interests had so perverted the implementation of the PFDA that they had negated any positive effects of the law. The administrative changes, he argued, resulted in the approval of many additives that Wiley thought were harmful.

Long before the publication of the book, Wiley had divided everyone involved with the early history of the PFDA into two competing camps. "Practically every one who knows the history of the food law must find himself more or less prejudiced," he wrote in 1910, "either with the views which I have endeavored to maintain or those which concede such large liberties to manufacturers and distributors."[47] To Wiley, you were either for his position or against it—even though his position had changed over time. However, even if Wiley eventually won the argument over whether a crime had occurred, he identified the wrong criminal. Food manufacturers, supported by their allies in the federal bureaucracy, could not have continued to produce the lines of products that Wiley found suspect if not for a decision from the United State Supreme Court.

The court's decision in *United States v. The Lexington Mill and Elevator Company* came down in February 1914, two years after Wiley had left government service, and its effects extended far beyond just flour. The case began, at Wiley's initiative, in 1909, when the government seized 625 sacks of bleached flour that had been shipped from the Lexington Mill and Elevator Company of Lexington, Nebraska, to Missouri. Under the Pure Food and Drug Act the government had the right to seize the flour because it had traveled across state lines and because Wiley had convinced the a US attorney that it had been adulterated in the bleaching process by the chemical residues left over and had been misbranded as white flour.[48]

The court found unanimously in favor of the mill: it affirmed the original jury's decision that the bleaching process did not add enough nitrites for the effect to be injurious under the language of the Pure Food and Drug Act. More important, the decision allowed the government wide discretion in determining how it wanted to enforce the law, although there had to be a reasonable connection between the substance it wanted to ban and some harm. The court determined that the minimal amount of nitrites left over from the Alsop process were clearly not harmful under the terms of the PFDA.[49]

The decision came down to an interpretation of a clause in the Pure Food and Drug Act which stated that the government could ban additives "which may prove harmful to health." The court interpreted "may" in that clause as reflecting the discretionary nature of the law. In other words, Congress meant to leave it the government's discretion whether or not it would prosecute cases under the law depending upon the level of injury a particular substance caused. Although nitrates might be harmful in large quantities, the Supreme Court said it was incumbent on the government to prove that the amount of nitrates found in a typical serving of bread baked from this flour would cause harm. It couldn't.[50]

That decision not only permitted a bleaching process that Wiley saw as an unhealthful adulteration but also put a final end to his interpretation of how the PFDA should be enforced. Permitting harmful substances in food, even in tiny quantities, made it impossible to carry out Wiley's vision of excluding chemicals of every kind. If manufacturers could add ingredients that could cause injury, then future litigation was destined to center on how much of an injurious ingredient was acceptable rather than whether the substance was injurious or not. The Department of Agriculture could have tried to bring cases against bleached flour manufacturers on a case-by-case basis, but it would have been impossible to stop all the bleached flour then circulating in commerce on this basis.[51]

When the Lexington Mill decision came out, Wiley did his best to preserve the possibility of a chemical-free food supply. He called for Congress to strike the suspect clause in the PFDA entirely. By removing any discretion as to whether a substance was harmful, Wiley sought to force the government to prosecute all foods with potentially harmful substances—just as he had originally imagined. Wiley wrote, "Into our butter they may put a few parts per million of a poisonous coal-tar dye; into the milk a few parts per million of poisonous formaldehyde; into the bread a few parts per million of a poisonous nitrous acid; into the baking powder a few parts per million of poisonous arsenic."[52] This argument was completely disingenuous as there was still a bureaucracy in place to prevent precisely this eventuality. Wiley simply differed with that bureaucracy over how much of particular additives made a food poisonous.

In reality, the court's interpretation of the PFDA squared nicely with the intentions of the law's framers. Near the end of the decision, Justice William R. Day, who delivered the opinion of the court, quoted Senator Weldon Heyburn, one of the original sponsors of the law. "As to the use of the term 'poisonous,'" the senator explained on the Senate floor before the law's passage, "let me state that everything which contains poison is not poison. It depends on the quantity and the combination."[53] The government could have brought cases against all food additives if it deemed them all sufficiently harmful, but nothing compelled it to do so. Wiley called the exercise of this court-mandated federal government discretion a "crime against the food law," but in fact it was just a conflict of regulatory visions, which the chemist lost.

In the final 1919 settlement of the Lexington Mill case, the government agreed to drop the charge that residues of the bleaching process in flour were hazardous to health. The government took possession of the original 625 sacks of flour and destroyed them. This outcome maintained the precedent about how to interpret the Pure Food and Drug Act but eliminated the precedent with respect to bleached flour. In response to that settlement, the Department of Agriculture laid down new, more precise rules about the circumstances under which the bleaching of flour would be allowed. Any bleaching methods that impaired the quality of the flour were disallowed. By then, in any case, safer methods of flour bleaching had been developed. The quest for such methods was a consequence of Wiley's crusade against bleached flour. The result was better-quality white flour for all, thanks to the original initiative of Harvey Wiley.[54]

Of course, Wiley didn't see things this way. He thought the Bureau of Chemistry was giving millers an open invitation to keep injecting dangerous substances into the American food supply.[55] Yet in terms of limiting the spread of bleached flour, Wiley had already won. The prosecution, which Wiley had arranged and publicized, highlighted the risks of bleached flour, cutting demand and making it harder for millers to make any money from the practice. Consumption of bleached flour dropped considerably.[56] Still, Wiley was convinced that he had lost the war.

CHAPTER FOURTEEN

THE

GOOD

HOUSEKEEPING

YEARS

"**D**R. WILEY MOVES ABOUT AS VIGOROUSLY** as men fifty years his junior," gushed his editors at *Good Housekeeping* when he visited them in New York City for an interview in 1920. At the time, Wiley was seventy-six years old. "He is a very little bald, a very little stooped, diminishing his height of six-feet-one," explained the reporter who wrote the magazine's profile. "Broad, two hundred and thirty-five pounds in weight, rather athletic seeming. He has a springy step. He carries his round, strong-featured, well-shaped head a little forward, as a fighter does."[1] Such descriptions of Wiley were common in his later years. His diet and constant activity were always cited as the traits that kept him young. The age of his much-younger wife would occasionally merit a mention as well.

Toward the end of his life, Wiley's longevity became something of an advertisement for the diet advice he had been giving for years. "One's attitude toward life is highly important in prolonging life," explained a reporter who interviewed Wiley in the mid-1920s. "Young in spirit, of course, is this eighty-two-years-young scientist and world-renowned authority on human nutrition. What he preaches, he practices, hence his extraordinary physical and mental vigor, that many a man twenty or thirty years younger might envy."[2] Wiley's youthful image made him seem a more reliable authority on human nutrition than he might otherwise have been.

Harvey Wiley maintained a busy schedule as long as he could, with few concessions made to his age apart from the occasional midday nap. As long as he was capable of work, he was determined to keep doing so.[3] As late as 1926, he worked from twelve to sixteen hours each day. On most days he walked two miles to his office and back. He expressed a strong desire to keep living even after his health ceased to be as strong as it once was.[4]

Despite his laudatory press clippings, the truth about Wiley's declining years was more complicated than most people knew. For the first seven years following his retirement from government, Wiley continued touring the country on the lecture circuit. By 1921 he had mostly stopped because of poor eyesight and the decline in his hearing. That same year, he had an operation for cataracts that left him unable to do much reading. Nevertheless, he kept up upon a substantial correspondence with readers and friends, just as he had when he worked for the government, with the assistance of a substantial secretarial staff.[5]

During his time with *Good Housekeeping,* Wiley walked two miles to his office and back every day whenever he was in Washington. As his eyesight and the traffic got worse, the chemist increasingly found himself in precarious situations while in transit. One day, according to a story that circulated among his friends, he found himself caught in traffic and only saved himself from fatal injury by leaping to the curb. When he recovered, he blurted to an onlooker, "There only two kinds of people: the quick and the dead."[6] While intended to illustrate Wiley's wit, this story also demonstrated Wiley's considerable pride and increasing frailty. Even if Harvey Wiley had followed his own dietary advice to the letter, he could not halt the inevitable decline of old age.

Wiley worked for *Good Housekeeping* from the time he left government service in 1912 right up until his death in 1930. There he oversaw a chemical laboratory that tested a wide range of home products. When not fulfilling his duties for *Good Housekeeping*, Wiley spent time with his new family. He fathered two children with his wife, Anna: Harvey Wiley Jr. in 1912 and John Preston Wiley in 1914.[7] The birth of Wiley's first son was a media event, not just because of the father's age but because of how the Wileys planned to feed the child. Interviewed in the *Washington Times* after the birth, Wiley said, "The first thing he did was to stick out his fists, close his eyes and yell for pure food."[8] Upon the occasion of his christening, that same newspaper, like many others, referred to the child as the "pure food baby."[9] Shortly after the child's birth, Wiley "pledged" his son's hand in marriage to the daughter of the food commissioner of Kentucky, generating still more adorable newspaper stories.[10]

Wiley's theories of diet and child rearing became fodder for his lectures and writings. "In bringing up my son, I have tried to make him healthy," he told one audience in 1914. "He has never tasted candy, cake or ice cream. He doesn't care for them. When he goes to parties he carries with him hard graham biscuits, which he eats while other children are eating sweets."[11] Calling Wiley's sons the "healthiest [babies] in the world," the *Evening Ledger* of Philadelphia reported in 1915, "The Wiley children are healthy because Dr. Wiley has clung to the belief that Nature is quite adequate to handle the situation if one only lets her alone. And the two Wiley children illustrate that the food expert is right."[12] Despite his complete lack of psychological training, Wiley often discussed baby and child-rearing issues in his *Good Housekeeping* column. He also took the occasion of the birth of his son to advocate in favor of breastfeeding.[13]

Many food reformers during this era took an interest in the racist pseudo-science of eugenics, and Wiley did too.[14] Over the course of many public appearances during the 1910s, Wiley occasionally strayed from his usual subject of food purity and expressed support for racial ranking, sterilization of "imbeciles" and the insane, or other racist arguments then being normalized in some scientific circles.[15] "I advocate the public instruction of eugenics," he told a Utah reporter in 1913, "but not to children. This subject should be taught to parents. Children are to be the beneficiaries in generations to come."[16]

Wiley's most extensive remarks on eugenics came in an October 1922 *Good Housekeeping* article entitled "The Rights of the Unborn," though the word "eugenics" does not appear in the article. He wrote, "I believe that it

FIGURE 14.1 Anna Kelton Wiley and her two children, John and Harvey Wiley Jr., c. 1920. *Courtesy Library of Congress*

will be necessary for the state to exercise control over marriage to a much greater degree than has yet been done."[17] Wiley's flirtation with eugenics indicates an underlying racism, but that racism was never central to his work as a food reformer. Protecting consumers was the primary goal of his career, and he didn't make distinctions between one set of consumers and another. His interest in eugenics was rather a reflection of his willingness to speak and write about science of which he had little understanding. Wiley was prone to follow scientific fads of all kinds—whether right or wrong—because he wanted to appear to understand more science than he actually did. His willingness to leave the realm of food left him open to what in retrospect seem like serious lapses of judgment.

Press attention to the birth of Wiley's children extended to his wife for the first time since they had gotten married. After her marriage Anna became president of the Consumer's League of Washington, DC, and continued her work as a suffragist. In matters related to the home, she could be quite deferential. "I am quite willing to permit the public to know me as Dr. Wiley's wife," Kelton Wiley told one interviewer, "though I have some individual opinions and a few fads and fancies of my own. Still my interest has been almost absorbed by the vital questions with which my husband's name is associated."[18] Despite her other duties, she willingly described herself as a housekeeper of their multiple residences. She also set herself up in the home to act as Dr. Wiley's private secretary.[19] Certainly, her husband spent much more time at home so that he could be with his family than he did when he worked for the Department of Agriculture.

Nevertheless, Anna Kelton Wiley's life as an advocate for women had a strong impact on the marriage. She testified in Congress in support of bills to certify garments that were made in humane conditions (invariably by women workers) and in support of a parcel post system to allow rural women to receive the products they needed to live a more modern life.[20] In November 1917 Anna made headlines when she was arrested while picketing the White House as part of a long series of peaceful protests conducted by the National Woman's Party to get President Wilson to change his mind about the woman's suffrage amendment.[21] That whole year her husband had been receiving letters from jailed suffragettes describing the horrible food they received in captivity. Wiley, in turn, publicized the dangers these foods posed.[22] His wife stayed in jail for only five days and said later that this was the highlight of her life.[23] She spent most of her days in Washington managing the home while her husband went to work running a lab that tested food for impurities.

———

As the Good Housekeeping Institute's director of food, sanitation, and health, Wiley led a small office in Washington, DC, that answered between fifty and seventy-five letters a day.[24] He had a full chemical laboratory at his disposal, although this time the lab was for commercial purposes. The magazine, which already had a famous "Seal of Approval," created a special seal, "Tested and Approved by the Bureau of Food, Sanitation, and Health," for foods and other goods that Wiley determined to be pure.[25] Wiley argued that doing the same kind of work he had done at the Bureau of Chemistry but in the private sector freed him from the kind of censorship imposed by political concerns.[26]

Wiley no longer tried to give the impression that he still did chemistry. Instead, he claimed that the work for the magazine was done under his "immediate supervision" and that he put in a full day of work every day.[27] In fact, his responsibilities there left him plenty of time to give public speeches, write books, and spend time with his family. "*Good Housekeeping* has concluded with me what I call a very liberal agreement," Wiley wrote one of his many friends in Indiana shortly after leaving the Bureau of Chemistry, "by means of which I keep my offices in Washington and have academic freedom along the whole line with liberty to go upon the lecture platform as much as I please, provided I do not neglect my editorial work."[28]

A clause in Wiley's contract allowed him to require the magazine to reject advertising from companies whose products did not meet his standards. In one of his earliest years at the magazine, *Good Housekeeping* rejected $196,000 out of $240,000 worth of advertising for drugs and cosmetics on Wiley's orders.[29] Over seventeen years, Wiley instructed the magazine

to reject more than a million dollars in advertising revenue. In his autobiography, Wiley argued that this function alone took up a considerable
amount of his time.[30]

This practice reflected Wiley's decidedly outdated conception of what
people should and should not eat. Wiley worried primarily about whether
a particular food was pure, not whether it was nutritious or even healthy.
Therefore foods like Jell-O and Cream of Wheat, which had little in the
way of nutrients, came to bear the seal of approval that originated in Wiley's
lab. While Wiley did not necessarily have a direct hand in any particular
endorsement, such was the risk associated with working for a magazine that
depended on advertising revenues from food manufacturers.[31] At a time
when researchers were just discovering the existence of vitamins and their
importance to a healthy diet, Wiley continued to preach his older doctrine
of eating foods that were "simple and as near to nature as possible."[32] Wiley's
suspicions of processed food would make him popular with food faddists
long after his death, but they marked him as seriously out of step with other
food scientists during the last decades of his long life.

In most issues of *Good Housekeeping* (published monthly), Wiley contributed a column, and sometimes several. He also answered readers' questions. When his wife asked him how he came up with new things to write
about, he replied that "if he lived to be one hundred he would never exhaust
the reservoir of information he had stored up."[33] Such confidence explains
why Wiley often strayed far from matters having strictly to do with pure
food. In his January 1916 column, for example, he endorsed the complete
elimination of tobacco on health grounds—a position taken by Henry Ford
and Thomas Edison but few other prominent Americans. Wiley worried
not only about the health effects of smoking, but about all the money spent
on tobacco that might otherwise go to living a more pleasant and enjoyable
life. "The readers of GOOD HOUSEKEEPING ought to consider the propriety of
consistently discouraging such an expensive, useless and dangerous habit,"
he wrote. "Their boys and girls ought to be told the truth about tobacco and
the havoc it works."[34] Wiley had the power to force the magazine to reject
tobacco advertising, despite the serious financial consequences. Here is one
instance where science eventually vindicated Wiley completely.

Nevertheless, many of Wiley's columns were backward looking in two senses. They revisited pure food questions from his career in government—usually when Congress or the Supreme Court actions touched upon a particular debate from that time. And some were almost anti-modern in outlook. In December 1924 Wiley wrote a column about the future of the United States and its food supply. In it, he decried not only the globalization of food production but also the very idea of food processing. "There is one fundamental fact with regard to food which should always be kept in view," he wrote, "namely, that the sooner after maturity the food is consumed, and the less change that is worked upon it before consumption, the more nutritious and wholesome it is."[35] While true to some extent, this sentiment ignored the fact that people had been processing foods by pickling or drying them for thousands of years. Wiley's fear of industrial processing and poor understanding of working-class budgets left his conception of pure food out of reach for many consumers.

Wiley did his best to stay in touch with the concerns of his overwhelmingly female middle-class readership by answering their letters (with the help of his staff). He came to call this "the most valuable and certainly dominating activity of the Bureau's work." In one year, his office received and answered about 10,000 letters. The questions predominantly involved diet, health, and child-rearing issues.[36] However, as Wiley himself admitted, many of the questions he received were frivolous, and even some of the questions he answered in print were just plain weird. At various times he answered questions about "nose shapers," whether potted plants were appropriate for a school classroom, and whether bats were dangerous.[37]

Many of the letters he received, as Wiley put it, "do not enter at all into my activities."[38] While freely admitting that he was not a practicing medical doctor, Wiley still answered questions on medical topics.[39] In December 1923 Wiley listed the most popular topics of the letters he received: "the feeding of infants, the feeding of older children, reducing weight, increasing weight, constipation, diet in pregnancy and lactation."[40] None of these had anything to do with chemistry, and they were only incidentally connected to the subject of pure food. Although Wiley recognized the limitations of his expertise, his published answers exhibited the same certainty that he had always shown on food-related issues.

———

Even though Wiley had left government, he never really left politics and was deeply involved in the 1912 presidential election. Republicans in Indiana approached Wiley about running for governor that year. He declined. The Prohibition Party wanted to nominate Wiley for the presidency that year. He declined that opportunity as well. A group of Democrats, led by Wiley's friend Albert Sydney Burleson, asked if they could submit Wiley's name for consideration for vice president. Not being a Democrat, he turned down that offer too.[41] However, Wiley supported the Democratic ticket in other ways. In doing so, he began a campaign to besmirch the reputations of his former bureaucratic enemies that would last the rest of his life.

Harvey Wiley had been a Republican since the 1860s, shortly after the creation of that party. While he was still nominally a member of the Republican Party, his retirement from government service freed him to support and vote for a Democratic presidential candidate for the first time. Wiley wrote on behalf of Governor Woodrow Wilson for a publication called *The Democratic Text-Book*. He helped lead a national organization of Republicans for Wilson. He became vice president of the Wilson National Progressive Republican League. He also brought his expertise on health issues to a feminist organization committed to supporting the Democratic ticket. Perhaps most important, Wiley barnstormed on behalf of Wilson for a month during the fall campaign. At his own expense he traveled throughout Indiana (with a few stops in Pennsylvania, Ohio, and Massachusetts) giving speeches that were not so much pro-Wilson as anti-Roosevelt. By charging that former president Theodore Roosevelt—running that year on the Progressive Party ticket—had destroyed the pure food law by appointing the Remsen Board to limit its effects, Wiley almost single-handedly made pure food an issue in that election.[42]

The issue did not work in Roosevelt's favor. Roosevelt wanted to claim credit for that popular law, but Wiley objected strenuously, and his attacks were personal. "Mr. Roosevelt," he wrote at the height of the campaign, "by reason of his attitude toward the pure food and drug act abandoned the consumers of the country to the rapacity of a few mercenary manufacturers."

After explaining how Roosevelt began what he would later call a "crime against the pure food law," Wiley noted that the incumbent, William Howard Taft, was even more culpable. Citing his whiskey decision, Wiley accused the Republican of throwing "the mighty weight of the executive office to the support of the worst lot of adulterators that ever disgraced a country."[43] No wonder he crossed party lines in order to support Wilson.

When Wilson won the election, Wiley sent a letter suggesting that the previous administrations' executive orders with respect to the enforcement of the pure food law be overturned. The new president never acted.[44] Despite his work on behalf of Wilson's election, the president did not pick Wiley for a job in his administration. While Wiley might have seemed like an ideal candidate to serve in the US Food Administration, the agency charged with managing food rationing during World War I, this possibility did not work out. Wiley made a number of suggestions for managing the wartime food supply, but a feud with Herbert Hoover, who headed the agency, over the nutritional content of whole wheat likely kept him from serving.[45]

Unable to enter the new administration, Wiley toured on the Chautauqua and Lyceum speaking circuits, crisscrossing the country for about seven years, telling enraptured audiences about the danger of a wide variety of adulterated foods. He visited small towns in Midwestern states with thriving Chautauqua venues, like Nebraska, many times. Late in life, Wiley believed he had spoken in every state in the union at that time except Texas.[46] Although he had given a few speeches on the Chautauqua circuit before leaving government service, these lecture tours were longer and more draining for a man of almost seventy. By the beginning of the 1920s, he lectured only occasionally.[47]

Whenever Wiley gave public speeches, pure food was the topic that most interested his audiences. "Dr. Harvey W. Wiley will fight the enemies of pure food from the lecture platform," read a *Chicago Post* preview of one tour. "Freed from the entanglements of departmental red tape and etiquette, the veteran fighter is planning to carry the fight to the people and his program includes cities from coast to coast."[48] The usual title for his speech when he toured was "The Public Health: Our Greatest Asset," but in fact Wiley never used a set speech. He would speak off the cuff about all manner of

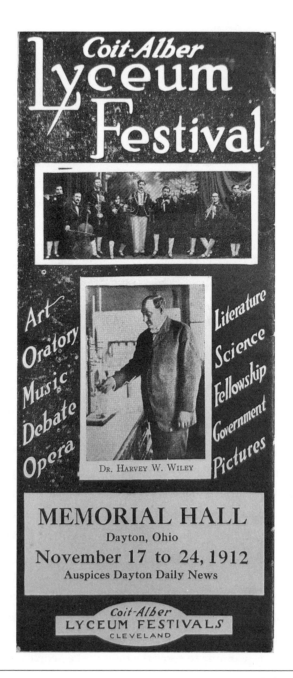

FIGURE 14.2 A program from one of Harvey Wiley's many speaking tours following his government service.

Harvey Wiley Papers, Library of Congress, Box 212. Courtesy Library of Congress.

health-related issues. Initially he shied away from recounting his fight for pure food from his time serving in government, but because this subject generally got the strongest reaction from the crowd, he touched on the past more and more over time.[49] "The lecture was livened throughout by humorous and witty interludes, which drove home the point of his arguments in a most convincing manner," noted the reviewer of a California speech.[50] Wiley's speaking skill was not surprising given his extensive experience addressing audiences around the country and the world during his years of government service.

Wiley, who had signed contracts with multiple speaking bureaus, made a great deal of money giving these speeches.[51] In the early years of his new career, when he was still a large draw, Wiley earned $1,575 in just a nine-day stretch touring the Midwest.[52] (Recall that his salary had been $5,000 a year when he left government service.) Public speaking was also an effective way for the chemist to stroke his now considerable ego. The promotional material for an Iowa appearance called Wiley "one of the greatest benefactors of the human race."[53] As much as he loved his family, they couldn't provide the kind of attention offered by a large, sympathetic crowd. One early Chautauqua speech attracted "several thousand people" according to the next day's paper.[54]

Wherever he spoke, Wiley's lectures invariably received tremendous coverage in the local press. Some of his statements in these lectures seem so shameless, at least in retrospect, that it is easy to imagine he made them to attract attention. "Three-quarters of the children who die are killed by love. Love is the greatest assassin," he said in 1914.[55] In early 1913 he claimed that half the children in the United States were starving.[56] In speeches during World War I, he said, "Kill all your pet dogs and cats"—to make more food available for the war effort—"but save their hides."[57] Whenever a comment of Wiley's attracted a headline, the story accompanying it would remind readers of his work in support of the pure food law, helping Wiley secure credit for what he increasingly perceived as his legacy.

In his last years, when his traveling slowed, Wiley spent every summer with his family on his farm near Bluemont, Virginia. He had bought the place in 1909 as an investment, and it paid off handsomely. He had the old farmhouse restored and began to run a dairy there. By 1915 it produced 110 gallons of milk a day, all of which he shipped to market in the Washington, DC, area. He raised hogs and grew corn, clover, alfalfa, cowpeas, rye, and oats. He farmed according to what he had learned from his extensive lifelong reading on the practice of agriculture rather than what he had learned working for his father when he was much younger.[58] (In 1924 he purchased another farm. This one, with 1,400 orange trees, was in Florida, where he wanted to spend his winters.)[59]

For Wiley, farm work was place to relive the positive aspects his childhood lifestyle without quite as much hard work. "The life of the Wiley family reproduces the simplicity of Dr. Wiley's boyhood as far as modern living conditions make it practicable," reported an interviewer in 1920.[60] This was particularly true with respect to the family's diet. The family ate only grains milled in small batches to preserve the brown parts, all straight from the farm. They grew their fruits and vegetables and cured their own meats, which they ate year-round. Harvey and Anna rarely ate sweets, and when they did the boys didn't get any. Following another of Wiley's ideas formed in battle with food manufacturers, the children were forbidden to drink tea or coffee.[61]

In 1927 the agricultural appropriation act divided the Bureau of Chemistry into the Bureau of Chemistry and Soils and the Food and Drug Administration. Wiley mistook this action as a further degradation of his old office's authority to enforce the Pure Food and Drug Act. He was worried that the division was done in secret and that a new civil service test would be imposed upon employees there.[62] In fact, with the passage of the Food, Drug and Cosmetic Act of 1938, what was left of Wiley's old office would only become stronger.

Nevertheless, this action inspired Wiley to write and publish *The History of a Crime against the Food Law*.[63] By telling the story of the struggle over passing and enforcing the Pure Food and Drug Act entirely from his own point of view, Wiley inevitably affected the historiography of those events. Wiley not only outlived many of his pure food movement contemporaries, he remained in the public eye longer, so nobody was around to dispute his assessment of the enforcement of the law over which he now claimed paternity. The book was part of a broader effort by Wiley and his allies to put the chemist squarely on the right side of history. Working from within the government, went the gist of this narrative, Wiley set himself up as a consumer advocate so that he could represent the interests of ordinary people who held no sway in Washington. Unable to act on the dictates of this perspective inside of the government, Wiley moved outside of government so that he could help more people and not have his voice stifled.

There are elements of truth in this assessment. For example, Wiley managed to do an enormous amount of good while writing for *Good Housekeeping*, beyond the useful health advice he dispensed in his Question-Box column. Much of his work actually resembled that of the muckraking journalists of an earlier era. In the January 1914 issue of the magazine, he denounced a weight-loss product called Get-Slim.[64] In the July 1914 issue, he challenged the effectiveness of mineral waters that were marketed as medicinal.[65] In the May 1923 issue, he challenged a faith healer.[66]

Wiley's pioneering opposition to tobacco further demonstrates his strong identification with consumers. In 1911 he predicted that tobacco would disappear from public places within fifteen years because of the smell and inconvenience it inflicted upon others.[67] By 1920, having left government service and cultivated a following of upper-middle-class readers, Wiley had decided that tobacco in all forms should be discarded. "If the land that is devoted to the culture of tobacco is devoted to the culture of useful foods," he wrote in response to a reader question, "it would do much to lessen the acuteness of the problem of feeding the world."[68] This was more than four decades before the release of the landmark 1964 surgeon general's report that declared tobacco a health hazard, and even today few people would go so far as to suggest destroying the tobacco crop entirely. Nevertheless, this was the logical extension of Wiley's belief that the government had a duty to completely remove harmful food products from the market.

Wiley's recommended response to the problem of harmful ingredients in foods reflects this same path of escalation. His initial purpose in pursuing pure food legislation was to inform consumers of the ingredients in the foods they purchased so they could make informed choices. But when he decided that particular food additives had adverse effects on people's health, he came to believe that the way the government enforced the Pure Food and Drug Act did not do enough to protect consumers. Upon leaving government, he made definitive judgments and passed them on to consumers so they could avoid products with ingredients that he thought should be banned.[69] Even if customers had access to impure foods, as long as they kept track of Wiley's judgments they would come to no harm. Following Wiley's model, the Good Housekeeping Institute continues to carry out this mission today.[70]

Unchecked by political concerns, Wiley was far more outspoken in the pages of *Good Housekeeping* than he had been in all the articles he wrote while working for the federal government. It was during this time that his role as a consumer advocate most closely resembled the role assumed by consumer advocates engaged in today's struggle over food issues. Harvey Wiley was among the first people to recognize that consumers could change what products were available to them entirely through the collective choices they made when buying food. This may be Wiley's most far-reaching legacy.

WILEY'S LEGACY

HARVEY WILEY PUT GREAT EMPHASIS ON the importance of food choice in promoting longevity. Adulterated or misbranded food, he argued, made it harder for people to make the kinds of smart food choices that would help them live as long as they might if they ate pure food instead.[1] In 1901 Wiley wrote an article for *Everybody's* magazine on how to eat, as usual making no mention of how any particular food tasted. The article began by discussing how to achieve a balanced ratio of foods in order to prolong life. It continued, "I am not a believer in the doctrine of going away from the table hungry. One object of eating is to satisfy hunger, because hunger is the natural mentor which tells the wants of the system. Satisfaction of hunger, however, is not gluttony. The dangers from overeating are not so much in the kinds of food employed as in the amounts of them consumed."[2] This kind of diet advice, with its emphasis on personal responsibility, now seems quite modern.

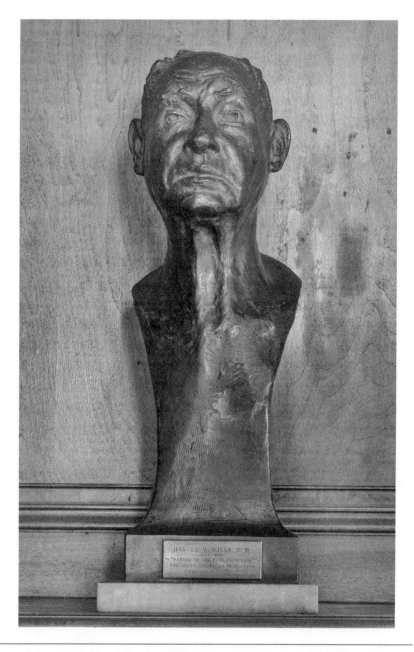

FIGURE C.I Bronze bust of Harvey Wiley sculptured in 1927 by Gutzon Borglum, best known for his work carving Mount Rushmore. Anna Kelton Wiley donated the original bust to Wiley's beloved Cosmos Club in 1950.

Bruce White Photography. Courtesy the Cosmos Club.

Despite such sentiments, Wiley had trouble following his own diet advice. Known among his friends for favoring ten-course meals, Wiley was confronted by a reporter in a Pennsylvania Avenue restaurant in July 1908. Rather than consuming the light summer diet he recommended, Wiley was dining on crab, a large steak, and a special salad. "It's true I'm not following my own directions," Wiley explained, "but then you know a pure food inspector sometimes has to do things that are distasteful." The reporter finished the story by noting that Wiley "pushed his chair back from the table, folded his hands across his stomach and smiled."[3] Wiley must have recognized that this kind of story could threaten his well-cultivated reputation as an expert on diet and nutrition, but such stories persisted. "He has a fine appetite—a remarkable appetite considering all the unpleasant and terrifying things he knows about foodstuffs," a California paper quipped in 1911.[4] However, Wiley's tendency to gorge himself at the table does not necessarily mean that he didn't believe his own recommendation not to do so.

The frequency and passion with which Wiley dispensed diet advice suggest that he believed that drinking alcohol and consuming large meals were indeed unhealthy. He did both of these things anyway. This pattern of behavior demonstrates that Harvey Wiley recognized his own complicated feelings about what he chose to eat. Wiley wanted to live longer, but he also loved eating. Sometimes the second priority contradicted the first. The fact that Wiley failed to follow his own strict advice may be the most modern thing about him.

Harvey Wiley's career did much to popularize the notion that what we eat can kill us. By singling out particular ingredients for complete eradication from the food supply, he made people worry about what their food might be doing to them—not just immediately but in the long term. Some of his attempts to determine what Americans could eat under the regime created by the Pure Food and Drug Act (PFDA) were less misguided than others, and there was excellent reason to ban some of the ingredients that Wiley railed against. Copper sulfate (to make canned green beans greener) and formaldehyde are both dangerous in minute quantities and have no legitimate purpose in food. Wiley's great mistake was to treat every food ingredient as if it were as poisonous as these two. He never absorbed the idea that thresholds exist for particular substances under which people can consume those ingredients safely, or that the existence of those ingredients in the food supply might serve a valid purpose, like making food cheaper or more convenient.

Wiley opposed most preservatives and other additives—artificial flavors, the Alsop process, caffeine in Coca-Cola, or sodium benzoate in absolutely anything—not because he favored inconvenience or expensive foods, but because he considered these substances unnatural in those foods, even if they came from other natural sources. Over time, he came to believe that anything unnatural was also unhealthy, at least for some members of the population. He favored not only "natural" substances but also "natural" processes—hence his attachment to straight whiskey (which was aged through a natural process) over rectified whiskey (which shortchanged the natural aging process and could be easily produced in a laboratory).

Because of his adherence to natural ingredients above all other concerns, Harvey Wiley's brand of consumer populism was deeply conservative. Unlike other Progressive Era reformers, Wiley saw the real problem as modernization itself. He came to support the PFDA—which was progressive in the way it aligned government with the interests of consumers to fix a corrupt food-provisioning system—to fix a problem related to modernization. But by standing against most changes that made food cheaper and more convenient, Harvey Wiley stood against not only the excesses of modern food processing but also many of its benefits.

Wiley offered simple answers to difficult questions about what substances should be acceptable in the modern food supply. His definition of adulteration was far too narrow for a nation that had accepted the mass production of food as a legitimate aim. No one likes poison in their food, but most people, including most consumers, were unwilling to adopt Wiley's strict standard for what the government should do about food ingredients that risked the health of consumers in any way, shape, or form. Unable to impose his will on the structure charged with enforcing the PFDA, he argued desperately that failing to adopt his standard was a mistake. "Natural" sounds easy to define, but it is not, and Wiley's vast body of writing on food issues serves as a reminder of that fact. The more sophisticated our ability to manipulate food, the harder it becomes to escape this principle.

Rather than trying to find consistency in Harvey Wiley's evolving definition of "natural" food, it is best to understand Wiley's philosophy of food
by recognizing his increasingly low tolerance for risk. "Foods," as Wiley
explained in 1904, "are prepared for the whole people, the strong and the
weak, and they should be safe-guarded that no added substance should be
permitted which could work an injury on the least resistant."[5] Yet, as Wiley
himself recognized, plenty of foods that he himself enjoyed could create at
least a tiny injury for someone. Imagine that the United States had made
Harvey Wiley's philosophy the basis of its food policy. Gluten would not be
an acceptable ingredient because some people have celiac disease. Planters
could not sell peanuts because some people have allergies. Wiley's criteria for judging the acceptability of additives were based on an unattainable
goal, and the government officials who opposed his interpretation of the
Pure Food and Drug Act understood this because they saw that their constituencies included more than just the weakest consumers.

Still, Wiley recognized the relationship between diet and health at a time
when this link was far from obvious to most scientists, let alone most people.
Despite their impracticality, Harvey Wiley's warnings attracted attention
because eating is an intimate act: taking something from outside the body
and putting it inside. Wiley thus turned food selection into a life-or-death
matter to most Americans for the first time. Of course, Wiley wanted consumers to recognize him—not industry, not industry's representatives inside
the federal government—as the final arbiter of what was pure and what was
not. That did not happen. Yet he did succeed in providing the ideological
underpinnings for broad government intervention in the nation's food supply.

———

In late 1929 Harvey Wiley fell ill and never really recovered. On June 3, 1930,
the chemist testified at a hearing about the importation of substandard ergot,
a drug that was supposed to help control bleeding in mothers immediately
after childbirth. Wiley, obviously very sick, began his testimony with a long
history of the Pure Food and Drug Act and the usurpation of the Bureau of
Chemistry's role in the enforcement of that legislation. When the chair of

the committee reminded him of the actual purpose of the hearing, Wiley admitted that he was not prepared to speak on that subject. That was the last time Harvey Wiley was seen in public.[6] He died of heart failure on June 30, 1930, at eighty-five years of age.[7] Wiley's autobiography (written with substantial anonymous assistance from a journalist) was released posthumously later that year.[8]

Because of his service in the Civil War, Harvey Wiley is buried at Arlington National Cemetery. Near the top, the headstone reads "Father of the Pure Food Law," a label that surfaced long before Wiley died.[9] From the beginning of the Poison Squad experiments until his retirement from government in 1912, Harvey Wiley worked hard to pass and enforce legislation that ensured the purity of the American food supply. After the passage of the PFDA, he worked to shape how that law was enforced. The PFDA was not just a landmark in the history of eating, but a major step toward an increased role for government in American life. Wiley's efforts to enforce that law along the lines he wanted changed the American diet for the better.

Nonetheless, calling Wiley the "Father of the Pure Food Law" is misleading. Wiley didn't write the law. He didn't even like the compromise law that eventually passed Congress and got President Theodore Roosevelt's signature. Furthermore, had Wiley stayed at Purdue his entire career, there is no question that some kind of pure food law would have passed after the turn of the twentieth century. In a 1908 statement he drafted as part of a campaign to get himself nominated for the Nobel Prize in Chemistry, Wiley anonymously described his work this way: "He instigated and conducted the work of the Department of Agriculture in the examination of the adulteration of food and drugs, a work that led directly to the formation of public opinion which resulted in the enactment of the Food and Drugs Act of June 30, 1906."[10] While Harvey Wiley never won the Nobel Prize for Chemistry, this self-serving passage is a fairly apt description of Wiley's activities on behalf of that legislation.

In 1960 Anna Kelton Wiley started a campaign to get her deceased husband elected to the Hall of Fame for Great Americans, a statuary hall in the Bronx where busts of many famous individuals reside.[11] These elections occurred every five years. "Unfortunately," explained one of the letters sent to garner support for his election, "the movement which was started by Dr. Wiley was so successful that the average American no longer is aware of the fact that his food and drugs are protected by a small organization which he was largely responsible in establishing."[12] Only the top three vote getters would be inducted into the hall; Wiley came in eighteenth. The winners that year were Thomas Edison, Henry David Thoreau, and the composer Edward MacDowell.[13]

This unsuccessful campaign sought to convince voters that Harvey Wiley was solely responsible for the passage of the Pure Food and Drug Act.[14] The attempt collapsed, however, under the weight of the chemist's curious and contradictory legacy. Wiley wanted to claim credit for a law that he revered at the time of his death but that he had seen as a compromise at the time of its passage. Toward the end of his life Wiley passionately argued not that the PFDA was irretrievably broken but that had it never been adequately enforced. The PFDA had a good reputation at this time, but so did many other pieces of reform legislation that passed Congress during the Progressive and New Deal Eras.

More important, by the time Anna Kelton Wiley tried to get her late husband enshrined in the Hall of Fame for Great Americans, the laws governing food purity and safety in America had changed significantly. After a new panic over food impurity during the 1930s, Congress passed the Food, Drug, and Cosmetic Act of 1938 (FD&C Act), which was much stronger than its 1906 predecessor. This new law not only included the food standards that had been explicitly left out of previous legislation but also prohibited false food advertising and codified the safe tolerances for various poisons. By offering specific definitions of terms like "misbranding" and "adulteration," it became the foundation of subsequent criminal prosecution of food fraud in America. On the drug side, it allowed the FDA to issue regulations formally differentiating over-the-counter from prescription drugs.[15] Anna Kelton Wiley justifiably believed that her late husband would have approved of the FD&C Act overall.[16]

Later food safety measures probably would have elicited a mixed reaction from the chemist. The 1958 Food Additives Amendment allowed the Food and Drug Administration for the first time to examine the health effects of food additives before they entered the food supply. As was already the case with drugs, manufacturers had to submit proof of "reasonable certainty in the minds of competent scientists that the substance is not harmful under intended conditions of use." The Delaney Clause, which was part of that same amendment, stated that "no additive shall be deemed safe if it is found to induce cancer when ingested by man or animal." While the amendment itself recognized that there was a threshold of acceptable risk to consumers that society could accept, the Delaney Clause, like Wiley himself, did not. This mixed message to manufacturers and consumers has resulted in a chaotic food safety situation ever since.[17]

Even though the FDA has gradually accumulated more power through legislation like this, it has used that power in very different ways than it did when Harvey Wiley worked for the Department of Agriculture. Despite Wiley's bluster over food additives, the Bureau of Chemistry's approach to enforcing the Pure Food and Drug Act was always far more educational than punitive. The law's most important early successes involved cases where producers decided not to challenge the decisions of the Bureau of Chemistry or the Board of Food and Drug Inspection in court (as with milk) or where producers changed the formula of their product to avoid prosecution (as with ketchup and some nostrums). That approach is now outdated: educational measures cannot stop all food-borne illnesses or prevent impure goods from being imported into the country as part of an increasingly globalized food system.[18]

———

"If they had left me alone, food adulteration in this country would be only a memory and not a menace, as it is today," Wiley quipped while touring the country in 1913.[19] That assessment was wrong. Food adulteration happens in any modern provisioning system in which producers and consumers are separated by both physical space and multiple intermediaries. The financial incentives for producers to cheat is too great, and the risk of punishment for being caught, even when penalties are harsh, is mitigated by the difficulty of finding the exact place along a complicated supply chain where the adulteration occurred.[20] Moreover, as long as nobody dies, food adulteration remains both difficult and expensive to detect.

Wiley's strict definition of food purity actually reduced the likelihood of his eliminating adulteration. It would have been hard enough to end the deceptive practices of partial substitutions, as with honey or the watering down of milk. Yet by the end of his government career, Wiley wanted to treat anything that did not appear naturally in any given food as an adulteration even if the substance being added was itself natural and known to consumers, like the caffeine in Coca-Cola. Public support for this position varied considerably with respect the type of food or drink in question. Wiley's vision of a food system based entirely on nature often ran smack into the reality that people seldom considered the cumulative health effects of unknown food additives to be their primary concern.

Wiley's ideas about food and food processing are an excellent example of how people who use the words "pure" and "food" together seldom mean the same thing. More than one definition of purity was circulating in both scientific and political circles before and after the passage of the Pure Food and Drug Act. Rather than imposing our own conception of pure food, it is worth exploring the precise ideas that historical actors and consumers brought to this struggle. Some people considered some processed foods to be pure if they had no objection to the effects of that processing. Other people found processed foods acceptable, even if not "pure," because of the advantages they possessed with respect to availability or taste. Nevertheless, Wiley opposed many kinds of food processing on principle.

Indirectly recognizing the opposition to his vision, Wiley advocated for legislation and an enforcement regime that would have made these choices for consumers. But not all of his opponents were intent on poisoning America. Many were just food producers who had different definitions of pure food, and in many cases their conceptions of pure food have held up better than Wiley's. They were also closer to the spirit under which the Pure Food and Drug Act originally passed Congress. Wiley designed his strategy for implementing the PFDA to mitigate the practices that make food adulteration likely, but he was not solely in charge. While he never achieved the goals for the American diet that he once sought, his aspirations still did much to shape what manufactures added to foods and how they process them to this day.

Sodium benzoate was never outlawed, but Wiley encouraged ketchup makers to cease using it. Coca-Cola is the world's most popular soda, and thanks to Wiley it is now made with less caffeine. Borax remains legal as a preservative for meat, but Wiley's first Poison Squad experiment encouraged packers to stop using it as soon as better methods of preservation became available. Although Wiley failed in his attempt to eliminate rectified whiskey, he nonetheless laid down the reasoning for eliminating medicinal whiskey over the long run. Wiley led "milk crusades" that helped clean up urban dairies across the country. All of these and other similar changes improved the health of the American people, and they deserve historical recognition. While this version of his legacy is not quite as impressive as the one in which Wiley is the sole "Father of the Pure Food Law," it has the advantage of being true.

As he pursued his ideals, Harvey Wiley was wrong about all kinds of science-related questions. He was incorrect about the health effects of many preservatives during the Poison Squad experiments. In some of his wrong ideas (especially with respect to non-food-related issues like hair growth or eugenics), Harvey Wiley recalls the 1840s food faddist Sylvester Graham—now best known as the eponym of the graham cracker but really something of a crackpot who nonetheless commanded a large following. About other issues, mostly related to chemistry, Wiley was correct. Even before he entered the private sector, it is easy to see him as a prototype for the modern consumer advocate Ralph Nader (despite Wiley's tendency to accept gifts from companies he was in charge of regulating). Notably, Wiley managed to pioneer the role of consumer advocate while working inside the federal government.

In the course of these efforts, Harvey Wiley convinced many Americans that modern food processing had become a problem in need of a solution rather than a benefit of modernization. "For about eleven years," explains the historian Harvey Levenstein, "the public had heard the highly respected official watchdog of food safety repeatedly warn that food processors were using poisons in their products. The long-term effects of this, while impossible to gauge, could not have been negligible."[21] In this manner, Wiley's ideas about purity became part of the culture and remain so now. Harvey Wiley's struggles to popularize those ideas at the turn of the twentieth century offer us important perspective as we continue to wrestle with the challenge of maintaining "purity" in an age of even greater industrial food production.

Despite all the attention that Wiley drew to his work, it is important to remember that there was a pure food movement before Harvey Wiley became famous. Food-related muckraking predates the Poison Squad experiments and postdates them too. This helps explain why Upton Sinclair remains a far better known figure than Harvey Wiley. It is even possible that the PFDA could have had a greater effect without Wiley because food producers may not have felt the need to mobilize against the idea of one man's controlling what they could put into their food. Apart from Wiley, there was a remarkable consensus over the need to end deception and ban obviously poisonous ingredients (like formaldehyde) from the country's food supply. Wiley played an important role in mobilizing public opinion for the cause of pure food, but to treat him as the sole leader of those efforts is a mistake derived from Wiley's own misleading accounting of his life and work.

When evaluating Harvey Wiley's entire career, it is best not to use the same criteria that he did. What Wiley saw as a "crime against the food law" was actually a compromise needed to successfully implement a piece of legislation that balanced a wide array of competing interests. To see Harvey Wiley's primary legacy as the Pure Food and Drug Act of 1906 not only does an injustice to every other pure food advocate of that era but ignores the chemist's extraordinary impact on the manufacture and marketing of foodstuffs of all kinds. Wiley was a significant figure in the history of American eating because of his considerable influence on what we eat and how we think about food in general. While these achievements were not enough to get Wiley enshrined in the Hall of Fame of Great Americans, the fruits of his efforts confront us every day at the supermarket and on our plates.

ACKNOWLEDGMENTS

THE IDEAL SITUATION FOR A HISTORIAN is to do a lot of research, become an expert on its subject in the process, then write a book about it. That did not happen in this case. I did the research, wrote a draft manuscript, and still wasn't sure what everything meant. This is where being a part of a community of scholars can be so helpful. For years, I "talked Wiley" with people I knew well, people I had just met at conferences, and even people who knew nothing about Harvey Wiley but had a lot of interesting things to say about the history of food. This book is the result of all those encounters, deliberate and random, and I am grateful that chance helped me deliver such a better-informed result.

This is my third book with Johns Hopkins University Press. I never would have imagined such a thing happening when they deservedly rejected the manuscript that came from my dissertation, but I remain delighted that things have worked out between us over time. While everybody there has been delightful to collaborate with for more than a decade now, I want to single out Greg Britton and my editor, Laura Davulis, who saved me from my own worst impulses, for their support.

I first encountered Harvey Wiley while researching the history of refrigeration for those earlier two books, so it should come as no surprise that many of my thanks are repeats from those earlier projects. For example, Katy Handley and Jane Townsend again offered me their spare rooms when

I needed them. Here at Colorado State University–Pueblo, Kenny McKenzie remains an interlibrary loan superstar. Fawn-Amber Montoya (now of James Madison University), Doug Eskew, Jason Saphara, Jonathan Poritz, and Donna Souder Hodge are entirely responsible for keeping me sane while doing my day job, thereby making this kind of research and writing possible whenever I can find the time.

Suzanne Junod was particularly helpful at the beginning of this project. Rachel Nellis, the archivist for the Cosmos Club, sent me some great information about Wiley right near its end. Stephanie Frost of the Cosmos Club shepherded my request to use a picture of Gutzon Borglum's Wiley bust through the permission process there. Other useful archival help came from Jennifer Duplaga at Hanover College and Jim Stimpert in Special Collections at Johns Hopkins University. I am also thankful that the University of Denver is so welcoming to anyone interested in using their databases of historical newspapers, as I used them a lot during the course of this project.

Some historians I know from Twitter regularly post the number of words they write on any particular day. That would never work for me because I always write and rewrite and rewrite until I decide it's done. Sometimes I know when a section is done. Sometimes I need the help of somebody who knows that subject better than I do. Special thanks on this front go out to Gary Patterson, Linda Civitello, and especially the three anonymous reviewers who read my first draft for Johns Hopkins University Press. Both Nadia Berenstein's dissertation and her journalism have been particularly helpful to me given our interest in such similar subjects. I am so grateful for her help sorting things out that I thought I understood but didn't and for inspiring me to rewrite large chunks of this book. Without the reading list I got from Xaq Frohlich, the chapter on drugs here simply would not have been possible. Benjamin Cohen let me see his book, *Pure Adulteration: Cheating on Nature in the Age of Manufactured Food*, while it was still in page proofs. This immeasurably improved chapters two, three, and four.

Melanie DuPuis alerted me to the relationship between food purity and eugenics. I'm not sure I would have noticed the evidence of that relationship in Wiley's life if I didn't know to go looking for it. Nicola Twilley and Cynthia Graber's *Gastropod* remains the only podcast that is professionally important to me. All sorts of little things I first heard about there have ended up in this manuscript. However, since the books they happened to be promoting ended up in the notes, their influence is not adequately reflected there. I am also grateful to John Coupland, Roger Horowitz, and Maureen Ogle for their general encouragement.

I wrote two different short overviews of Harvey Wiley's contributions to the way America eats for the American Chemical Society and the Humanities Center at Texas Tech University. In the process of shepherding those to publications, Mary Virginia Orna and Dorothy Chansky expertly edited early versions of two chapters from this work. The Department of History, the Provost's Office, and the College of Humanities and Social Sciences at Colorado State University–Pueblo offered me so many small grants to help with research at various stages of this project that I lost count of the number long ago. I am grateful for my employer's unflagging support of all of my numerous research projects.

This book is dedicated to John Milton Cooper Jr., whose enthusiasm for and encyclopedic knowledge of everything related to late nineteenth- and early twentieth-century American history made this study possible long before I ever decided to write it.

NOTES

SELECTED ARCHIVAL REPOSITORIES have been identified by the
following abbreviations:

AKWP   Anna Kelton Wiley Papers, Manuscripts Division,
       Library of Congress, Washington, DC

FDA–NARA   Records of the Food and Drug Administration,
       Record Group 88, National Archives and Records
       Administration, College Park, MD

HWP LoC   Harvey Wiley Papers, Manuscripts Division, Library
       of Congress, Washington, DC

HWP NARA   General Records of Dr. Harvey Wiley and Records
       Relating to Other Bureau Matters, 1901–1910, Records
       of the Food and Drug Administration, Record Group
       88, National Archives and Records Administration,
       College Park, MD

HWP PU   Harvey W. Wiley Papers, Virginia Kelly Karnes
       Archives, Purdue University, West Lafayette, IN

IRP   Ira Remsen Papers, Sheridan Libraries Special Collec-
       tions, Johns Hopkins University, Baltimore, MD

INTRODUCTION. WHO WAS HARVEY WILEY?

1 The other six men started getting borax on January 23, 1903. They would go through the same regimen that the first subjects did.

2 Most of the details on the experiment are from H. W. Wiley, *Boric Acid and Borax*, pt. 1 of *Influence of Food Preservatives and Artificial Colors on Digestion and Health,* US Department of Agriculture, Bureau of Chemistry, Bulletin 84 (Washington, DC: Government Printing Office, 1904). Some of the details come from newspaper accounts.

3 For a good overview of the borax experiment, see Dr. H. W. Wiley, "Methods of Studying the Effect of Preservatives and Other Substances Added to Foods upon Health and Digestion," *Journal of the Franklin Institute* 157 (March 1904): 161–78. In the documentation for this book, I have reproduced Harvey Wiley's name and title as they appeared in the various original sources. Sometimes, for example, Wiley included his medical degrees in his byline for popular articles. Sometimes he included his PhD. Sometimes he included both. If Wiley's name is not written on the document being cited (as in the carbon copies of his letters in the Harvey Wiley Papers at the Library of Congress), I list the author simply as "Harvey Wiley."

4 At the time it was passed, the Pure Food and Drug Act was known simply as the Food and Drugs Act. In this work I use the modern name for the law, even though it is an anachronism, to prevent confusion.

5 The Food and Drug Administration did not get that name until 1930, the year Wiley died.

6 Edwin Björkman, "Our Debt to Dr. Wiley," *World's Work* 19 (January 1910): 12443.

7 Arthur Wallace Dunn, "Dr. Wiley and His Work," *Good Housekeeping* 54 (May 1912): 593n.

8 Rene Bache, "Wonders Done by Wiley," *Los Angeles Times*, April 24, 1910, IM518.

9 W. D. Bigelow, "Harvey Washington Wiley," *Science* 72 (September 26, 1930): 312.

10 Edward H. Beardsley, *The Rise of the American Chemistry Profession, 1850–1900* (Gainesville: University of Florida Press, 1964), 28.

11 Harvey Wiley, "Economy of Nutrition," *Good Housekeeping* 60 (February 1915): 218.

12 Fred B. Linton, "Federal Food and Drug Laws: Leaders Who Achieved Their Enactment and Enforcement," *Food and Drug Law Journal* 50 (1995; originally published in 1949): 9.

13 Wiley's autobiography is Harvey W. Wiley, *An Autobiography* (Indianapolis: Bobbs-Merrill, 1930). The two major biographies of Wiley are Oscar E. Anderson Jr., *The Health of a Nation: Harvey W. Wiley and the Fight for Pure Food* (Chicago: University of Chicago Press, 1958), and Deborah Blum, *The Poison Squad: One Chemist's Single-Minded Crusade for Food Safety at the Turn of the Twentieth Century* (New York: Penguin, 2018). For more on the historiography surrounding Wiley, see the Essay on Sources.

14 E. Melanie DuPuis, *Dangerous Digestion: The Politics of American Dietary Advice* (Berkeley: University of California Press, 2015), 136.

CHAPTER ONE. INDIANA

1 Harvey Wiley, "After Fifty Years," c. 1923, 1, Box 72, AKWP.

2 Dr. Harvey W. Wiley, "The Rights of the Unborn," *Good Housekeeping* 75 (October 1922): 32; William Lloyd Fox, "Harvey W. Wiley: Formative Years" (PhD diss., George Washington University, 1960), 1–3; "Preston P. Wiley," unmarked Indiana newspaper clipping, c. 1895, Box 211, HWP LoC; Harvey W. Wiley, *Harvey W. Wiley: An Autobiography* (Indianapolis: Bobbs-Merrill, 1930), 15; Oscar E. Anderson Jr., *The Health of a Nation: Harvey W. Wiley and the Fight for Pure Food* (Chicago: University of Chicago Press, 1958), 2–3. Only two of the boys survived to adulthood.

3 Dr. Harvey W. Wiley, "What Women Have Done for Me," *Good Housekeeping* 80 (February 1925): 84, 114.

4 Fox, "Formative Years," 11n33.

5 Philip J. Hilts, *Protecting America's Health: The FDA, Business, and One Hundred Years of Regulation* (Chapel Hill: University of North Carolina Press, 2003), 13.

6   Wiley, *Autobiography*, 24.

7   Harvey W. Wiley, "The Education of a Backwoods Hoosier," *Indiana Magazine of History* 24 (June 1928): 82.

8   Wiley, *Autobiography*, 24, 35–36.

9   Wiley, *Autobiography*, 18–21, 50, 26; William MacHarg, "Speaking of Dr. Wiley . . . ," *Good Housekeeping* 70 (April 1920): 28.

10   E. W. Davidson, "The 'Father of the Pure Food Law,'" *Washington Post*, October 13, 1929, Davidson, SM12; Wiley, *Autobiography*, 50, 63.

11   Fox, "Formative Years," 9.

12   Robert J. Gordon, *The Rise and Fall of American Growth* (Princeton, NJ: Princeton University Press, 2016), 39–41.

13   Anderson, *Health of a Nation*, 3.

14   J. L. Heid, "Dr. Wiley," *Co-Operation for Profit* 7 (September 1927): 6; Wiley, *Autobiography*, 41.

15   Wiley, *Autobiography*, 36.

16   A. Y. Moore, *History of Hanover College* (Indianapolis: Hollenbeck Press, 1900), 7, 93–94; William McKee Dunn, *Early History of Hanover College* (Madison, IN: Courier Company, 1883), 12–15.

17   Fox, "Formative Years," 49.

18   William MacHarg, "Speaking of Dr. Wiley . . . ," *Good Housekeeping* 70 (April 1920), 28; James G. Morrow, "Dr. Wiley Was His Own Cook," *New York Tribune*, November 8, 1908, C8; *Washington Times*, July 17, 1911, 7; *Indianapolis Star*, September 4, 1911, 5.

19   Wiley, *Autobiography*, 67–74; William L. Fox, "Corporal Harvey W. Wiley's Civil War Diary," *Indiana Magazine of History* 51 (June 1955): 140; Fox, "Formative Years," 42.

20   Fox, "Civil War Diary," 141–42, 155.

21   Bill Price, "You Can Live on Eleven Cents per Day or Feast for Fifty," *Washington Times*, December 26, 1919, 18.

22   Wiley, *Autobiography*, 71–74; Fox, "Formative Years," 41–42.

23   Fox, "Formative Years," 23.

24   Harvey Wiley, untitled unpublished excerpt from his autobiography, Box 185, HWP LoC.

25   Wiley, untitled unpublished excerpt.

26   Anderson, *Health of a Nation*, 11.

27   Edward H. Beardsley, *The Rise of the American Chemistry Profession, 1850–1900* (Gainesville: University of Florida Press, 1964), 28.

28   Wiley, *Autobiography*, 94–95; Anderson, *Health of a Nation*, 9–11.

29   David Oshinsky, *Bellevue: Three Centuries of Medicine and Mayhem at America's Most Storied Hospital* (New York: Anchor Books, 2016), 68–69.

30   Anderson, *Health of a Nation*, 11.

31   Fox, "Formative Years," 62.

32   H. W. Wiley, M.D., "The Relation of the Physician to the Education of the People," *Indiana Journal of Medicine* 4 (September 1873): 200–201.

33   Wiley, "What Is Wanting," *Indiana Journal of Medicine* 4 (April 1874): 535.

34   William Lloyd Fox, "The Harvard Days of Dr. Harvey W. Wiley," *Harvard Alumni Bulletin* 59 (September 29, 1956): 19–20. Despite having completed college at Hanover, he did not get a graduate degree at Harvard. Wiley's PhD in chemistry came from Hanover College in 1872. That small school had no PhD programs at that point, so that doctorate, like the doctor of laws degree Hanover awarded Wiley in 1895, was honorary. Wiley never received a PhD in chemistry based on actual coursework. With few options for advanced study in chemistry in America at that time, many chemists relied on practical experience rather than graduate training as the basis for their jobs. Nevertheless, this point is conspicuously absent in Wiley's autobiography.

35   Anderson, *Health of a Nation*, 14; Fox, "Formative Years," 101.

36   Harvey W. Wiley, "The Education of a Backwoods Hoosier," *Indiana Magazine of History* 24 (June 1928): 93.

37   Wiley, *Autobiography,* 3–8; Fox, "Formative Years," 113, 108.

38   Fox, "Harvard Days," 22; Fox, "Formative Years," 114.

39   Wiley, *Autobiography*, 112.

40   Wiley, *Autobiography*, 117–25, 149.

41   Anderson, *Health of a Nation*, 17.

42   William Murray Hepburn and Louis Martin Sears, *Purdue University: Fifty Years of Progress* (Indianapolis: Hollenbeck Press, 1925), 59, 44.

43 Harvey Wiley, "Remarks Made at Purdue Banquet at New York on December 7, 1907," 5, Box 190, HWP LoC.

44 Joanne Mendes, "Harvey W. Wiley papers, 1878–2003" [Finding Aid], Purdue University Libraries, Archives and Special Collections, https://archives.lib.purdue.edu/repositories/2/resources/163.

45 Harvey Wiley, "Chapter II" in *Autobiography* draft, 10, Box 212, HWP LoC.

46 Anderson, *Health of a Nation*, 18.

47 Anderson, *Health of a Nation*, 18.

48 *Annual Report of the Board of Trustees of Purdue University*, December 31, 1880, 105, in *Annual Reports of Purdue University, 1873/74–1881/82* (Lafayette, IN: Purdue University, 1876–84).

49 Harvey Wiley as quoted in Hilts, *Protecting America's Health,* 16.

50 Hepburn and Sears, *Purdue University*, 54.

51 Wiley, "Chapter II," 16.

52 *Second Report of Purdue University for Two Years Ending June 30, 1876* (Indianapolis: Sentinel, 1876), 37–54.

53 Anderson, *Health of a Nation*, 18; *Annual Report of the Board of Trustees* [. . .], 1874, 16.

54 *Fourth Annual Report of Purdue University for the Academic Year Ending June 30, 1878* [. . .] (Indianapolis: Indianapolis Journal Company, 1879), 45.

55 H. W. Wiley to William M. Hepburn, January 2, 1924, 2, Box 1, HWP PU.

56 Untitled Wiley notes, Box 1, HWP PU.

57 *Purdue Experiment,* January 19, 1908, Box 1, HWP PU.

58 Hepburn and Sears, *Purdue University*, 177.

59 Wiley, "Remarks," 8–9; Wiley, *Autobiography*, 127.

60 Fox, "Formative Years," 159.

61 Anderson, *Health of a Nation*, 5–7; Wiley, *Autobiography*, 27.

62 Harvey Wiley, Diary, April 21, 1863, Box 213, HWP LoC.

63 Harvey Wiley, "Gleanings from Harvard Diary," Box 72, AKWP.

64 Harvey Wiley, Diary, Saturday, October 26, 1878, Box 213, HWP LoC. Emphasis in original.

65   H. A. Huston, *Debris* (Purdue yearbook), 1908, Box 1, HWP PU.

66   Unsigned note to Harvey Wiley, 1875, Box 10, HWP LoC.

67   Wiley as quoted in Fox, "Formative Years," 85.

68   Fox, "Formative Years," 83; Harvey Wiley to Sarah Fletcher, July 6, 1869, Box 11, HWP LoC.

69   Harvey Wiley to Sarah Fletcher, December 30, 1870, Box 11, HWP LoC.

70   Harvey Wiley to Sarah M. Fletcher, December 13, 1871, Box 11, HWP LoC. Emphasis in original.

71   Sarah Fletcher to Harvey Wiley, February 24 (no year), Box 11, HWP LoC.

72   "Bertie" to Harvey Wiley, June 9, c. 1872, Box 10, HWP LoC.

73   Mamie Hall to Harvey Wiley, September 20, 1879, Box 10, HWP LoC.

CHAPTER TWO. HONEY

1   William Lloyd Fox, "Harvey W. Wiley: The Formative Years" (PhD diss., George Washington University, 1960), 204.

2   Bob Kriebel, "Bicycle Has Proud History on Greater Lafayette Streets," *Lafayette Journal and Courier*, May 8, 1994, Box 1, HWP PU.

3   H. A. Huston, "Dr. H. W. Wiley," *Debris* (Purdue yearbook), 1908, Box 1, HWP PU.

4   Harvey Wiley, "Remarks Made at Purdue Banquet at New York on December 7, 1907," 10–11, Box 190, HWP LoC.

5   Harvey W. Wiley, *An Autobiography* (Indianapolis: Bobbs-Merrill, 1930), 157.

6   James G. Morrow, "Dr. Wiley Was His Own Cook," *New York Tribune*, November 8, 1908, C8.

7   Wiley, *Autobiography*, 157–58.

8   Morrow, "Dr. Wiley Was His Own Cook," C8.

9   Wiley, *Autobiography*, 158.

10   Ex-Professor [Harvey Wiley], "College Professors," letter to the editor, *The Nation* 36 (June 21, 1883): 530.

11 Wiley, *Autobiography*, 159.

12 Oscar E. Anderson Jr., *The Health of a Nation: Harvey W. Wiley and the Fight for Pure Food* (Chicago: University of Chicago Press, 1958), 27–29.

13 Fox, "Formative Years," 202.

14 Fox, "Formative Years," 218–19; Anderson, *Health of a Nation*, 29–30.

15 Ex-Professor [Wiley], "College Professors," 530.

16 Daniel T. Rodgers, *Atlantic Crossings: Social Politics in a Progressive Age* (Cambridge, MA: Belknap Press of Harvard University Press, 1998), 62.

17 Frederic J. Cheshire, "The President's Address: The Early History of the Polariscope and the Polarizing Microscope," *Journal of the Royal Microscopical Society* 43 (March 1923): 14.

18 Anderson, *Health of a Nation*, 20–21; Fox, "Formative Years," 188–89.

19 Harvey W. Wiley, *Principles and Practices of Agricultural Analysis,* vol. 3, *Agricultural Products* (Easton, PA: Chemical Publishing Co., 1897).

20 Jim Thompson, "The Polariscope: A Useful Tool for Judging Honey," *Bee Culture*, April 20, 2017, http://www.beeculture.com/the-polariscope/.

21 *Fourth Annual Report of Purdue University for the Academic Year Ending June 30, 1878* (Indianapolis: Indianapolis Journal Company, 1879), 248.

22 Wiley, *Autobiography*, 150.

23 Professor Harvey W. Wiley, "Glucose and Grape-Sugar," *Popular Science Monthly* 19 (June 1881), 254.

24 Harvey Wiley to Professor A. J. Cook, June 15, 1892, 3, Box 3, HWP LoC.

25 *American Bee Journal* 18 (April 19, 1882): 243.

26 Honey Producers' League, "The Wiley Honey Lie," privately published, c. 1904, 3, Box 215, HWP LoC.

27 Honey Producers' League, "Wiley Honey Lie," 5–6.

28 George E. Walsh, "Honey and Bee Keeping," *Scientific American* 77 (September 1897): 167.

29 Harvey Wiley to Professor A. J. Cook, June 7, 1892, Box 3, HWP LoC.

30 Untitled clipping in scrapbook, Box 110, AKWP.

31 Natasha Geiling, "The Science behind Honey's Eternal Shelf Life," Smithsonian.com, August 22, 2103, http://www.smithsonianmag.com /science-nature/the-science-behind-honeys-eternal-shelf-life-1218690/.

32   Lucy M. Long, *Honey: A Global History* (London: Reaktion, 2017), 53.

33   Long, *Honey*, 46.

34   Walsh, "Honey and Bee Keeping," 167.

35   Deborah Jean Warner, *Sweet Stuff: An American History of Sweeteners from Sugar to Sucralose* (Washington, DC: Smithsonian Institution Scholarly Press, 2011), 174.

36   Harvey Wiley, "Adulterated Food and Drinks," typescript, c. 1904, Box 2, "Articles and Lectures of Harvey Wiley, 1890–1906," Records of the Bureau of Agricultural and Industrial Chemistry, Record Group 97, National Archives and Records Administration, College Park, MD.

37   Wiley, *Autobiography*, 151–52.

38   H. W. Wiley, *Sugar, Molasses and Sirup, Confections, Honey and Beeswax*, pt. 6 of *Food and Food Adulterants*, US Department of Agriculture, Division of Chemistry, Bulletin No. 13 (Washington, DC: Government Printing Office, 1892), 746.

39   National Academy of Sciences, *Report of the National Academy of Sciences for the Year 1884* (Washington, DC: Government Printing Office, 1884), 77, 84.

40   Mitchell Okun, *Fair Play in the Marketplace: The First Battle for Pure Food and Drugs* (Dekalb: Northern Illinois University Press, 1986), 224–25.

41   Wiley, *Autobiography*, 151–52.

42   Robert Packer, "Detecting Honey Adulteration," *Bee Culture*, April 20, 2017, http://www.beeculture.com/detecting-honey-adulteration/.

43   Jonathan W. White Jr., "Wiley Led the Way: A Century of Federal Honey Research," *Journal of the Association of Official Analytical Chemists* 70, no. 2 (1987), 181.

44   *American Bee Journal* 30 (July 14, 1892): 77.

45   White, "Wiley Led the Way," 181.

46   Clayton A. Coppin and Jack High, *The Politics of Purity: Harvey Washington Wiley and the Origins of Federal Food Policy* (Ann Arbor: University of Michigan Press, 1999), 52.

47   Richard Evershed and Nicola Temple, *Sorting the Beef from the Bull: The Science of Food Fraud Forensics* (London: Bloomsbury, 2016), 65.

48 Harvey Wiley to A. J. Cook, June 7, 1892, Box 3, HWP LoC.

49 Wiley, *Food and Food Adulterants*, 745.

50 *Washington Post*, April 19, 1897, 10.

51 Industrial Commission on Agriculture, *Report of the Industrial Commission on Agriculture* [. . .], vol. 11, *Adulteration of Food Products* (Washington, DC: Government Printing Office, 1901), 59.

52 Harvey Wiley to H. W. Collingswood, October 3, 1904, Box 1, Miscellaneous Records, 1877–1910, Records of the Bureau of Chemistry, FDA–NARA.

53 Harvey Wiley to R. M. Allen, January 20, 1906, Box 2, Miscellaneous Records, 1877–1910, Records of the Bureau of Chemistry, FDA–NARA.

54 Professor H. W. Wiley, "Mixed Sugars," *Science* 2 (September 24, 1881): 455.

55 *Indianapolis Star*, March 28, 1902, 6.

56 Benjamin R. Cohen, *Pure Adulteration: Cheating on Nature in the Age of Manufactured Food* (Chicago: University of Chicago Press, 2019), 151.

57 James D. Boyle, "Glucose and Starch Industry," in *Census of Manufactures: 1914* (Washington, DC: Government Printing Office, 1917), 3.

58 Wiley, *Autobiography*, 271; Harvey Wiley to Winfred Harper Cooley, February 3, 1912, Box 102, HWP LoC.

59 Alfred D. Chandler Jr., *The Visible Hand: The Managerial Revolution in American Business* (Cambridge: Belknap Press of Harvard University Press, 1977), 336.

60 *American Food Journal* 3 (February 15, 1908): 8.

61 Anderson, *Health of a Nation*, 205–6.

62 Wiley, *Autobiography*, 271.

63 Harvey Wiley to W. S. Wright, January 2, 1909, Box 76, HWP LoC.

64 C. A. Browne, *Chemical Analysis and Composition of American Honeys*, US Department of Agriculture, Bureau of Chemistry, Bulletin No. 110 (Washington, DC: Government Printing Office, 1908), 58.

65 Roy J. Barker, "Considerations in Selecting Sugars for Feeding to Honey Bees," *American Bee Journal* 117 (February 1977): 76–77.

66 Wiley, *Autobiography*, 151.

67 Warner, *Sweet Stuff*, 176.

68 *Gleanings in Bee Culture* 68 (January 1940): 37. Wiley's easy-to-
disprove assertion that honey manufacturers had grown to like him is a
good reason to look skeptically on Wiley's account of his own life.

69 *Washington Post*, April 19, 1897, 10.

70 Suzanne Rebecca White, "Chemistry and Controversy: Regulating
the Use of Chemicals in Foods, 1883–1959" (PhD diss., Emory
University, 1994), 186, 188.

71 Vlasta Pilizota and Nela Nedic Tiban, "Advances in Honey Adulteration Detection," *Food Safety Magazine* (August/September 2009),
http://www.foodsafetymagazine.com/magazine-archive1
/augustseptember-2009/advances-in-honey-adulteration-detection/.

72 Long, *Honey*, 134–35.

73 Larry Olmsted, *Real Food Fake Food: Why You Don't Know What You're
Eating and What You Can Do About It* (Chapel Hill, NC: Algonquin
Books, 2016), 257–58, Kindle.

CHAPTER THREE. SUGAR BEETS

1 Francis G. Caffey, *A Brief Statutory History of the United States Department of Agriculture* (Washington, DC: US Department of Agriculture, Office of the Solicitor, 1916), 3, 5.

2 Daniel Stone, *The Food Explorer: The True Adventures of the Globe-
Trotting Botanist Who Transformed What America Eats* (New York:
Dutton, 2018), 107.

3 William Lloyd Fox, "Harvey W. Wiley's Search for Sugar
Self-Sufficiency," *Agricultural History* 54 (October 1980): 516.

4 Harvey W. Wiley, *Harvey W. Wiley: An Autobiography* (Indianapolis:
Bobbs-Merrill, 1930), 50.

5 Wiley, *Autobiography*, 54.

6 *Fourth Annual Report of Purdue University for the Academic Year
Ending June 30, 1878* (Indianapolis: Indianapolis Journal Company,
1879), 248.

7 William Lloyd Fox, "Harvey W. Wiley; The Formative Years" (PhD
diss., George Washington University, 1960), 229, 236–37.

8   Harvey Levenstein, *Revolution at the Table: The Transformation of the American Diet* (Berkeley: University of California Press, 2002), 32.

9   Mike Wallace, *Greater Gotham: A History of New York City from 1898 to 1919* (New York: Oxford University Press, 2017), 5, 299.

10 Jessy Yancy, "What Is Sorghum?" *Farm Flavor*, February 7, 2013, http://farmflavor.com/at-home/seasonal-foods/what-is-sorghum/.

11 Peter Collier, Ph.D., *Sorghum: Its Culture and Manufacture* [. . .] (Cincinnati: Robert Clarke and Co., 1884), 1.

12 Fox, "Formative Years," 238.

13 Professor H. W. Wiley, "Sorghum: Its Success and Value," 170, Box 1, HWP PU.

14 Fox, "Formative Years," 517–19.

15 Wiley, *Autobiography*, 179.

16 James G. Morrow, "Dr. Wiley Was His Own Cook," *New York Tribune*, November 8, 1908, C*.

17 C. A. Browne, "Wiley—The Chemist," in "In Memorium: Harvey Washington Wiley," Association of Official Agricultural Chemists, 1930, 8, Box 211, HWP LoC.

18 Fox, "Formative Years," 271–72.

19 Oscar E. Anderson Jr., *The Health of a Nation: Harvey W. Wiley and the Fight for Pure Food* (Chicago: University of Chicago Press, 1958), 35.

20 *Report of the Commissioner of Agriculture for the Years 1881 and 1882* (Washington, DC: Government Printing Office, 1882), 25.

21 Herbert Myrick, *The American Sugar Industry* (New York: Orange Judd Company, 1899), 102.

22 Wiley quoted in Fox, "Formative Years," 268.

23 Fox, "Formative Years," 520–22.

24 H. W. Wiley, *The Sugar Beet Industry: The Culture of the Sugar Beet and the Manufacture of Beet Sugar*, US Department of Agriculture, Division of Chemistry, Bulletin No. 27 (Washington, DC: Government Printing Office, 1890), 169; Wiley, *Autobiography*, 178.

25 H. W. Wiley, *Experiments with Sugar Beets in 1890*, US Department of Agriculture, Division of Chemistry, Bulletin No. 30 (Washington, DC: Government Printing Office, 1891), 79.

26 Harvey W. Wiley, *Experiments with Sugar Beets in 1893*, US Department of Agriculture, Division of Chemistry, Bulletin No. 39 (Washington, DC: Government Printing Office, 1894), 8–9.

27 H. W. Wiley, "Our Sugar Supply," December 9, 1886, *Bulletin of the Chemical Society of Washington*, no. 2 (1887): 24.

28 Those tops usually got fed to cattle near the sugar beet–processing factory.

29 Technically, the farmers owned their own fields, but finding labor for harvesting was a prerequisite for any farmers who were considering taking on sugar beets as their main crop.

30 Myrick, *American Sugar Industry*, 125.

31 C. W. Hamburger, *The Beet Grower's Manual* (Chicago: Columbia Printing Company, 1901), 47–48.

32 H. W. Wiley, *Special Report on the Sugar Beet Industry* (Washington, DC: Government Printing Office, 1898), 178.

33 Dr. Harvey Wiley, M.D., "Who Pays the Wages?" *Good Housekeeping* 79 (October 1924): 84.

34 United States Department of the Treasury, *Synopsis of Decisions of the Treasury Department* [. . .] (Washington, DC: Government Printing Office, 1898), 982.

35 US Department of Agriculture, *Annual Reports of the Department of Agriculture for the Fiscal Year Ended June 30, 1904* (Washington, DC: Government Printing Office, 1904), 234.

36 Harvey W. Wiley, "The True Meaning of the New Sugar Tariff," *Forum* (February 1898): 693.

37 Sidney W. Mintz, *Sweetness and Power: The Place of Sugar in Modern History* (New York: Penguin, 1985), 188.

38 US Customs and Border Protection, "Did You Know . . . CBP Supported Sweet Standards?" https://www.cbp.gov/about/history/did-you-know/sweet-standards, accessed November 14, 2017.

39 *American Economist* 70 (September 8, 1922), 103.

40 *American Sugar Industry and Beet Sugar Gazette* 11 (January 1909), 6.

41 Scott Miller, *The President and the Assassin: McKinley, Terror, and Empire at the Dawn of the American Century* (New York: Random House, 2011), 230, 335.

42 Fox, "Formative Years," 265–66, 269, 276–77.

43 Anderson, *Health of a Nation*, 102.

44 William L. Altdorfer, "Wonderful Growth of the Government's Pure Food Factory," *Washington Evening Star*, November 5, 1911, 51.

45 Harvey W. Wiley, *Foods and Their Adulteration* (Philadelphia: P. Blakiston's Son & Co., 1907), 471. With the advent of high-fructose corn syrup in the early 1970s, sugar would become still cheaper. High-fructose corn syrup now makes up 36 percent of the average American's sugar consumption of 22.7 teaspoons a day. Rich Cohen, "Sugar Love (A Not So Sweet Story)," *National Geographic* (August 2013), https://www.nationalgeographic.com/magazine/2013/08/sugar-love/.

46 R. H. McDowell and N. E. Wilson, *Sugar Beets: Notes for 1897*, Bulletin No. 37, Nevada State University Agricultural Experiment Station (December 1897), 13.

47 Untitled historical manuscript, 46, Series 5, Box 2, Great Western Sugar Company Papers, Records of the Great Western Sugar Company, Archives and Special Collections, Colorado State University, Fort Collins, CO.

48 W. D. Bigelow, "Harvey Washington Wiley," *Science* 72 (September 26, 1930): 311.

49 See, for example, Hamburger, *Beet Grower's Manual*, 20.

50 US Department of Agriculture, Economic Research Service, "Background: Sugar and Sweeteners," April 28, 2017, https://www.ers.usda.gov/topics/crops/sugar-sweeteners/background.aspx#hfcs, accessed July 3, 2017.

51 Judson C. Welliver, "The Mormon Church and the Sugar Trust," *Hampton's Magazine* 24 (January 1910): 82.

52 Donna J. Wood, *Strategic Uses of Public Policy: Business and Government in the Progressive Era* (Marshfield, MA: Pitman, 1986), 231.

53 Jose Aguayo, "*Los Betabeleros* (The Beetworkers)," in *La Gente: Hispano History and Life in Colorado*, ed. Vincent C. De Baca (Denver: Colorado Historical Society, 1998), 106.

54 *Washington Herald*, August 25, 1912, 7.

55 Mildred Morris, "Sugar Jags Are Speeding U.S. to a Premature Grave," *Grand Forks (ND) Evening Times*, December 19, 1913, 11.

56 Bill Price, "You Can Live on Eleven Cents per Day or Feast for Fifty," *Washington Times*, December 26, 1919, 18.

57 Richard Evershed and Nicola Temple, *Sorting the Beef From the Bull: The Science of Food Fraud Forensics* (London: Bloomsbury, 2016), 244.

58 Levenstein, *Revolution at the Table*, 32–33.

59 Benjamin R. Cohen, *Pure Adulteration: Cheating on Nature in the Age of Manufactured Food* (Chicago: University of Chicago Press, 2019), 156.

60 *Washington Times*, July 24, 1914, 7.

61 Harvey Wiley to Magnus Swenson, January 2, 1900, Box 1, Miscellaneous Records, 1877–1910, FDA–NARA.

62 Fox, "Formative Years," 289.

63 Harvey Wiley to John Arbuckle, June 23, 1894, Box 4, HWP NARA.

64 Guilford L. Spencer and Ervin Edgar Ewell, *Tea, Coffee, and Cocoa Preparations*, pt. 7 of *Foods and Food Adulterants*, US Department of Agriculture, Division of Chemistry, Bulletin No. 13 (Washington, DC: Government Printing Office, 1892).

65 Fox, "Formative Years," 289–92.

66 Harvey Wiley to Engineers Department, Office of the District Commissioners, October 9, 1900, Box 1, Miscellaneous Records, 1877–1910, FDA–NARA.

67 Harvey Wiley to Charley Rich, December 11, 1900, Box 1, Miscellaneous Records, 1877–1910, FDA–NARA.

68 Harvey Levenstein, *Fear of Food: A History of Why We Worry about What We Eat* (Chicago: University of Chicago Press, 2012), 180n4.

69 Fox, "Formative Years," 379–82; Harvey Wiley to the Marsden Company, December 6, 1901, Box 7, HWP NARA.

70 Harvey Wiley to M. Swanson, October 26, 1901, 2, Box 7, HWP NARA.

CHAPTER FOUR. ADULTERATED FOOD

1 Harvey Wiley as quoted in Philip J. Hilts, *Protecting America's Health: The FDA, Business, and One Hundred Years of Regulation* (Chapel Hill: University of North Carolina Press, 2003), 40.

2 Harvey W. Wiley, *Harvey W. Wiley: An Autobiography* (Indianapolis: Bobbs-Merrill, 1930), 200–201.

3 Oscar E. Anderson Jr., *The Health of a Nation: Harvey W. Wiley and the Fight for Pure Food* (Chicago: University of Chicago Press, 1958), 165.

4 Wiley begins the first chapter of his book *The History of a Crime against the Food Law* with a close recounting of the very last Congressional hearing on the subject. He skips his activities before 1900 because those did not help him reinforce his image as a crusading chemist. His autobiography also contains little coverage of the pre–Poison Squad fight for a pure food law because Wiley's ardor for the cause of pure food grew over time. Only later did Wiley and the historians who wrote about him begin to project that reputation backward. See Harvey W. Wiley, M.D., *The History of a Crime against the Food Law* (Washington, DC: Harvey W. Wiley, 1929), 1.

5 William Lloyd Fox, "Harvey W. Wiley: The Formative Years" (PhD diss., George Washington University, 1960), 303.

6 Mitchell Okun, *Fair Play in the Marketplace: The First Battle for Pure Food and Drugs* (Dekalb: Northern Illinois University Press, 1986), 3.

7 James Harvey Young, *Pure Food: Securing the Passage of the Pure Food and Drug Act of 1906* (Princeton, NJ: Princeton University Press, 1989), 106.

8 Harvey Wiley to Dr. W. W. Vinnedge, February 27, 1906, Box 2, Miscellaneous Records 1877–1910, Records of the Bureau of Chemistry, FDA–NARA.

9 F. Leslie Hart, "Adulteration of Food before 1906," *Food, Drug, Cosmetic Law Journal* 7 (January 1952): 7–8, 11–12.

10 Bee Wilson, *Swindled: From Poison Sweets to Counterfeit Coffee: The Dark History of Food Cheats* (London: John Murray, 2008), 1.

11 Thomas H. Hoskins, M.D., *What We Eat: An Account of the Most Common Adulterations of Food and Drink* (Boston: T. O. H. P. Burnham, 1861), iv.

12 Benjamin R. Cohen, *Pure Adulteration: Cheating on Nature in the Age of Manufactured Food* (Chicago: University of Chicago Press, 2019), 187–92.

13 Okun, *Fair Play in the Marketplace*, 153–54.

14 Marc T. Law, "The Origins of State Pure Food Regulation," *Journal of Economic History* 63 (December 2003): 1103.

15 Ilyse D. Barkan, "Industry Invites Regulation: The Passage of the Pure Food and Drug Act of 1906," *American Journal of Public Health* 75 (1985): 20.

16 A. S. Mitchell, "Wiley–The Pioneer," Organization of Official Agricultural Chemists, "In Memoriam: Harvey Washington Wiley," 1930, xi–xii, Box 211, HWP LoC.

17 W. R. M. Wharton, "Evolution," *Food, Drug, Cosmetic Law Quarterly* 1 (September 1946): 352.

18 Wiley, *Autobiography*, 198–99.

19 Okun, *Fair Play in the Marketplace*, 283.

20 Edwin Björkman, "Our Debt to Dr. Wiley," *World's Work* 19 (January 1910): 12446.

21 See, for example, the chemist Charles Drew's summary of his work in the pages of the *Saint Paul Daily Globe*, March 17, 1889, 8.

22 Aaron Bobrow-Strain, "White Bread Bio-Politics: Purity, Health, and the Triumph of Industrial Baking," *Cultural Geographies* 15 (2008): B20.

23 Joy Santlofer, *Food City: Four Centuries of Bread-Making in New York* (New York: W. W. Norton, 2017), 89.

24 Santlofer, *Food City*, 89–93.

25 Lochner v. New York, 198 U.S. 45 (1905). This case, which created the idea of liberty of contract, limited the ability of states and the federal government to regulate workplaces under the Constitution's Commerce Clause. It also explains why the Pure Food and Drug Act, passed the next year, could only regulate the purity of food that traveled across state lines.

26 A. Hunter Dupree, *Science in the Federal Government: A History of Policies and Activities to 1940* (Cambridge, MA: Belknap Press of Harvard University Press, 1957), 178.

27 Young, *Pure Food*, 103, 105.

28 Alex J. Wedderburn, *Report on the Extent and Character of Food and Drug Adulteration* (Washington, DC: Government Printing Office, 1894), 9–10.

29   H. W. Wiley, *Lard and Lard Adulterations,* pt. 4 in *Food and Food Adulterants,* US Department of Agriculture, Division of Chemistry, Bulletin No. 13 (Washington, DC: Government Printing Office, 1889), 405, 409, 476–77.

30   Wiley, *Lard and Lard Adulterations,* 506.

31   Donna J. Wood, "The Strategic Use of Public Policy: Business Support for the 1906 Food and Drug Act," *Business History Review* 59 (Autumn 1985): 405.

32   *Indianapolis Journal,* May 11, 1896, 8.

33   C. A. Browne, "Wiley–The Chemist," in Association of Official Agricultural Chemists, viii, Box 211, HWP LoC. See also Harvey W. Wiley, *Principles and Practice of Agricultural Analysis,* 3 vols. (Easton, PA: Chemical Publishing Company, 1897).

34   Anderson, *Health of a Nation,* 90–92; *Annual Reports of the Secretary of Agriculture for the Fiscal Year Ended June 30, 1897: Miscellaneous Reports* (Washington, DC: Government Printing Office, 1897), 33.

35   Dupree, *Science in the Federal Government,* 179.

36   Anderson, *Health of a Nation,* 82.

37   H. W. Wiley, "The Adulteration of Food," *Journal of the Franklin Institute* 137 (April 1894): 286–87.

38   *Journal of Proceedings of the National Food and Drug Congress,* Columbian University Hall, Washington, DC, March 2–5, 1898: 4, 7.

39   Young, *Pure Food,* 128.

40   *Journal of Proceedings,* 12–16.

41   Fox, "Formative Years," 367.

42   H. W. Wiley, M.D., Ph.D. "Food Adulteration in Its Relation to the Public Health," *Medical Age* 19 (April 10, 1901): 249.

43   Fox, "Formative Years," 230; Anderson, *Health of a Nation,* 82.

44   "The Fiftieth Anniversary of the Founding of the Cosmos Club, 1878–1928" (Washington, DC, 1929), 15, 17. Thank you to Rachel Nellis, the archivist at the Cosmos Club, for sending me a scan of Wiley's membership card and a link to a scan of the Club's Fiftieth Anniversary booklet.

45   James G. Morrow, "Dr. Wiley Was His Own Cook," *New York Herald Tribune,* November 8, 1908, C8; Harvey Wiley to George H. Oyster Jr.,

November 4, 1908, Box 69, HWP LoC; "Fiftieth Anniversary," 17.

46 "Fiftieth Anniversary," 18.

47 Harvey Wiley to B. W. Cole, April 13, 1900, Box 1, Miscellaneous Records, 1877–1910, Records of the Bureau of Chemistry, FDA–NARA.

48 "Why, dear Mama, I am getting along as nicely as if I had a dozen wives," wrote Wiley to his mother in 1883. Fox, "Formative Years," 284.

49 Fox, "Formative Years," 285–86.

50 Anderson, *Health of a Nation,* 81.

51 Arthur Wallace Dunn, "Dr. Wiley and Pure Food," pt. 2, *World's Work* 23 (November 1911): 32.

52 Katherine Graves Busbey, "Mrs. Harvey W. Wiley: The Notable Wife of the Great Champion of Pure Food," *Good Housekeeping* 54 (April 1912): 544.

53 Wiley, *Autobiography,* 194–96.

54 Anderson, *Health of a Nation,* 242; Fox, "Formative Years," 288.

55 Deborah Blum, *The Poison Squad: One Chemist's Single-Minded Crusade for Food Safety at the Turn of the Twentieth Century* (New York: Penguin, 2018), 72–73.

56 Edward H. Beardsley, *The Rise of the American Chemistry Profession, 1850–1900* (Gainesville: University of Florida Press, 1964), 28–30.

57 Fox, "Formative Years," 278–79, 294.

58 Clayton Coppin, "James Wilson and Harvey Wiley: The Dilemma of Bureaucratic Entrepreneurship," *Agricultural History* 64 (Spring 1990): 167, 169.

59 Fox, "Formative Years," 386.

CHAPTER FIVE. MEAT

1 James Harvey Young, *Pure Food: Securing the Federal Food and Drugs Act of 1906* (Princeton, NJ: Princeton University Press, 1989), 137–39.

2 Robert W. Merry, *President McKinley: Architect of the American Century* (New York: Simon and Schuster, 2017), 354–55.

3 Joshua Specht, *Red Meat Republic: A Hoof-to-Table History of How Beef Changed America* (Princeton, NJ: Princeton University Press, 2019), 222–23.

4   Donna J. Wood, *Strategic Uses of Public Policy: Business and Government in the Progressive Era* (Marshfield, MA: Pitman, 1986), 75.

5   Harvey Levenstein, *Fear of Food: A History of Why We Worry about What We Eat* (Chicago: University of Chicago Press, 62–63.

6   Deborah Blum, *The Poison Squad: One Chemist's Single-Minded Crusade for Food Safety at the Turn of the Twentieth Century* (New York: Penguin, 2018), 67.

7   Young, *Pure Food*, 152.

8   Harvey Wiley, "Report of the Bureau of Chemistry for the Period beginning July 1, 1897, ending June 30, 1905 [Draft]" c. 1905, 1–3, Box 199, HWP LoC.

9   Oscar E. Anderson Jr., *The Health of a Nation: Harvey W. Wiley and the Fight for Pure Food* (Chicago: University of Chicago Press, 1958), 105–6.

10   Harvey Wiley, "Report of the Bureau of Chemistry for the Period beginning July 1, 1897, ending June 30, 1905," c. 1905, 2–3, Box 199, HWP LoC. See also *Report of the Secretary of Agriculture 1906* (Washington, DC: Government Printing Office, 1906), 60–63.

11   H. W. Wiley, M.D., *Food Adulteration in Its Relation to the Public Health* (Columbus, OH: Berlin Printing Company, 1900), 8–9.

12   Fred B. Linton, "Federal Food and Drug Laws: Leaders Who Achieved Their Enactment and Enforcement," *Food and Drug Law Journal* 50 (1995; originally published in 1949): 10.

13   "Testimony of Harvey W. Wiley before the Federal Trade Commission," New York, NY, October 14, 1924, 2777, Box 198, HWP LoC.

14   Frank G. Carpenter, "Uncle Sam's Eating House and Its Tests of Pure Foods," *Richmond Times-Dispatch*, July 29, 1906.

15   US Department of Agriculture, *Report of the Secretary of Agriculture 1903* (Washington, DC: Government Printing Office, 1903), 53–54.

16   Harvey W. Wiley, *History of a Crime against the Food Law* (Washington, DC: Harvey W. Wiley, 1929), 61. The articles are not signed. Wiley first revealed the name of the author in this self-published book.

17 *Washington Post*, December 23, 1902, 4.

18 Suzanne Rebecca White, "Chemistry and Controversy: Regulating the Use of Chemicals in Foods, 1883–1959" (PhD diss., Emory University, 1994), 9.

19 Anderson, *Health of a Nation*, 152.

20 *Washington Post*, March 25, 1903, 2.

21 *Washington Post*, January 24, 1903, 2.

22 US Food and Drug Administration, "William Carter Poison Squad (FDA005)," Flickr, October 27, 2011, https://www.flickr.com /photos/fdaphotos/6800851132/in/photolist-mdru9D-dwKT5R -bHfmXz-brYhPj-bESARx-boNKBd-bESvpa-bmY971-bzSYDR -8t7TMm-8t4SKt/, accessed April 26, 2019.

23 Linton, "Federal Food and Drug Laws," 10–11.

24 *San Francisco Call*, June 22, 1903.

25 H. W. Wiley, M.D., *Boric Acid and Borax*, pt. 1 of *Influence of Food Preservatives and Artificial Colors on Digestion and Health*, US Department of Agriculture, Bureau of Chemistry, Bulletin 84 (Washington, DC: Government Printing Office, 1904), 255.

26 Wiley, *Boric Acid and Borax*, 7.

27 White, "Chemistry and Controversy," 8.

28 Oscar Liebreich, *Effects of Borax and Boracic Acid on the Human System* (London: J. & A. Churchill, 1899), 1–2.

29 *Manufacturer and Builder* 1 (January 1871): 13.

30 *New York Sun*, June 26, 1892, 8.

31 Pacific Coast Borax Company, *Borax, the Magic Crystal* (Oakland, CA: Pacific Coast Borax Company, 1913), 22–23.

32 Gilbert Bailey, *The Saline Deposits of California*, California State Mining Bureau, Bulletin No. 24 (Sacramento, 1902): 38–40.

33 *Encyclopedia Americana*, vol. 6, ed. Frederick Converse Beach (New York: Scientific American, 1903–1905), s.v. "Borax."

34 Pacific Coast Borax Company, "From the Desert, through the Press, into the Home" (San Francisco, 1895), 7.

35 William Cronon, *Nature's Metropolis: Chicago and the Great West* (New York: W. W. Norton, 1991), 229–30, 239.

36 Harvey W. Wiley, M.D., *Food and Its Adulteration*, 3rd ed. (Philadelphia: P. Blakiston and Sons, 1917), 37.

37 Young, *Pure Food*, 153.

38 Upton Sinclair, *The Jungle* (New York: Doubleday, Page & Company, 1906), 161.

39 H. W. Wiley, M.D., "The Food Law and the Experts," Convention of State Dairy and Food Departments, Hartford, CT, July 18, 1906, 19, Box 3, Articles and Lectures of Harvey Wiley, 1890–1906, Records of the Bureau of Agricultural and Industrial Chemistry, Record Group 97, National Archives and Records Administration, College Park, MD.

40 Wiley, *Food and Its Adulteration*, 37–38.

41 Harvey W. Wiley, *Harvey W. Wiley: An Autobiography* (Indianapolis: Bobbs-Merrill, 1930), 219. Of course, the public knew that Wiley worked for the Department of Agriculture, not the Smithsonian, but it may have been more difficult to work that agency's name into the rhyme scheme.

42 *Washington Evening Star*, November 12, 1905, 6.

43 *Washington Evening Star*, July 22, 1903, 7.

44 "Testimony of Harvey Wiley in Benzoate of Soda Evidence," Volume 4, August 1910, Filed April 27, 1912, Box 235, HWP LoC.

45 US House of Representatives, Committee on Interstate and Foreign Commerce, *The Pure-Food Bills* [. . .] (Washington, DC: Government Printing Office, 1906), 277.

46 *American Druggist and Pharmaceutical Record* (April 10, 1905): 211.

47 Edwin G. Boring, "The Nature and History of Experimental Control," *American Journal of Psychology* 67 (December 1954): 573.

48 *American Food Journal* 1 (October 1906): 17.

49 Wiley, *Autobiography*, 218.

50 US House of Representatives, *The Pure-Food Bills*, 277.

51 *New York Tribune*, June 17, 1903, 1.

52 H. H. Langdon, "A Criticism of Dr. Wiley's Anent the Use of Borax," *What-to-Eat* 22 (January 1907): 7; *American Food Journal* 1 (October 1906): 17.

53 Philip J. Hilts, *Protecting America's Health: The FDA, Business, and One Hundred Years of Regulation* (Chapel Hill: University of North Carolina Press, 2003), 39.

54 *American Food Journal* 4 (February 15, 1909): 17.

55 *Washington Evening Star*, July 22, 1903, 7.

56 N. J. Travis and E. J. Cocks, *The Tincal Trail: A History of Borax* (London: Harrap, 1984), 107.

57 Dr. Graham Lusk to *Medical Record* in *American Food Journal* 7 (February 15, 1912): 37.

58 Wiley, *Boric Acid and Borax*, 252, 254.

59 See Leibreich, *Effects of Borax and Boracic Acid,* 3.

60 Jack C. Fisher, "Wiley's Poison Squad," American Council on Science and Health, December 4, 2002, http://www.acsh.org/news/2002/12/04/wileys-poison-squad.

61 Harvey Levenstein, *Fear of Food: A History of Why We Worry about What We Eat* (Chicago: University of Chicago Press, 2012), 66; Harvey Wiley, "What Pure-Food Laws Are Doing for Our People," 23, Box 63, HWP LoC.

62 Two similar sets of experiments, one conducted by the Referee Board of Consulting Scientific Experts (or Remsen Board) and one conducted by the Coca-Cola Company, will be discussed in subsequent chapters. The author Richard Swiderski has also found experiments structured in ways similar to Wiley conducted at the University of Illinois in 1910, Hahnemann Medical College in 1911, and the New York Homeopathic College in 1927. While not all of these experiments were dubbed "poison squads," they attracted attention because of the compelling notion that the test subjects were somehow harming their health for the sake of advancing knowledge—as the filmmaker Morgan Spurlock did in his thirty-day diet of McDonald's food in his 2004 movie, *Supersize Me*. See Richard Swiderski, *Poison Eaters: Snakes, Opium, Arsenic, and the Lethal Show* (Boca Raton, FL: Universal Publishers, 2010), 246–49, 253.

63 "Testimony of Harvey W. Wiley before the Federal Trade Commission," 2777. He also tested copper sulfate and saltpeter the same way, but the secretary of agriculture prevented publication of those results under pressure from the food manufacturers. See White, "Chemistry and Controversy," 9.

64 Harvey W. Wiley, Ph.D., LL. D., "Studying the Effect of Preservatives on Health," *The Independent*, July 30, 1903, 1795, Box 3, Miscellaneous Records, 1877–1910, FDA–NARA.

65 Anderson, *Health of a Nation*, 221.

66 Wiley, "What Pure-Food Laws Are Doing for Our People," 19.

67 *National Provisioner* 58 (March 2, 1918): 18.

68 *American Food Journal* 11 (June 1916): 258.

69 Hipolite Egg Company v. United States 220 U.S. 45 (1911). By the time its case got before the Supreme Court, the Hipolite Egg Company had conceded that borax was a harmful additive. Its challenge to the Pure Food and Drug Act was under the Constitution's Commerce Clause.

70 A simple Google search produces many examples of the Material Safety Data Sheet for borax (like this one: https://omsi.edu/sites/all /FTP/files/kids/Borax-msds.pdf). The limited risks described therein apply only to workplaces. Consumers who encounter borax face even less trouble.

71 Clayton A. Coppin and Jack High, *The Politics of Purity: Harvey Washington Wiley and the Origins of Federal Food Policy* (Ann Arbor: University of Michigan Press, 1999), 55–56.

72 Young, *Pure Food*, 228.

CHAPTER SIX. PURE FOOD

1 International Pure Food Congress, *Journal of the National Proceedings of State Food and Dairy Departments*, September 26 to October 1, 1904, 149.

2 Deborah Blum, *The Poison Squad: One Chemist's Single-Minded Crusade for Food Safety at the Turn of the Twentieth Century* (New York: Penguin, 2018), 140.

3 Anna Zeide, *Canned: The Rise and Fall of Consumer Confidence in the American Food Industry* (Berkeley: University of California Press, 2018), 30.

4 Blum, *Poison Squad,* 140.

5 "The history of the pure food movement is the history of Harvey W. Wiley," explained Gabriel Kolko in his 1963 revisionist classic on the entire Progressive Era, *The Triumph of Conservatism*. Kolko argued

that starting in 1898, "the food reform movement was essentially supported by the food industry itself, directed by Wiley, and represented a desire of major food interests to set their own houses in order and protect themselves from more unscrupulous associates." Gabriel Kolko, *The Triumph of Conservatism: A Reinterpretation of American History, 1900–1916* (New York: Quadrangle, 1963), 108–9. Kolko, however, not only gets the date wrong for when Harvey Wiley became an important figure in the pure food movement, but also greatly overestimates Wiley's influence on the precise content of the final legislation.

6   The classic example here is H. J. Heinz. See Donna J. Wood, "The Strategic Use of Public Policy: Business Support for the 1906 Food and Drug Act," *Business History Review* 59 (Autumn 1985), 419–20.

7   F. B. Linton, "Wiley—The Man," in Association of Official Agricultural Chemists, *In Memoriam: Harvey Washington Wiley* (Association of Official Agricultural Chemists, 1930), xx, Box 211, HWP LoC.

8   William Atherton Du Puy, "The Guardian of Ninety Million Stomachs: Dr. Harvey W. Wiley of the Bureau of Chemistry," *Scientific American* 105 (July 29, 1911): 95.

9   James Wilson to William Howard Taft (stamped), August 2, 1911, 3, File 1756, William Howard Taft Papers, Manuscripts Division, Library of Congress, Washington, DC.

10 Roosevelt as quoted in Clayton A. Coppin and Jack High, *The Politics of Purity: Harvey Washington Wiley and the Origins of Federal Food Policy* (Ann Arbor: University of Michigan Press, 1999), 87.

11 H. W. Wiley, M.D., *Sulphurous Acid and Sulphites*, pt. 3 in *Influence of Food Preservatives and Artificial Colors on Digestion and Health*, US Department of Agriculture, Bureau of Chemistry, Bulletin No. 84 (Washington, DC: Government Printing Office, 1907).

12 H. W. Wiley, M.D., *Benzoic Acid and Benzoates*, pt. 4 in *Influence of Food Preservatives and Artificial Colors on Digestion and Health*, US Department of Agriculture, Bureau of Chemistry, Bulletin No. 84 (Washington, DC: Government Printing Office, 1908).

13 H. W. Wiley, M.D., *Formaldehyde*, pt. 5 in *Influence of Food Preservatives and Artificial Colors on Digestion and Health*, US Department of

Agriculture, Bureau of Chemistry, Bulletin No. 84 (Washington, DC: Government Printing Office, 1908).

14   US House of Representatives, Committee on Interstate and Foreign Commerce, *The Pure-Food Bills* [. . .] (Washington, DC: Government Printing Office, 1906), 254–55, 252.

15   *New York Sun*, April 2, 1905, 3.

16   H. W. Wiley, "The Influence of Preservatives in Foods on the Public Health," 2, Box 189, HWP LoC.

17   Coppin and High, *Politics of Purity*, 67.

18   James Harvey Young, *Pure Food: Securing the Pure Food and Drugs Act of 1906* (Princeton, NJ: Princeton University Press, 1989), 185.

19   Fran Moffett and Maggie Sullivan, "Alice Lakey, 1857–1935," in *Past and Promise: Lives of New Jersey Women,* ed. The Women's Project of New Jersey (Syracuse, NY: Syracuse University Press, 1997), 161.

20   Young, *Pure Food*, 185–86.

21   *Washington Post*, February 28, 1906, 5.

22   Young, *Pure Food*, 180–81.

23   United States Department of Agriculture, "Standards of Purity for Food Products," Office of the Secretary, Circular No. 10, November 20, 1903, Box 189, HWP LoC.

24   Harvey Wiley, "The Pure Food Law Is in Peril," *Good Housekeeping* 76 (June 1923): 186.

25   Suzanne Rebecca White, "Chemistry and Controversy: Regulating the Use of Chemicals in Food, 1883–1959" (PhD diss., Emory University, 1994), 26.

26   Arthur P. Greeley, *The Food and Drugs Act* (Washington, DC: John Byrne, 1907), 23–24; Clayton A. Coppin and Jack High, "Umpires at Bat: Setting Food Standards by Government Regulation," *Business and Economic History* 21 (1992): 109–10.

27   Coppin and High, "Umpires at Bat," 110.

28   Oscar E. Anderson Jr., *The Health of a Nation: Harvey W. Wiley and the Fight for Pure Food* (Chicago: University of Chicago Press, 1958), 177.

29   Young, *Pure Food*, 267.

30   Hipolite Egg Co. v. United States, 220 U.S. 45 (1911).

31 Coppin and High, "Umpires at Bat," 109.

32 "The Food and Drugs Act, June 30, 1906," in Greeley, *Food and Drugs Act*, 77–79.

33 Oscar E. Anderson Jr., "The Pure-Food Issue: A Republican Dilemma, 1906–1912," *American Historical Review* 61 (April 1956): 552. This arrangement is the origin of terrific names for legal cases like *United States v. Forty Barrels & Twenty Kegs of Coca-Cola*.

34 "The Food and Drugs Act," in Greeley, *Food and Drugs Act*, 75.

35 "The Food and Drugs Act," in Greeley, *Food and Drugs Act*, 74–75.

36 Harvey W. Wiley, M.D., *The History of a Crime against the Food Law* (Washington, DC: Harvey Wiley, 1929), 93.

37 Harvey Wiley to F. N. Barrett, July 6, 1906, Box 2, Miscellaneous Records, 1877–1910, Records of the Bureau of Chemistry, FDA–NARA.

38 On the other hand, if standards had been in place when Wiley was trying to enforce the Pure Food and Drug Act, there is no guarantee that Wiley's standards would have been the best ones possible for the health of the consumer. The lack of standards for judging the purity of foods became an issue only if the companies targeted by the Department of Agriculture decided to test in court the Bureau of Chemistry's decision about whether a product was adulterated or not.

39 Harvey W. Wiley, *Harvey W. Wiley: An Autobiography* (Indianapolis: Bobbs-Merrill, 1930), 232.

40 W. T. Bigelow, "The Detail of the Enforcement of the Food and Drugs Act," *Yearbook of the Department of Agriculture 1907*, Box 190, HWP LoC; Paul B. Dunbar, "Memories of Early Days of Federal Food and Drug Law Enforcement," *Food Drug and Cosmetic Law Journal* 14 (February 1959): 96; James Wilson, "Report of the Secretary," November 27, 1908, in *Yearbook of the Department of Agriculture 1908* (Washington, DC: Government Printing Office, 1909), 82–83.

41 W. R. M. Wharton, "Its Inspection Evolution," *Food Drug and Cosmetics Law Quarterly* 1 (September 1946): 357; Dunbar, "Memories of Early Days," 121, 94.

42 James Harvey Young, "From Oysters to After-Dinner Mints: The

Role of the Early Food and Drug Inspector," *Journal of the History of Medicine and Allied Sciences* 42 (1987): 34–35.

43 Blum, *Poison Squad*, 152, 150.

44 Roger W. Weiss, "The Case for Federal Meat Inspection Examined," *Journal of Law and Economics* 7 (October 1964): 110–11.

45 *National Provisioner* 35 (July 7, 1906): 16.

46 Coppin and High, *Politics of Purity*, 82.

47 Anderson, *Health of a Nation*, 196. According to Anderson, Wiley's greatest contribution to the legislation was "the inspired generalship he offered" rather than any particular piece of research or legislative action.

48 Arthur Wallace Dunn, "Dr. Wiley and Pure Food," pt. 1, *World's Work* 22 (October 1911): 14960–61.

49 Harvey Wiley, "Address Delivered at the Annual Dinner of the Atlas Club," December 14, 1906, 4–5, Box 60, HWP LoC.

50 The promotional literature for Wiley's tour on the Lyceum speaking circuit immediately following his retirement from government service in 1912 described him as "the sponsor for and writer of what is known as the Pure Food Bill enacted into a law several years ago by Congress." See Anderson, *Health of a Nation*, 307n41; "Coit-Alber Lyceum Festival Banner Program," Memorial Hall Dayton Ohio, 1912, Box 211, HWP LoC.

51 US House of Representatives, 62nd Congress, Second Session, "Expenditures in the Department of Agriculture," H.R. Rep. No. 249 (January 2, 1912), 5.

52 James Harvey Young, *The Medical Messiahs: A Social History of Health Quackery in Twentieth-Century America* (Princeton, NJ: Princeton University Press, 1967), 95.

CHAPTER SEVEN. WHISKEY

1 Harvey Wiley as quoted in *American Druggist and Pharmaceutical Review* (April 10, 1905): 211.

2 *New York Sun*, April 2, 1905, 3.

3 *Deseret Evening News*, April 21, 1905, 5.

4 *American Druggist and Pharmaceutical Review* (April 10, 1905): 211.

5   Harvey Wiley to Dr. H. Schweitzer, April 21, 1905, Box 2, Miscellaneous Records, 1877–1910, Records of the Bureau of Chemistry, FDA–NARA.

6   *San Francisco Call*, July 19, 1911, 6.

7   Harvey Levenstein, *Fear of Food: Why We Worry about What We Eat* (Chicago: University of Chicago Press, 2012), 168n4.

8   *New York Evening Post*, February 13, 1909, 1.

9   *Washington Post*, August 16, 1908, SM4.

10 Harvey Wiley to James E. Tower, February 19, 1909, Box 76, HWP LoC.

11 *New York Evening Post*, February 13, 1909, 1.

12 *Washington Post*, August 16, 1908, SM4.

13 Harvey Wiley to W. H. Hough, March 7, 1905, Box 2, Miscellaneous Records, 1877–1910, Records of the Bureau of Chemistry, FDA–NARA.

14 Harvey Wiley to J. W. McCulloch, October 4, 1901, Box 7, HWP LoC.

15 Fermenting different grains results in different but related products like bourbon or rye. In this case, the argument was about the exact definition of what could be marketed as traditional scotch whiskey.

16 H. Parker Willis, "What Whiskey Is," *McClure's* 34 (April 1910): 687–88; Raymond Sokolov, *Fading Feast: A Compendium of Disappearing Regional Foods* (New York: E. P. Dutton, 1983), 93–94.

17 Harvey Wiley, Untitled Whiskey Memo, May 1910, 1–4, Box 211, HWP LoC; Willis, "What Whiskey Is," 688.

18 Clayton A. Coppin and Jack High, *The Politics of Purity: Harvey Washington Wiley and the Origins of Federal Food Policy* (Ann Arbor: University of Michigan Press, 1999), 53. Coppin and High have also written extensively about whiskey in numerous articles. My analysis of the whiskey issue in this chapter depends heavily on their research and insights.

19 Harvey Wiley to H. W. Thomas, February 1, 1904, Box 8, HWP LoC.

20 *Washington Post*, February 28, 1906, 5.

21 *New York Times*, July 13, 1911, 2.

22 Ironically, one of the whiskey producers that sent bottles to his home was Green River Whiskey, a blended whiskey producer. Wiley thought

it was straight whiskey, demonstrating that he could not tell the difference between them. See Coppin and High, *Politics of Purity*, 78.

23 *Washington Post*, February 28, 1906, 5.

24 Coppin and High, *Politics of Purity*, 113–14.

25 Melissa Alexander, "Bottled-in-Bond: A Brief History," Bourbon & Banter, June 12, 2015, https://www.bourbonbanter.com/banter/bottled-in-bond-a-brief-history/#.WeJ5KxNSy9Y.

26 J. W. Gayle, "Bottling Whiskey in Bond," *Western Druggist* 26 (March 1904): 126.

27 Harvey Wiley to F. F. Gilmore, March 9, 1904, 2, 4, Box 1, Miscellaneous Records, 1877–1910, Records of the Bureau of Chemistry, FDA–NARA.

28 *New York Tribune*, November 11, 1908, 2.

29 Harvey W. Wiley, "Whisky," 196, Box 211, HWP LoC.

30 Harvey Wiley, "Statement in regard to Reported Address on Alcohol and Whisky," n.d., Box 209, HWP LoC.

31 Willis, "What Whiskey Is," 689.

32 Reports of Committees of the House of Representatives, "Whiskey Trust Investigation," H.R. Rep. No. 2601 (1892–93), 73.

33 Jack High and Clayton A. Coppin, "Wiley and the Whiskey Industry: Strategic Behavior in the Passage of the Pure Food Act," *Business History Review* 62 (Summer 1988): 291.

34 Hiram Walker & Sons, *A Plot against the People*, 3rd ed. (March 1911). This argument is the entire premise of the pamphlet. Although the pamphlet was issued by the makers of Canadian Club whiskey, it includes extensive excerpts from government documents demonstrating Wiley's changing positions on this issue. See also *American Food Journal* 4 (February 15, 1909): 16; Coppin and High, *Politics of Purity*, 73.

35 H. M. Hough to James Wilson, December 3, 1906, 2, Box 209, HWP LoC.

36 Coppin and High, *Politics of Purity*, 68.

37 Deborah Blum, *The Poison Squad: One Chemist's Single-Minded Crusade for Safety at the Turn of the Twentieth Century* (New York: Penguin, 2018), 166.

38 Harvey Wiley to H. A. Scovell, March 30, 1905, Box 2, Miscellaneous Records, 1877–1910, Records of the Bureau of Chemistry, FDA–NARA.

39 Wilson excerpted in Harvey W. Wiley, M.D. *The History of a Crime against the Food Law* (Washington, DC: Harvey Wiley, 1929), 108.

40 Coppin and High, *Politics of Purity*, 101.

41 Wiley, *History of a Crime*, 111.

42 Willis, "What Whiskey Is," 696–98.

43 Charles J. Bonaparte to Theodore Roosevelt, February 19, 1909, 6, Box 72, HWP LoC.

44 James Wilson to William Howard Taft, stamped August 2, 1911, 8–11, File 1756, William Howard Taft Papers, Manuscripts Division, Library of Congress, Washington, DC.

45 Coppin and High, *Politics of Purity*, 114–15.

46 Franklin MacVeagh, James Wilson, and Charles Nagel, "Food Inspection Decision No. 113," US Department of Agriculture, February 16, 1910, 1.

47 William Howard Taft, "What Is the Meaning of the Term 'Whiskey' under the Pure Food Act?" 3, 6, Box 209, HWP LoC.

48 Hiram Walker & Sons, *Plot against the People*, 21.

49 Harvey W. Wiley, M.D., "The Food Law and 'Nigger Gin,'" *Good Housekeeping* 57 (November 1913): 693, 696. Not coincidentally, Wiley made this claim at about the same time he became enamored with the new racist pseudoscience of eugenics. For more on that topic, see chapter 14.

50 Harvey W. Wiley, M.D., *The Lure of the Land: Farming after Fifty* (New York: Century, 1915), 70.

51 "The Food and Drugs Act, June 30, 1906," in Arthur P. Greeley, *The Food and Drugs Act* (Washington, DC: John Byrne, 1907), 76.

52 "Physicians," unidentified newspaper clipping, c. 1920, Box 129, HWP LoC. There is much more on the *Pharmacopeia* in chapter 10.

53 Harvey W. Wiley, M.D., "Why I Believe in Prohibition," *Good Housekeeping* 62 (May 1916): 644.

54 Harvey Wiley, *History of a Crime*, 152.

55 Harvey Wiley, M.D., letter to the editor, *Manufacturers Record*, March 22, 1922, in *The Prohibition Question: Viewed from the Economic and Moral Standpoint*, 2nd ed. (Baltimore: Manufacturers Record Publishing Company, 1922), 15.

56 H. Parker Willis, "Secretary Wilson's Record III: Pure Food," *Collier's* 49 (April 6, 1912): 11.

57 Megan Gambino, "During Prohibition, Your Doctor Could Write You a Prescription for Booze," *Smithsonian*, October 7, 2013, http://www.smithsonianmag.com/history/during-prohibition -your-doctor-could-write-you-prescription-booze-180947940/.

58 Reid Mitenbuler, *Bourbon Empire: The Past and Future of American Whiskey* (New York: Penguin, 2015), 185–86.

59 Kayleigh Kulp, "Don't Be a Single-Malt Scotch Snob," Daily Beast, updated April 14, 2017, https://www.thedailybeast.com /dont-be-a-single-malt-scotch-snob.

60 Jake Emon, "An Absurdly Complete Guide to Understanding Whiskey," Eater, August 13, 2015, https://www.eater.com/drinks/2015 /8/13/9113965/whiskey-guide?utm_campaign=eater.social&utm_ medium=weekendsocial&utm_source=twitter&utm_content=eater.

CHAPTER EIGHT. ENFORCEMENT

1 Nadia Berenstein, "Flavor Added: The Sciences of Flavor and the Industrialization of Taste in America" (PhD diss., University of Pennsylvania, 2018), 24.

2 Berenstein, "Flavor Added," 13n58, 23.

3 Alois von Isakovics to Harvey Wiley, May 5, 1905, Flavoring Extracts: 1900–1908, Food Standards Committee, Correspondence and Reports, 1897–1938, FDA–NARA. I got my copy of this letter from Nadia Berenstein and am using her citation, although my quotation from that letter here is different from hers.

4 Mark Kurlansky, *Milk! A 10,000-Year Food Fracas* (New York: Bloomsbury, 2018), 140.

5 Ai Hisano, "'Eye Appeal Is Buy Appeal': Business Creates the Color of Foods, 1870–1970" (PhD diss., University of Delaware, 2016), 60, 47–49.

6   Harvey Wiley to J. E. Blackburn, September 29, 1909, Box 76, HWP
     LoC.

7   Berenstein, "Flavor Added," 111.

8   Oscar E. Anderson Jr., *The Health of a Nation: Harvey W. Wiley and the
     Fight for Pure Food* (Chicago: University of Chicago Press, 1958), 204.

9   "Memorandum of Rules of Procedure" in "Executive Sessions 1 to
     25," and Minutes of Executive Sessions, September 17, 1907, Box 4,
     Records of Executive Sessions, 1907–1913, Records of the Board of
     Food and Drug Inspection, FDA–NARA.

10   F. L. Dunlap to Harvey Wiley, July 9, 1909, Box 205, HWP LoC.

11   Anderson, *Health of a Nation,* 204; Harvey W. Wiley, M.D., *The History
     of a Crime against the Food Law* (Washington, DC: Harvey Wiley, 1929),
     157–58.

12   James Wilson to Dr. H. W. Wiley, April 24, 1907, in US House of
     Representatives, 62nd Congress, Second Session, "Expenditures in the
     Department of Agriculture," H.R. Rep. No. 249 (January 2, 1912), 9.

13   Paul B. Dunbar, "Memories of Early Days of Federal Food and Drug
     Law Enforcement," *Food Drug and Cosmetics Law Journal* 14 (February
     1959): 101.

14   Frederick Dunlap, "Memorandum for Dr. Wiley," September 14,
     1909, 321–350, Box 7, Hearings, 1907–1915, Records of the Board of
     Food and Drug Inspection, FDA–NARA. Emphasis in original.

15   US Department of Agriculture, *Influence of Saccharin on the Nutrition
     and Health of Man*, Report No. 94 (Washington, DC: Government
     Printing Office, 1911), 62.

16   Fred B. Linton, "Federal Food and Drug Laws: Leaders Who Achieved
     Their Enactment and Enforcement," *Food and Drug Law Journal* 50
     (1995; originally published in 1949): 15.

17   Clayton A. Coppin and Jack High, *The Politics of Purity: Harvey Wash-
     ington Wiley and the Origins of Federal Food Policy* (Ann Arbor: Univer-
     sity of Michigan Press, 1999), 155–56.

18   Anderson, *Health of a Nation*, 233. For an example, see George McCabe,
     Memorandum for Dr. Wiley, June 5, 1910, Box 205, HWP LoC.

19   Linton, "Federal Food and Drug Laws," 15.

20 Frederick Dunlap, "Memorandum for the Board of Food and Drug Inspection," July 12, 1909, Box 3, Seizure Cases, 1908–1912, Records of the Board of Food and Drug Inspection, FDA–NARA.

21 Wiley, *History of a Crime*, 159–60.

22 H. W. Wiley, "Testing the Foods," *National Magazine* 30 (June 1909): 278.

23 Board of Food and Drug Inspection, Hearing No. 298, May 8, 1909, 1–21, Box 6, Hearings, 1907–1915, 231–320, Records of the Board of Food and Drug Inspection, FDA–NARA.

24 Board of Food and Drug Inspection, Hearing No. 298, May 8, 1909, 8.

25 Kurlansky, *Milk!*, 162, 170.

26 Robert J. Gordon, *The Rise and Fall of American Growth* (Princeton, NJ: Princeton University Press, 2016), 220.

27 Deborah Blum, *The Poison Squad: One Chemist's Single-Minded Crusade for Food Safety at the Turn of the Twentieth Century* (New York: Penguin, 2018), 23–24.

28 Wiley, *History of a Crime*, 238.

29 Blum, *Poison Squad*, 61–62.

30 Frank G. Carpenter, "The Great American Stomach," *Deseret Evening News*, July 28, 1906, 21.

31 H. W. Wiley, M.D., *Formaldehyde*, pt. 5 in *Influence of Food Preservatives and Artificial Colors on Digestion and Health*, US Department of Agriculture, Bureau of Chemistry, Bulletin No. 84 (Washington, DC: Government Printing Office. 1908), 1497–99.

32 Anderson, *Health of a Nation*, 257.

33 James Wilson, "Report of the Secretary," in *Yearbook of the United States Department of Agriculture* (Washington, DC: Government Printing Office, 1910), 39, 100.

34 Harvey Wiley, "Progress and Regress under the Food Law," *Good Housekeeping* 55 (October 1912): 544. While successful, the Bureau of Chemistry was limited in its impact on the constraints mandated by the PFDA. Because the law applied only to goods that entered into interstate commerce, it could test only the products of dairies that sold their milk

to cities in different states. See James Harvey Young, "From Oysters to After-Dinner Mints: The Role of the Early Food and Drug Inspector," *Journal of the History of Medicine and Allied Sciences* 42 (1987): 49.

35 Board of Food and Drug Inspection, Hearing 231, March 5, 1909, 1–11, Box 6, Hearings, 1907–1915, 231–320, Records of the Board of Food and Drug Inspection, FDA–NARA. Ironically, despite the numerous problems that the Bureau of Chemistry found with milk, Wiley eventually came out against milk pasteurization because "it would paralyze the efforts to secure a pure milk supply"—namely, a supply that was clean enough that anyone could safely consume milk in raw form, as nature intended. Harvey Wiley to William Dinwiddie, July 12, 1910, Box 82, HWP LoC.

36 *Washington Evening Star*, December 31, 1911, 7.

37 James Wilson to Congressman Ralph Moss, July 24, 1911 in US House of Representatives, 62nd Congress, Second Session, "Expenditures in the Department of Agriculture," H.R. Rep. No. 249 (January 2, 1912), 13; Anderson, *Health of a Nation*, 210. Herter died in 1910 and was replaced by Theobald Long of Harvard.

38 *New York Times*, August 3, 1911, 2.

39 Wilson to Moss, 13.

40 Harvey W. Wiley, *Harvey W. Wiley: An Autobiography* (Indianapolis: Bobbs-Merrill, 1930), 244.

41 *Canner and Dried Fruit Packer* 27 (November 5, 1908): 719.

42 James Wilson to William Howard Taft, stamped August 2, 1911, 6, File 1756, William Howard Taft Papers, Manuscripts Division, Library of Congress, Washington, DC.

43 Dr. Harvey W. Wiley, "A Page from My Autobiography," *Good Housekeeping* 81 (November 1925): 292.

44 See, for example, H. C. Moffatt to Carl L. Alsberg, April 14, 1914, Box 140, "Records Relating to the Use of Sulphur Dioxide [. . .]," 1911–1913, Records of the Referee Board of Consulting Scientific Experts, FDA–NARA.

45 See, for example, John Long to Ira Remsen, April 21, 1909, Box 5, Series I: Correspondence, IRP.

46 Ira Remsen to C. R. Miller, March 9, 1909, Box 5, Series I: Corre-
    spondence, IRP.

47 E. E. Smith to C. A. Herter, November 25, 1908, Box 5, Series I: Cor-
    respondence, IRP.

48 Coppin and High, *Politics of Purity*, 128.

49 Ira Remsen to John Long, February 11, 1910, Box 5, Series I: Corre-
    spondence, IRP.

50 Ira Remsen to John Long, January 14, 1910, Box 5, Series I: Corre-
    spondence, IRP.

51 Board of Food and Drug Inspection, Hearing No. 231, March 5, 1909,
    9, Box 6, Hearings, 1907–1955, 231–320, Records of the Board of Food
    and Drug Inspection, FDA–NARA.

CHAPTER NINE. SACCHARIN AND KETCHUP

1   I use the terms "sodium benzoate" and "benzoic acid" interchangeably
    here (as many people did at the time) even though the substances are
    slightly different.

2   Dwight Eschliman and Steve Ettinger, *Ingredients: A Visual Exploration
    of 75 Additives and 25 Food Products* (New York: Regan Arts, 2015), 154.

3   W. D. Bigelow, "Some Common Methods of Preserving Food—II,"
    Western Druggist 23 (December 1901): 672.

4   Bee Wilson, *Swindled: From Poisoned Sweets to Counterfeit Coffee—The
    Dark History of the Food Cheats* (London: John Murray, 2008), 203–4.

5   Harvey W. Wiley, M.D., *The History of a Crime against the Food Law*
    (Washington, DC: Harvey Wiley, 1929), 62–66.

6   Clayton A. Coppin and Jack High, *The Politics of Purity: Harvey Wash-
    ington Wiley and the Origins of Federal Food Policy* (Ann Arbor: Uni-
    versity of Michigan Press, 1999), 123; US House of Representatives,
    Committee on Interstate and Foreign Commerce, *The Pure-Food
    Bills* [. . .] (Washington, DC: Government Printing Office, 1906), 252.
    Wiley's position did not make sense because it defeated the entire
    purpose of preservatives. Giving consumers the choice to add a
    flavorless, not particularly harmful preservative would do nothing to
    affect whether the food in question had been preserved successfully

by the time it got to them. This stance, when applied across the broad
spectrum of food science, would have made the mass production of
any perishable food impossible.

7   H. W. Wiley, *General Results of the Investigation Showing the Effect of
    Benzoic Acid and Benzoates upon Digestion and Health*, United States
    Department of Agriculture, Bureau of Chemistry Circular No. 39,
    July 20, 1908, 2.

8   James Harvey Young, "The Science and Morals of Metabolism: Cat-
    sup and Benzoate of Soda," *Journal of the History of Medicine and Allied
    Sciences* 23 (January 1968): 95.

9   Derek Lowe, "Sodium Benzoate Nonsense," *In the Pipeline* (blog),
    Science Translational Medicine, June 24, 2017, http://blogs.sciencemag.org
    /pipeline/archives/2017/07/24/sodium-benzoate-nonsense.

10 Young, "Science and Morals of Metabolism," 95.

11 K. B. Lehman, "Most Recent Investigations of the Determination,
    Preservative Action and the Admissibility of the Use of Benzoic
    Acid," *Science* 35 (April 13, 1912): 577–78.

12 US Department of Agriculture, *The Influence of Sodium Benzoate on
    the Nutrition and Health of Man*, Report No. 88 (Washington, DC:
    Government Printing Office, 1909): 88–89.

13 *Macon Daily Telegraph*, March 29, 1909, 2.

14 Lehman, "Most Recent Investigations," 580.

15 Ira Remsen to Russell Chittenden, May 11, 1910, Box 5, Series I:
    Correspondence, IRP.

16 Harvey W. Wiley, *An Autobiography* (Indianapolis: Bobbs-Merrill,
    1930), 244–45.

17 James Wilson to William Howard Taft, stamped August 2, 1911,
    5, Box 1756, William Howard Taft Papers, Manuscripts Division,
    Library of Congress, Washington, DC.

18 Harvey Wiley to Daniel R. Lucas, May 8, 1909, Box 75, HWP LoC.

19 Young, "Science and Morals of Metabolism," 100.

20 Memorandum for Mr. [Frederick] Dunlap, March 29, 1909, Box 73,
    HWP LoC.

21 *New York Times*, August 27, 1909, 2.

22   Young, "Science and Morals of Metabolism," 103.

23   Harvey Wiley to F. N. Barrett, March 11, 1909, Box 74, HWP LoC.

24   That derivative is toluene. See *Buffalo Sanitary Bulletin* 10 (September 30, 1917): 90; Albert E. Leach, *Food Inspection and Analysis* (New York: John Wiley and Sons, 1907), 673. See also US Department of Agriculture, *Report of the Secretary of Agriculture 1891* (Washington, DC: Government Printing Office, 1892), 180.

25   Harvey W. Wiley, M.D., "Bitter-Sweet," *Good Housekeeping* 57 (November 1912): 690.

26   Carolyn de la Peña, *Empty Pleasures: The Story of Artificial Sweeteners from Saccharin to Splenda* (Chapel Hill: University of North Carolina Press, 2010), 19.

27   De la Peña, *Empty Pleasures*, 19–20.

28   *Louisiana Planter and Sugar Manufacturer* (September 3, 1904): 161. "Saccharin" was commonly spelled "saccharine" at that time.

29   H. W. Wiley, M.D., "Saccharin in Food Products," *Pure Products* 1 (June 1905): 283.

30   Harvey Wiley to George P. McCabe, January 13, 1908, Box 70, HWP LoC.

31   Wiley, *History of a Crime*, 163.

32   US Department of Agriculture, *Influence of Saccharin on the Nutrition and Health of Man*, Report No. 94 (Washington, DC: Government Printing Office, 1911), 8.

33   US Department of Agriculture, *Influence of Saccharin*, 17.

34   *Spice Mill* 35 (May 1912): 394.

35   Wiley, *History of a Crime*, 399.

36   "Why Saccharin Is Not a Substitute for Sugar," *Practical Druggist* 32 (December 1914): 534.

37   James Wilson and Charles Nagel, "Saccharin in Food," February 29, 1912, in 58 Cong. Rec. 7411 (1919).

38   *Washington Times*, August 1, 1922, 4.

39   Wiley, *History of a Crime*, 398–99.

40   Deborah Blum, *The Poison Squad: One Chemist's Single-Minded Crusade for Food Safety at the Turn of the Twentieth Century* (New York: Penguin, 2018),

280. Many years later Wiley's position against saccharin made something of a resurgence. In 1970 a study from the University of Wisconsin Medical School linked saccharin consumption to bladder cancer in rats. The Food and Drug Administration removed saccharin from its list of safe additives in 1972. When the FDA moved to ban saccharin completely, both saccharin producers and 44 million American consumers vehemently objected since, at that time, saccharin was the only artificial sweetener on the market. Congress intervened and asked for more study before the FDA acted. In 2000 the government took saccharin out of limbo, stating that the earlier studies on rats were not good models of human digestion. See Jesse Hicks, "The Pursuit of Sweet," *Distillations,* May 2, 2010, https://www.sciencehistory.org/distillations /magazine/t he-pursuit-of-sweet; de la Peña, *Empty Pleasures*, 142–75.

41 Executive Session of the Board of Food and Drug Inspection, January 3, 1908, Box 4, Minutes of Executive Sessions, 1907–1913, Records of the Board of Food and Drug Inspection, FDA–NARA.

42 Amy Bentley, "How Ketchup Revolutionized How Food Is Grown, Processed and Regulated," *Smithsonian Magazine*, June 4, 2018, https:// www.smithsonianmag.com/innovation/how-ketchup-revolutionized -how-food-is-grown-processed-regulated-180969230/; Andrew F. Smith, *Pure Ketchup: A History of America's National Condiment With Recipes* (Columbia: University of South Carolina Press, 1996), 12–18.

43 Smith, *Pure Ketchup*, 34–35, 45.

44 Bentley, "How Ketchup Revolutionized."

45 Donald Gilliland, "Make Ketchup like Henry Heinz Used to Make," *Pittsburgh Post-Gazette*, October 13, 2017, http://www.post-gazette.com /life/food/2017/10/13/Heinz-ketchup-octagon-bottle-keystone-recipe -pure-food/stories/201710160007.

46 Smith, *Pure Ketchup*, 43, 86, 95–97.

47 Gabriella M. Petrick, " 'Purity as Life': H. J. Heinz, Religious Sentiment and the Beginning of the Industrial Diet," *History and Technology* 27 (March 2011): 43.

48 The economic historians Clayton Coppin and Jack High make much of Wiley's relationship with Heinz, suggesting that the company

used the chemist to gain a competitive advantage over other ketchup makers; Coppin and High, *Politics of Purity*, 124. In service of this argument, Coppin and High write that "Wiley's unqualified con-demnation of preservatives did not occur until 1906 when he was informed that Heinz could produce a catsup without benzoate of soda, the preservative most often used in catsup"; *Politics of Purity*, 79. This is, however, an oversimplification of Wiley's position. Here's a paraphrase of Wiley from 1907, after he had supposedly unqualifiedly condemned preservatives in ketchup: "The ordinary person in good health might use tomato ketchup for a long period of years without any deleterious effect whatever; however, to a person having any kid-ney trouble, benzoate of soda might prove a deadly poison"; "Ketchup Manufacturers Puzzled," *California Fruit Grower* (March 16, 1907): 7. Wiley consistently wanted to ban preservatives for everyone in order to protect the vulnerable. The forcefulness of his attempts to do so may have strengthened over time, but his position was not affected one way or another by Heinz's formula.

49 Sebastian Mueller to H. W. Wiley, October 7, 1908, Box 69, HWP LoC.

50 Gilliland, "Make Ketchup."

51 Coppin and High, *Politics of Purity*, 124.

52 H. W. Wiley, "Letter of Transmittal," in A. W. Bitting, *Experiments on the Spoilage of Tomato Ketchup*, US Department of Agriculture, Bureau of Chemistry, Bulletin No. 119 (Washington, DC: Government Print-ing Office, 1909), 3.

53 Charles F. Loudon to "Mr. Chairman" [Wiley?], 1908, Box 207, HWP LoC.

54 Sebastian Mueller to H. W. Wiley, October 7, 1908, Box 207, HWP LoC.

55 *American Food Journal* (January 15, 1909): 23.

56 Malcolm Gladwell, "The Ketchup Conundrum," *New Yorker*, Septem-ber 6, 2004, https://www.newyorker.com/magazine/2004/09/06/the-ketchup-conundrum.

57 René Bache, "Shall Pure Food Be Pure?" *Technical World Magazine* 11 (April 1909): 165.

58 John Brownlee, "How 500 Years of Weird Condiment History Designed the Heinz Ketchup Bottle," Fast Company, December 21, 2013, https://www.fastcodesign.com/1673352/how-500-years-of -weird-condiment-history-designed-the-heinz-ketchup-bottle.

59 Bitting, *Experiments on Spoilage*, 13.

60 Harvey W. Wiley, *Foods and Their Adulteration*, 2nd ed. (Philadelphia: P. Blakiston's Son and Co., 1911), 317.

61 Gladwell, "Ketchup Conundrum."

62 Smith, *Pure Ketchup*, 87.

63 US House of Representatives, *The Pure-Food Bills*, 315.

64 Smith, *Pure Ketchup*, 109.

65 Bentley, "How Ketchup Revolutionized."

66 Eschliman and Ettinger, *Ingredients*, 154.

67 Mike Adams, *Food Forensics: The Hidden Toxins Lurking in Your Food and How You Can Avoid Them for Lifelong Health* (Dallas: BenBella Books, 2016), 198–99.

68 Center for Science in the Public Interest, "Sodium Benzoate" in "Chemical Cuisine," https://cspinet.org/eating-healthy/chemical -cuisine#sodiumb, accessed October 6, 2018.

CHAPTER TEN. DRUGS

1 Board of Food and Drug Inspection, Hearing No. 584, August 2, 1910, 1–31, Box 14, Hearings, 1907–1915, 546–606, Records of the Board of Food and Drug Inspection, FDA–NARA.

2 Board of Food and Drug Inspection, Hearing No. 584, August 2, 1910, 22–24.

3 *Washington Herald*, February 21, 1917, 4.

4 Philip J. Hilts, *Protecting America's Health: The FDA, Business, and One Hundred Years of Regulation* (Chapel Hill: University of North Carolina Press, 2003), 23.

5 H. W. Wiley, "The United States Food and Drugs Act: Its Effect on the Composition of Medicine," *Pharmaceutical Journal* 78 (January 19, 1907): 56.

6 Donna J. Wood, *Strategic Uses of Public Policy: Business and Government*

in the Progressive Era (Marshfield, MA: Pitman Publishing, 1986), 79–80.

7   John Swann, "The Formation and Early Work of the Drug Laboratory, USDA Bureau of Chemistry," *Apothecary's Cabinet* No. 9 (Fall 2005): 1–2.

8   H. W. Wiley, A.M., M.D., LL. D., "Drugs and Their Adulterations and the Laws Relating Thereto," *Washington Medical Annals* 2 (1903): 219.

9   Swann, "Formation and Early Work," 2–3.

10 Lyman F. Kebler, *Adulterated Drugs and Chemicals*, US Department of Agriculture, Bureau of Chemistry, Bulletin No. 80 (Washington, DC: Government Printing Office, 1904): 7.

11 James Harvey Young, *The Toadstool Millionaires: A Social History of Patent Medicines in America before Federal Regulation* (Princeton, NJ: Princeton University Press, 1961): 233–34.

12 Young, *Toadstool Millionaires*, 219–22.

13 Congress of the United States, "Food and Drugs Act," June 30, 1906 (Washington, DC: Government Printing Office, 1908), 9–10.

14 Peter Temin, *Taking Your Medicine: Drug Regulation in the United States* (Cambridge, MA: Harvard University Press, 1980), 32. See also Clayton A. Coppin and Jack High, *The Politics of Purity: Harvey Washington Wiley and the Origins of Federal Food Policy* (Ann Arbor: University of Michigan Press, 1999), 97.

15 James Wilson, "Formula on the Label of Drugs," Board of Food and Drug Inspection Decision No. 53, 5, January 28, 1907.

16 L. F. Kebler, *The Harmful Effects of Acetanilid, Antipyrine, and Phenacetin*, US Department of Agriculture, Bureau of Chemistry, Bulletin No. 126 (Washington, DC: Government Printing Office, 1909): 7.

17 Board of Food and Drug Inspection, Hearing No. 469, February 15, 1910, 1–4, Box 11, Hearings, 1907–1915, 461–510, Records of the Board of Food and Drug Inspection, FDA–NARA.

18 James Harvey Young, *The Medical Messiahs: A Social History of Health Quackery in Twentieth-Century America* (Princeton, NJ: Princeton University Press, 1967), 4–6.

19 Young, *Medical Messiahs*, 6–12.

20 John Queeny to the Secretaries of Commerce and Labor, June 12, 1908, Box 1, Reports: Labeling of Acephenetidin, Records of the Bureau of Chemistry, FDA–NARA.

21 Fredcrick Dunlap to the Attorney General of the United States, December 14, 1908, Box 1, Reports: Labeling of Acephenetidin, Records of the Bureau of Chemistry, FDA–NARA.

22 Kebler, *Harmful Effects of Acetanilid, Antipyrine, and Phenacetin,* 5; John Toedt, Darrell Koza and Kathleen Van Cleef-Toedt, *Chemical Composition of Everyday Products* (Westport, CT: Greenwood Press, 2005), 68.

23 United States Department of Agriculture, Board of Food and Drug Inspection, Notice of Judgments Nos. 54–55, Food and Drugs Act, April 17, 1909, 2; North Dakota Agricultural Experiment Station, *Special Bulletin* 2 (August 1913): 301–2.

24 H. W. Wiley, "Report of the Chemist," September 1, 1911, in *Annual Reports of the Department of Agriculture, 1911* (Washington, DC: Government Printing Office, 1912), 423.

25 George McCabe to Harvey Wiley, January 29, 1910, Box 81, HWP LoC.

26 Harvey Wiley, "Memo for the Solicitor," July 20, 1910, 5, Box 205, HWP LoC.

27 George McCabe to Harvey Wiley, September 6, 1910, Box 81, HWP LoC.

28 Coppin and High, *Politics of Purity,* 155.

29 Harvey W. Wiley, *An Autobiography* (Indianapolis: Bobbs-Merrill, 1930), 239.

30 Harvey Wiley, "Memorandum for the Solicitor," July 23, 1910, Box 205, HWP LoC.

31 Coppin and High, *Politics of Purity,* 155.

32 George McCabe to Harvey Wiley, September 6, 1910, Box 81, HWP LoC.

33 *Washington Post,* April 27, 1911, 1.

34 *Chicago Tribune,* April 29, 1911, 7.

35 *Washington Post,* June 18, 1911, C11.

36 "Pure Food and Drugs Act," in Arthur P. Greeley, *The Food and Drugs Act* (Washington, DC: John Byrne, 1907), 76.

37 Harvey Wiley to W. J. Woodruff, March 25, 1920, Box 129, HWP LoC.

38 Joseph P. Remington, "Speech at Dinner Given in Honor of Harvey W. Wiley," April 9, 1908, Box 211, HWP LoC.

39 Linette A. Parker, "Legal Standards for Drugs," *American Journal of Nursing* 22 (July 1922): 809.

40 Wiley, "Drugs and Their Adulterations," 206.

41 Harvey Wiley to Dr. N. S. Davis, December 12, 1910, Box 81, HWP LoC.

42 Harvey Wiley to J. P. Remington, September 23, 1910, Box 81, HWP LoC.

43 "The Living Fame of Harvey W. Wiley," Box 28, AKWP.

44 *St. Louis Post-Dispatch*, 30 June 1920, 3.

45 Parker, "Legal Standards for Drugs," 810.

46 Harry M. Marks, *The Progress of Experiment: Science and Therapeutic Reform in the United States, 1900–1990* (New York: Cambridge University Press, 1997), 11, 24–28.

47 United States v. Johnson, 221 US 488 (1911).

48 Temin, *Taking Your Medicine*, 33–34.

49 James Harvey Young, *Pure Food: Securing the Pure Food and Drugs Act of 1906* (Princeton, NJ: Princeton University Press, 1989), 117, 6–17.

50 Board of Food and Drug Inspection, Hearing 171, November 6, 1908, 7, Box 5, Hearings, 1907–1915, 156–230, Records of the Board of Food and Drug Inspection, FDA–NARA.

51 Harvey W. Wiley and Anne Lewis Pierce, "The Inherent 'No-Accountness' of Patent Nostrums," *Good Housekeeping* 59 (September 1914): 392.

CHAPTER ELEVEN. BLEACHED FLOUR AND BAKING POWDER

1 Bee Wilson, *Swindled: From Poison Sweets to Counterfeit Coffee— The Dark History of Food Cheats* (London: John Murray 2008), 85.

2 Karl Marx, *Capital* (New York: Charles H. Kerr and Company, 1906), 194n3.

3 Jennifer Jensen Wallach, *How America Eats: A Social History of U.S. Food and Cuisine* (Lanham, MD: Rowman and Littlefield, 2013), 145.

4 George Galloway, "The Pure Food and Drugs Act, June 30, 1906" (MA thesis, University of Iowa, 1909), 14–15.

5 C. B. Morison, "Why Bleached Flour? Part I," *Baking Technology* 1 (March 1922): 72–73.

6 H. W. Wiley, "The Chemistry of Wheat Flour by Dr. C. H. Bailey," *Science* 62 (December 4, 1925): 513.

7 J. H. Shepard, in United States Department of Agriculture, "Notice of Judgment No. 382, Food and Drugs Act: Adulterated and Mis-branded Bleached Flour," May 14, 1910, 11.

8 Suzanne Rebecca White, "Chemistry and Controversy: Regulating the Use of Chemicals in Foods, 1883–1959" (PhD diss., Emory University, 1994), 115.

9 Dr. H. W. Wiley, "Some Problems in the Milling Industry," September 25–27, 1907, Box 190, HWP LoC.

10 *Northwestern Miller* 72 (October 9, 1907): 90.

11 *Northwestern Miller* 72 (December 4, 1907): 589.

12 United States Department of Agriculture, *Annual Report of the Department of Agriculture for the Year Ending June 30, 1908* (Washington, DC: Government Printing Office, 1909), 467.

13 Oscar E. Anderson Jr., *The Health of a Nation: Harvey W. Wiley and the Fight for Pure Food* (Chicago: University of Chicago Press, 1958), 220–21. In his *The History of a Crime against the Food Law*, Wiley tells what he called "The Pathetic Story of Bleached Flour." That story begins in 1910, two years after all the players in the Department of Agriculture agreed to ban it. However, to tell a story in which the Board of Food and Drug Inspection was in agreement on anything would have undercut the thesis of the book. Harvey W. Wiley, M.D., *The History of a Crime against the Food Law* (Washington, DC: Harvey Wiley, 1929), 382.

14 Shepard, "Notice of Judgment No. 382," 13.

15 "Hearings on the Bleaching of Flour," November 19, 1908, 219, Box 4, Hearings, 1907–1915, 155, Records of the Board of Food and Drug Inspection, FDA–NARA.

16 James Wilson, "Food Inspection Decision No. 100," December 9, 1908, in *Food Inspection Decisions 1–212* (Washington, DC: Government Printing Office, 1905–24).

17 White, "Chemistry and Controversy," 24.

18 The difference between baking soda and baking powder is that the powder includes an agent to activate the baking soda.

19 Linda Civitello, *Baking Powder Wars: The Cutthroat Food Fight That Revolutionized Cooking* (Urbana: University of Illinois Press, 2017), 6–7; Ben Panko, "The Great Uprising: How a Powder Revolutionized Baking," *Smithsonian Magazine*, June 20, 2017, http://www.smithsonianmag.com /science-nature/great-uprising-how-powder-revolutionized-baking -180963772/; "Layton Case—Missouri Supreme Court," in A. Cressy Morrison, *The Baking Powder Controversy*, vol. 1 (New York: American Baking Powder Association, 1904), 773.

20 Civitello, *Baking Powder Wars*, 41, 46.

21 Donna J. Wood, *Strategic Uses of Public Policy: Business and Government in the Progressive Era* (Marshfield, MA: Pitman Publishing, 1986), 166.

22 Donna J. Wood, "The Strategic Use of Public Policy: Business Support for the 1906 Food and Drug Act," *Business History Review* 59 (Autumn 1985): 425.

23 Clayton A. Coppin and Jack High, *The Politics of Purity: Harvey Washington Wiley and the Origins of Federal Food Policy* (Ann Arbor: University of Michigan Press, 1999), 22.

24 Federal Trade Commission v. Royal Baking Powder Co., Brief for the Respondent, Docket No. 540, 1924, 5. Some baking powders mixed cream of tartar and phosphate, but for the purposes of this discussion they are grouped in with the cream of tartar powders, given that the most important distinction from Wiley's perspective was whether or not baking powder contained alum.

25 C. A. Crampton, *Foods and Food Adulterants, Part Fifth: Baking Powders*, United States Department of Agriculture, Division of Chemistry, Bulletin No. 13 (Washington, DC: Government Printing Office, 1889), 572.

26 Civitello, *Baking Powder Wars*, 77–78.

27 Civitello, *Baking Powder Wars*, 68, 73.

28 Coppin and High, *Politics of Purity*, 23.

29 Civitello, *Baking Powder Wars,* 113.

30 Crampton, *Foods and Food Adulterants,* 572.

31 Wiley had had close ties to cream of tartar interests before he became famous. On April 20, 1892, Wiley, then head of the Division of Chemistry at the United States Department of Agriculture, wrote a friend of his at the Royal Baking Powder Company, a firm in an industry over which his office had jurisdiction. "Things are going on here in about the same old way," he wrote, "and I am still as poor as a church mouse. I want you and [William] McMurtrie to get up some scheme to get me into an office where I can make some money as you are doing. I do not care what it is just so the remuneration is sufficient." Harvey Wiley to J. LeDow, April 20, 1892, Box 3, HWP LoC. On the one hand, this kind of request from a government official ought to be shocking. On the other hand, Harvey Wiley was already committing himself to the cause of pure food, and Royal Baking Powder had an image of purity that it wanted to protect. Just because Wiley hoped his association with Royal Baking Powder might make him some money does not necessarily mean that he was abandoning his cause.

32 A. Cressy Morrison, *The Baking Powder Controversy*, vol. 2 (New York: American Baking Powder Association, 1907), 1675–76.

33 Morrison, *Baking Powder Controversy*, vol. 2, 1748.

34 Industrial Commission on Agriculture, *Report of the Industrial Commission on Agriculture* [. . .], vol. 11 (Washington, DC: Government Printing Office, 1901), 134.

35 Morrison, *Baking Powder Controversy*, vol. 1, 144.

36 Harvey Wiley to J. McK. Cattel, June 26, 1902, 3, Box 7, HWP LoC.

37 United States War Department, *Report of the Philippine Commission*, vol. 8, *Report of the Director of Health* (Washington, DC: Government Printing Office, 1909), 81.

38 Harvey W. Wiley, *Harvey W. Wiley: An Autobiography* (Indianapolis: Bobbs-Merrill, 1930), 264.

39 Harvey W. Wiley, M.D., *Foods and Their Adulteration* (Philadelphia: P. Blakiston's Son and Co., 1907), 253–54.

40 Board of Food and Drug Inspection, Executive Session No. 101, December 15, 1908, Minutes of the Board of Food and Drug Inspection, 1907–1913, Box 4, Records of the Board of Food and Drug Inspection, FDA–NARA.

41 Secretary, "Memorandum for the Board of Food and Drug Inspection," October 20, 1909, Box 78, HWP LoC; Board of Food and Drug Inspection, Executive Session No. 119, March 19, 1909, Box 4, Records of the Board of Food and Drug Inspection, FDA–NARA.

42 Referee Board of Consulting Scientific Experts, "Alum in Foods," Bulletin of the US Department of Agriculture No. 103 (Washington, DC: Government Printing Office, 1914), 1, 7.

43 Harvey Wiley, "Memorandum for Mr. James Martin Miller," c. 1923, 2–3, Box 199, HWP LoC.

44 Harvey Wiley to James Wilson, February 16, 1912, 7, Box 205, HWP LoC.

45 Richard Wright, *Black Boy*, 60th anniversary ed. (New York: Harper Perennial, 2006), 103.

46 Harvey W. Wiley, M.D., "The Alum Jimmy at the Pure Food Door," *Good Housekeeping* 59 (September 1914): 393.

47 Civitello, *Baking Powder Wars*, 122–23.

48 Civitello, *Baking Powder Wars*, 136; Federal Trade Commission as quoted in Civitello, *Baking Powder Wars*, 136.

49 Federal Trade Commission v. Royal Baking Powder Co., 5, 39.

50 *New York Times*, May 28, 1926, 23; Civitello, *Baking Powder Wars*, 136–37; Calumet Baking Powder Company, *The Truth about Baking Powder* (Chicago: 1928), 19.

51 Testimony of Harvey W. Wiley, Federal Trade Commission, October 14, 1924, 2766–88, Box 198, HWP LoC.

52 Testimony of Harvey W. Wiley, 2771–72.

53 Harvey W. Wiley, "The Baking Powder Controversy," *Science* (August 17, 1928): 161.

54 *New York Times*, August 22, 1911, 3.

55 Civitello, *Baking Powder Wars*, 162.

56 *Hygeia* 18 (February 1940): 150.

57 "If Dr. Wiley had had his way," explains one friendly sketch of
the doctor posted online by a modern library of information about
organic food, "all of America's food would now be organic."
"Harvey Washington Wiley, MD [Biography]," Selene River Press,
https://www.seleneriverpress.com/historical /harvey-washington
-wiley-md-biography/?hilite=%22Wiley%22, accessed August 21, 2017.

CHAPTER TWELVE. COCA-COLA

1 F. B. Linton, "Wiley—The Man," in Association of Official Agricultural Chemists, "Harvey Washington Wiley: In Memorium," xix–xx,
Box 211, HWP LoC.

2 Linton, "Wiley—The Man," xx.

3 Rene Bache, "Wonders Done by Wiley," *Los Angeles Times*, April 24,
1910, IM518.

4 Paul B. Dunbar, "Memories of Early Days of Federal Food and Drug
Law Enforcement," *Food Drug and Cosmetics Law Journal* 14 (February
1959): 106.

5 Harvey Wiley to Irving Fisher, September 26, 1905, Box 2, Miscellaneous Records, 1877–1910, Records of the Bureau of Chemistry,
FDA–NARA.

6 Harvey Wiley to the *Metropolitan Magazine*, January 27, 1909, Box 75,
HWP LoC.

7 Wiley as quoted in H. L. Harris to the Editor of the *Springfield
Republican,* September 11, 1911, 2, Box 6, Series I: Correspondence,
IRP.

8 Harvey Wiley to R. B. Owens, Box 81, HWP LoC.

9 *Spokane Press*, December 18, 1906, 2.

10 Caroline Niernsee to Harvey Wiley, April 1908, Box 307, AKWP.
Caroline Niernsee signed her handwritten letters to Wiley "Pal."
However, one typewritten letter in her own name from her workplace
on the stationary of her employer, the Planters Manufacturing Company of Anniston, Alabama, is enough to reveal the identity of all
the letters signed that way. See Caroline Niernsee to Harvey Wiley,
May 4, 1908, Box 307, AKWP.

11 "Blanche [Thayer]" to Harvey Wiley, September 20, 1906, Box 304, AKWP. On Blanche residing in New York, see "Blanche" to Harvey Wiley, February 13, 1905, Box 303, AKWP. I found Blanche's last name in William Lloyd Fox, "Harvey W. Wiley: The Formative Years" (PhD diss., George Washington University, 1960), 207.

12 Roxie Olmsted, "Anna Kelton Wiley, Suffragist," History's Women, http://www.historyswomen.com/socialreformer/annkeltonwiley.html, accessed September 1, 2017. Anna's father, General John C. Kelton, a Civil War veteran and former adjutant general to the US Army, "died so poor that by his special request he was accorded only such a funeral as is given to the inmates of the Soldiers' Home, of which he died governor." *Washington Evening Star*, September 11, 1893, 5.

13 Arthur Wallace Dunn, "Dr. Wiley and His Work," *Good Housekeeping* 54 (May 1912): 5930.

14 Harvey W. Wiley, *Harvey W. Wiley: An Autobiography* (Indianapolis: Bobbs-Merrill, 1930), 281; Oscar E. Anderson Jr., *The Health of a Nation: Harvey W. Wiley and the Fight for Pure Food* (Chicago: University of Chicago Press, 1958), 242.

15 Josephine Kelton to Harvey Wiley, January 11, 1911, 5, Box 311, AKWP.

16 John William Leonard, ed., *Woman's Who's Who of America* (New York: American Commonwealth Company, 1915), 451. Those letters are all in Box 311, AKWP. Ironically, in one of those letters, Josephine told Harvey that Anna should never know of this correspondence.

17 Murray Carpenter, *Caffeinated: How Our Daily Habit Helps, Hurts, and Hooks Us* (New York: Penguin, 2014), 81.

18 Dwight Eschliman and Steve Ettinger, *Ingredients: A Visual Exploration of 75 Additives and 25 Food Products* (New York: Regan Arts, 2015), 26.

19 Lyman F. Kebler, "Soft Drinks Containing Caffeine and Extracts of Coca Leaf and Kola Nut," in *Report of Committee on Building of Model Houses* (Washington, DC: President's Homes Commission, 1908), 268–69.

20 H. W. Wiley, A.M., M.D., LL. D., "Drugs and Their Adulterations and the Laws Relating Thereto," *Washington Medical Annals* 2 (1903): 209.

21   Clayton A. Coppin and Jack High, *The Politics of Purity: Harvey Washington Wiley and the Origins of Federal Food Policy* (Ann Arbor: University of Michigan Press, 1999), 145.

22   H. W. Wiley, "Testing the Foods," *National Magazine* 30 (June 1909): 278.

23   *Chicago Daily Tribune*, June 25, 1904, 1.

24   United States House of Representatives, "Hearings Before the Committee on Agriculture . . . on Estimates of Appropriations [. . .]," Fifty-Ninth Congress, Second Session (Washington, DC: Government Printing Office, 1907), 261.

25   On the state of the cold storage industry at this precise time, see Jonathan Rees, *Refrigeration Nation: A History of Ice, Appliances, and Enterprise in America* (Baltimore: Johns Hopkins University Press, 2013), 99–112.

26   H. W. Wiley, "Use of Cold Storage," Senate Document No. 486, Sixty-First Congress, Second Session, 4.

27   *Proceedings: Fourth National Food Conservation Congress* (Indianapolis: National Conservation Congress, 1912), 326.

28   Wiley, "Uses of Cold Storage," 5.

29   Wiley, "Uses of Cold Storage," 5.

30   *Ice and Refrigeration* 43 (November 1912): 171.

31   Harvey Wiley as quoted in Anna Zeide, *Canned: The Rise and Fall of Consumer Confidence in the American Food Industry* (Oakland: University of California Press, 2018), 29–30.

32   Harvey Wiley, letter to the editor, *Journal of the American Medical Association* (May 22, 1912), Box 200, HWP LoC.

33   Mark Pendergrast, *For God, Country, and Coca-Cola* (New York: Charles Scribner's Sons, 1993), 112.

34   *American Bottler* 30 (April 15, 1910): 44.

35   The Coca-Cola Company, "History of Bottling," http://www.coca-colacompany.com/our-company/history-of-bottling, accessed October 27, 2017.

36   H. W. Wiley, M.D., "So-called Temperance Drinks," April 4, 1907, 9, 11, Box 190, HWP LoC.

37 "Executive Session 104 of the Board of Food and Drug Inspection," January 8, 1909, Minutes of Executive Sessions, 1907–1913, Box 4, Records of the Board of Food and Drug Inspection, FDA–NARA.

38 Pendergrast, *For God, Country, and Coca-Cola,* 114; Suzanne Rebecca White, "Chemistry and Controversy: Regulating the Use of Chemicals in Food, 1883-1959" (PhD diss., Emory University, 1994), 137–38.

39 United State Circuit Court of Appeals, United States, Appellant, v. Forty Barrels and Twenty Kegs of Coca-Cola, Appellee: Record Part One (c. 1911), 2. I used the copy of the charges and exhibits available on Google Books.

40 Pendergrast, *For God, Country, and Coca-Cola,* 119–21; Ludy T. Benjamin Jr., Anne M. Rogers, and Angela Rosenbaum, "Coca-Cola, Caffeine, and Mental Deficiency: Harry Hollingsworth and the Chattanooga Trial of 1911," *Journal of the History of Behavioral Sciences* (January 1991): 48.

41 *Pittsburg Journal* excerpted in *American Food Journal* 3 (March 15, 1908): 8.

42 *American Food Journal* 6 (October 15, 1911): 14.

43 Ludy T. Benjamin Jr., "Coca-Cola—Brain Tonic or Poison?" *Psychologist* 23 (November 1910): 943; Pendergrast, *For God, Country, and Coca-Cola,* 120.

44 White, "Chemistry and Controversy," 144.

45 United States Department of Agriculture, "Notice of Judgment No. 1455," May 27, 1912, 12.

46 *Chattanooga Times,* April 7, 1911, clipping in Anna Kelton Wiley scrapbook, Box 200, HWP LoC.

47 *American Food Journal* 6, April 15, 1911, 25.

48 *Lubbock Avalanche,* April 18, 1912, 11.

49 US Department of Agriculture, "Notice of Judgment No. 1455," 9.

50 *Colorado Transcript,* August 24, 1911, 6.

51 US House of Representatives, Committee on Interstate and Foreign Commerce, *The Pure Food and Drugs Act, Part 1* (Washington, DC: Government Printing Office, 1912), 461.

52 Harvey Wiley, letter to the editor, *Journal of the American Medical Association* (May 22, 1912), 5–6.

53 White, "Chemistry and Controversy," 147–48.

54 Circuit Court of Appeals, Sixth District, as excerpted in *Presbyterian of the South*, August 5, 1914, 18.

55 White, "Chemistry and Controversy," 149.

56 White, "Chemistry and Controversy," 149–150.

57 Pendergrast, *For God, Country, and Coca-Cola*, 124.

58 Pendergrast, *For God, Country, and Coca-Cola*, 124, 121, 450.

59 Harvey W. Wiley, M.D. *The History of a Crime against the Food Law* (Washington, DC: Harvey Wiley, 1929), 380–82.

60 Wiley, *History of a Crime*, 382.

61 Dr. Harvey W. Wiley, "A Job for the New Administration," *Good Housekeeping* (June 1925): 188.

CHAPTER THIRTEEN. RESIGNATION

1 *New York Times*, July 13, 1911, 2.

2 Charles W. Rauchway to Harvey Wiley, June 16, 1903, Box 51, HWP LoC.

3 *American Food Journal* 7 (June 15, 1912): 17.

4 Clayton A. Coppin and Jack High, *The Politics of Purity: Harvey Washington Wiley and the Origins of Federal Food Policy* (Ann Arbor: University of Michigan Press, 1999), 85–86.

5 Mark A. Sullivan to H. W. Wiley, January 23, 1906, Box 60, HWP LoC.

6 H. W. Wiley, M.D., *Salicylic Acid and Salicylates,* pt. 2 in *Influence of Food Preservatives and Artificial Colors on Digestion and Health*, US Department of Agriculture, Bureau of Chemistry Bulletin No. 84 (Washington, DC: Government Printing Office, 1906), 757.

7 For examples, see *Deseret Evening News*, April 21, 1905, 5, and *Richmond Times-Dispatch*, April 19, 1905, 3. Wiley's correspondence files include ample evidence that this charge was true. See, for example, Curtis Publishing Company to H. W. Wiley, November 13, 1906, Box 55, HWP LoC. This was a $100 payment for an article on headache remedies for *Ladies' Home Journal*.

8 See, for example, Blomoco Manufacturing Company to H. D. [*sic*] Wiley, October 22, 1904, Box 57, HWP LoC.

9 Harvey Wiley to Adolph Kern, Box 7, HWP LoC.

10 Alfred G. Bauer to H. W. Wiley, July 1, 1902, Box 50, HWP LoC.

11 Arthur Wallace Dunn, "Dr. Wiley and Pure Food," pt. 2, *World's Work* 23 (November 1911): 40.

12 For examples, see California Wine Association to Wiley, December 20, 1905, Box 59, HWP LoC; Du Vivier and Company to Wiley, December 22, 1905, Box 59, HWP LoC; J. H. Hunt to Wiley, April 15, 1910, Box 309, AKWP; and Harvey Wiley to F. H. Smith, April 2, 1910, Box 76, HWP LoC. Coppin and High (in *Politics of Purity*, 85) suggest that Wiley's gift taking waxed and waned over the course of his time in Washington. However, just these examples, drawn from Wiley's correspondence during the bitter struggles over the passage of the Pure Food and Drug Act and his role in its enforcement, threatened to seriously undermine his goals had they come to light at that time.

13 The vast majority of evidence documenting the gifts that Wiley received is in the letters that accompanied those gifts. There is no admission from Wiley that accepting these gifts was wrong except in one case, when a distiller sent a box of whiskey to his cousin William's apartment in New York City by mistake. "I do not feel I can accept gifts of this kind from parties whose cases I may be called upon to consider officially," he wrote in 1907. Yet he told the distiller to let his cousin keep the whiskey, and he looked forward to meeting William for a "tipple" the next time he was in the city. See Harvey Wiley to William H. Wiley, September 16, 1907, Box 64, HWP LoC.

14 Coppin and High, *Politics of Purity*, 83–84.

15 Dr. H. W. Wiley, "Address before the Sphinx Club," November 10, 1908, Box 190, HWP LoC.

16 Harvey Wiley to R. E. Armstrong, July 31, 1903, 2, Box 8, HWP LoC.

17 United States House of Representatives, "Hearings before the Committee on Agriculture [. . .] on Estimates of Appropriations [. . .]," Fifty-Ninth Congress, Second Session (Washington, DC: Government Printing Office, 1907), 248–49.

18 Harvey Wiley to Walter Wyman, July 8, 1904, 3–4, Box 57, HWP LoC.

19 Harvey Wiley to James Wilson, March 15, 1912, Box 105, HWP LoC.

20 Mary Tidd Read, "Wiley–The Boss," in Association of Official
    Agricultural Chemists, "In Memorium: Harvey Washington Wiley,"
    1930, xvii, Box 211, HWP LoC.

21 Snell Smith, "Dr. Wiley, Government Chemist," *American Review of
    Reviews* 37 (May 1908): 552.

22 Coppin and High, *Politics of Purity*, 90.

23 *New York Times*, July 13, 1911, 2.

24 Fred B. Linton, "Federal Food and Drug Laws: Leaders Who
    Achieved Their Enactment and Enforcement," *Food and Drug Law
    Journal* 50 (1995; originally published in 1949): 19.

25 *New York Times*, July 13, 1911, 2.

26 United States House of Representatives, "Expenditures in the
    Department of Agriculture," Report No. 249, January 2, 1912, 13,
    Sixty-Second Congress, Second Session; Judson C. Welliver, "Prob-
    ers Aghast as Dr. Wiley Lays Bear Plot Facts," *Washington Times*,
    August 16, 1911, 1, 9.

27 *New York Sun*, August 18, 1911, 4; *New York Sun*, August 17, 1911, 2.

28 Welliver, "Probers Aghast," 1.

29 *Washington Times*, September 15, 1911, 2.

30 *New York Times*, September 16, 1911, 3.

31 *New York Times*, March 16, 1912, 5.

32 *New York Times*, March 16, 1912, 1.

33 *New York Times*, March 16, 1912, 5.

34 *New York Times*, March 16, 1912, 5.

35 Anna Kelton Wiley, "Original Federal Food and Drugs Act of June
    30, 1906: Its Great Founder," *Food Drug and Cosmetic Law Quarterly* 1
    (September 1946): 321.

36 President, American Home Magazine Company, to Dr. Harvey W.
    Wiley, November 11, 1911, Box 74, AKWP.

37 Harvey Wiley to Dana T. Ackerly, February 22, 1912, Box 74, AKWP.

38 *New York Times*, April 26, 1912, 9.

39 See, for example, Cresta Blanca of California to Dr. Harvey W. Wiley,
    September 2, 1912, Box 106, HWP LoC.

40 *New York Times*, April 26, 1912, 9.

41   Coppin and High, *Politics of Purity*, 161.

42   *New York Times*, February 1, 1913, 13.

43   Oscar E. Anderson Jr., *The Health of a Nation: Harvey W. Wiley and the Fight for Pure Food* (Chicago: University of Chicago Press, 1958), 254.

44   *Atlanta Constitution*, February 8, 1914, 6.

45   *American Food Journal* 11 (January 1916): 4.

46   Harvey W. Wiley, M.D., *The History of a Crime against the Food Law* (Washington, DC: Harvey W. Wiley, 1929).

47   Harvey Wiley to S. N. D. North, November 5, 1910, Box 83, HWP LoC.

48   Aaron Bobrow-Strain, *White Bread: A Social History of the Store-Bought Loaf* (New York: Beacon Press, 2012), 66–67.

49   United States v. Lexington Mill and Elevator Company, 34 US 338 (1914); Suzanne Rebecca White, "Chemistry and Controversy: Regulating the Use of Chemicals in Food, 1883–1959" (PhD diss., Emory University, 1994), 132.

50   Bobrow-Strain, *White Bread*, 67. After the first Supreme Court decision, the government prosecuted Lexington Mill again and won solely on the grounds that bleaching inferior flour constituted misbranding. However, as Bobrow-Strain writes, "The bureau won that battle, but had already lost the war."

51   Bobrow-Strain, *White Bread*, 68.

52   Harvey Wiley, "The End of the Bleached Flour Case," *Good Housekeeping* 58 (June 1914): 833.

53   United States v. Lexington Mill.

54   C. B. Morison, "Why Bleached Flour? Part III," *Baking Technology* 1 (May 1922): 132–33.

55   Wiley, *History of a Crime*, 391.

56   Anderson, *Health of a Nation*, 236.

CHAPTER FOURTEEN. THE *GOOD HOUSEKEEPING* YEARS

1   William MacHarg, "Speaking of Dr. Wiley . . . ," *Good Housekeeping* 70 (April 1920): 27.

2   Elna Harwood Wharton, "Dr. Wiley's Recipe for Longevity," c. 1926, 1, Box 211, HWP LoC.

3 Harvey Wiley, "When Should One Stop Working?" *Good Housekeeping* 78 (February 1924): 151.

4 Wharton, "Dr. Wiley's Recipe," 3.

5 W. D. Bigelow, "Harvey Washington Wiley," *Science* 72 (September 26, 1930), 312.

6 Mary Tidd Read, "Wiley–The Boss," in Association of Official Agricultural Chemists, "In Memoriam: Harvey Washington Wiley," xviii, Box 211, HWP LoC. Read claimed that she could not vouch for the authenticity of this story but offered it up anyway because it felt true enough to her.

7 Harvey W. Wiley, *Harvey W. Wiley: An Autobiography* (Indianapolis: Bobbs-Merrill, 1930), 282.

8 *Washington Times*, May 16, 1912, 1.

9 *Washington Times*, February 23, 1913, 11.

10 See, for example, *Washington Evening Star*, May 23, 1912, 10.

11 *Washington Herald*, December 9, 1914, 12.

12 *Philadelphia Evening Public Ledger*, August 27, 1915, 8.

13 *St. Louis Post-Dispatch*, May 17, 1912, 1.

14 E. Melanie DuPuis, *Dangerous Digestion: The Politics of American Dietary Advice* (Berkeley: University of California Press, 2015): 78, 80.

15 Martin S. Pernick, "Eugenics and Public Health in American History," *American Journal of Public Health* 87 (November 1997): 1769–70.

16 *Logan* (UT) *Republican*, February 4, 1913, 2.

17 Dr. Harvey W. Wiley, "The Rights of the Unborn," *Good Housekeeping* 75 (October 1922): 32.

18 Margaret B. Downink, "Mrs. Harvey Wiley," *Los Angeles Times*, January 21, 1912, III20.

19 Katherine Graves Busbey, "Mrs. Harvey W. Wiley: The Notable Wife of the Great Champion of Pure Food," *Good Housekeeping* 54 (April 1912): 545.

20 Busbey, "Mrs. Harvey W. Wiley," 544–45.

21 *Washington Herald*, November 11, 1917, 3.

22 Helen Zoe Veit, *Modern Food, Moral Food: Self-Control, Science, and the Rise of Modern American Eating in the Early Twentieth Century* (Chapel

Hill: University of North Carolina Press, 2013), 98.

23   *New York Times*, January 7, 1964, 33.

24   Anna Kelton Wiley, "Original Federal Food and Drugs Act of June 30, 1906: Its Great Founder," *Food Drug and Cosmetic Law Quarterly* 1 (September 1946): 321.

25   *Good Housekeeping*, "The History of the Good Housekeeping Seal," October 1, 2011, http://www.goodhousekeeping.com/institute /about-the-institute/a16509/good-housekeeping-seal-history/, accessed September 26, 2017.

26   Wiley, *Autobiography*, 303.

27   H. W. Wiley, "An Interesting Letter from Dr. Wiley," *Pacific Pharmacist* 6 (September 1912): 120; Wiley, *Autobiography*, 324.

28   Harvey Wiley to W. E. Barnard, April 12, 1912, Box 106, HWP LoC.

29   *New York Times*, February 8, 1940.

30   Wiley, *Autobiography*, 304.

31   Harvey Levenstein, *Revolution at the Table: The Transformation of the American Diet* (Berkeley: University of California Press, 2003), 159.

32   Dr. Harvey W. Wiley, "Food Reconstruction," *Good Housekeeping* 68 (February 1919): 125.

33   Anna Kelton Wiley, "Its Great Founder," 321.

34   Harvey W. Wiley, M.D., "The Little White Slaver," *Good Housekeeping* 62 (January 1916): 94.

35   Dr. Harvey W. Wiley, "Looking Ahead," *Good Housekeeping* 79 (December 1924): 210.

36   Dr. Harvey W. Wiley, "A Little Bit of History," *Good Housekeeping* 77 (December 1923): 209.

37   Harvey Wiley, "Dr. Wiley's Question-Box," *Good Housekeeping* 68 (February 1919), 72; Harvey Wiley, "Dr. Wiley's Question-Box," *Good Housekeeping* 78 (April 1924): 94; Harvey Wiley, "Dr. Wiley's Question-Box," *Good Housekeeping* 83 (November 1926): 93.

38   Wiley, "A Little Bit of History," 209.

39   Harvey Wiley, "Dr. Wiley's Question-Box," *Good Housekeeping* 75 (July 1922): 94. Many of his columns carried the byline "Dr. Harvey Wiley, M.D." Sometimes the M.D. disappeared. In other instances,

Wiley had no byline at all, and such columns were simply labeled "Dr. Wiley's Department."

40 Wiley, "A Little Bit of History," 209.

41 Wiley, *Autobiography*, 299–300.

42 Oscar E. Anderson Jr., "The Pure-Food Issue: A Republican Dilemma, 1906–1912," *American Historical Review* 61 (April 1956): 550; *Washington Times*, August 30, 1912, 4.

43 Harvey W. Wiley, "Why Dr. Wiley Is for Wilson," *Holbrook* (AZ) *Argus*, October 15, 1912, 4. This article was almost certainly syndicated nationwide.

44 Wiley, *Autobiography*, 301–2.

45 Veit, *Modern Food, Moral Food*, 53–54.

46 Wiley, *Autobiography*, 309.

47 Oscar E. Anderson Jr., *The Health of a Nation: Harvey W. Wiley and the Fight for Pure Food* (Chicago: University of Chicago Press, 1958), 261; Wiley, *Autobiography*, 307.

48 *Lyceum News* 2 (April 1912): 2.

49 Anderson, *Health of a Nation*, 261.

50 *Los Angeles Times*, March 31, 1913, 112.

51 Wiley, *Autobiography*, 307.

52 Harvey Wiley to the White Entertainment Bureau, August 16, 1912, Box 108, HWP LoC.

53 "Dr. Harvey W. Wiley," n.d., Box 108, HWP LoC.

54 *New York Tribune*, July 16, 1910, 13.

55 *Washington Herald*, December 9, 1914, 12.

56 *Day Book*, January 29, 1913, 27.

57 Veit, *Modern Food, Moral Food*, 55.

58 E. I. D. Seymour, "Dr. Wiley and His Farm," *Country Life in America* 28 (August 1915): 19–21.

59 E. W. Davidson, "The 'Father' of the Pure Food Law," *Washington Post*, October 13, 1929, SM12.

60 MacHarg, "Speaking of Dr. Wiley," 129.

61 MacHarg, "Speaking of Dr. Wiley," 129; Wiley, *Autobiography*, 323–24.

62 Harvey W. Wiley, "Abolition of the Bureau of Chemistry," *Science* 65 (April 15, 1927): 371–72.

63 Anna Kelton Wiley, "Its Great Founder," 323.

64 Dr. Harvey W. Wiley and Anne Lewis Pierce, "Swindled Getting Slim," *Good Housekeeping* 58 (January 1914): 109–13.

65 Dr. Harvey W. Wiley, "The Mineral Water Humbug," *Good Housekeeping* 58 (July 1914): 107–114.

66 Dr. Harvey W. Wiley, "The Philosophy of Coué," *Good Housekeeping* 76 (May 1923): 84, 185–88.

67 *Washington Times*, July 7, 1911, 1.

68 Harvey Wiley, "Dr. Wiley's Question-Box," *Good Housekeeping* (July–August 1920): 71

69 H.W. Wiley, "The Pure Food Battle," in Harvey W. Wiley, M.D., *1001 Tests of Foods, Beverages and Toilet Accessories, Good and Otherwise* (New York: Hearst's International Library Co., 1914), xxvii.

70 *Good Housekeeping*, "About the Good Housekeeping Institute," September 1, 2011, http://www.goodhousekeeping.com/institute /about-the-institute/a16265/about-good-housekeeping-research -institute/, accessed October 6, 2017.

CONCLUSION. WILEY'S LEGACY

1 Dr. H. W. Wiley, "Chemistry and Longevity: Food in Its Relation to Individual and National Development," *Bulletin* (Hundred Year Club), no. 1, March 23, 1899, 4, 7.

2 Dr. H. W. Wiley, "What to Eat to Live Long," *Everybody's* 5 (July 1901): 51.

3 *Indianapolis Star*, July 29, 1908, 1.

4 *Lompoc Journal*, January 7, 1911, 6.

5 H. W. Wiley, "The Influence of Preservatives in Foods on the Public Health," New York Academy of Medicine, 1904, Box 189, HWP LoC.

6 Oscar E. Anderson Jr., *The Health of a Nation: Harvey W. Wiley and the Fight for Pure Food* (Chicago: University of Chicago Press, 1958), 276–78.

7 *New York Herald Tribune*, July 1, 1930, 21.

8 Anderson, *Health of a Nation*, 276–77.

9   Cora deForest Grant, "Mrs. Wiley Takes Up Husband's Mantle," *Washington Post Magazine*, October 19, 1930, 4. The inscription was placed there at Wiley's request. See E. W. Davidson, "The Father of the Pure Food Law," *Washington Post,* October 13, 1929, SM12.

10   Francis E. Hamilton (Wiley) "Statement," 1, January 4, 1909, Box 71, HWP LoC. Wiley explained that he authored that statement in Harvey Wiley to F. E. Hamilton, November 23, 1908, Box 68, HWP LoC.

11   The Hall of Fame for Great Americans was established in 1900, and its elections once received great attention. "But when the hall's host, New York University, sold its Bronx campus in 1973, the collection languished. The 98 busts tarnished, soot gathered, and the Hall of Fame slowly slipped into irrelevance. An election has not been held since 1976." See Sam Dolnick, "A Hall of Fame, Forgotten and Forlorn," *New York Times*, December 5, 2009, A17.

12   William Horowitz to Milton Altman, June 17, 1960, Box 28, AKWP.

13   "The Thirteenth Quinquennial Election 1960," Box 28, AKWP; Mrs. H. W. Wiley to Sabre Voelke and "Mr. Powers," February 25, 1962, Box 28, AKWP.

14   "The Living Fame of Harvey W. Wiley," c. 1960, Box 28, AKWP.

15   Courtney I. P. Thomas, *In Food We Trust: The Politics of Purity in American Food Regulation* (Lincoln: University of Nebraska Press, 2014), 25–26; Peter Temin, *Taking Your Medicine: Drug Regulation in the United States* (Cambridge, MA: Harvard University Press, 1980), 43, 4.

16   Anna Kelton Wiley, "Original Federal Food and Drugs Act of June 30, 1906: Its Great Founder," *Food Drug and Cosmetic Law Quarterly* 1 (February 1946): 322.

17   Nadia Berenstein, "How Activists Forced FDA to Blacklist 'Carcinogenic' Flavor Chemicals the Agency Says Are Safe," *New Food Economy*, October 18, 2018, https://newfoodeconomy.org /fda-carcinogenic-flavor-chemical-food-additive-lacroix-lawsuit/, accessed October 22, 2018.

18   Thomas, *In Food We Trust,* 33.

19   Mildred Morris, "Sugar Jags Are Speeding U.S. to a Premature Grave," *Grand Forks* (ND) *Evening Times*, December 19, 1913, 11.

20   Denis W. Stearns, "A Continuing Plague: Faceless Transactions and
     the Coincident Rise of Food Adulteration and Legal Regulation of
     Quality," *Wisconsin Law Review* (2014): 439.

21   Harvey Levenstein, *Fear of Food: A History of Why We Worry about
     What We* Eat (Chicago: University of Chicago Press, 2012), 73.
     Levenstein's book is a good place to see the ways that Wiley's ideas
     both evolved yet still remained recognizable over the course of the
     twentieth century.

ESSAY ON SOURCES

TOWARD THE END OF HIS LONG LIFE, Harvey Wiley published two auto-biographical works: the privately published *The History of a Crime against the Pure Food Law* (1928) and *Harvey W. Wiley: An Autobiography* (Bobbs-Merrill, 1930). Neither of them is particularly reliable. Both are greatly influenced by Wiley's anger at his failure to determine how the Pure Food and Drug Act would be enforced during the years 1907–1912—so much so that anything but the most non-controversial factual statements made in these works should require a second source in order to be believed (except, of course, for statements about Wiley's anger at these events as he looked back at them). This attitude is most apparent in *History of a Crime*. The *Autobiography* is really just a string of anecdotes that mostly have little or nothing to do with the central subject of Harvey Wiley's life—food. The parts that do consider food seldom reflect his thinking about the foods he struggled over at the time those struggles occurred. Yet this has not stopped those two works from becoming the most common sources for historians seeking to interpret Wiley's role in the passage and interpretation of the Pure Food and Drug Act.

Anyone interested in Wiley's life must compare Wiley's autobiographical works with his extensive papers housed at the Library of Congress in Washington, DC, as well as Wiley's other work-related archives. Many of his letter books, for example, are in the Records of the Food and Drug Administration at the National Archives in College Park, Maryland. You can also read what Wiley thought about food in the records of the Board of Food and Drug Inspection at the same location. Taken together, Wiley's communications offer a far different picture of his life from that given by the *Autobiography* or a *History of a Crime*. Even a cursory perusal of the archival record should undermine anyone's faith in what he wrote twenty years after the events documented in those files. Therefore, I have privileged the contemporary record over Wiley's reminiscences, as any careful historian should.

All of Wiley's letters, whether stored in folders or letter press books, blur the line between the personal and the professional. Wiley sent letters from his office to his family and friends. He sent personal letters to his professional contacts, many of whom became his friends. Letters he sent on behalf of the Cosmos Club and letters he sent on behalf of American consumers rest back to back in many of his files. A complete biography of Wiley must cross this same line between personal and professional back and forth many times to take in every aspect of his life. In my opinion, too much of the earlier work on Wiley concentrates on his political activities to the exclusion of everything else.

Of all the differences between this and earlier work about Wiley, access to multiple digitized newspaper and magazine archives may be the greatest. From the beginning of the Poison Squad experiments onward, Harvey Wiley's name appeared in newspapers constantly. Search for the terms "Harvey Wiley" or just "Dr. Wiley" in the Library of Congress's Chronicling America database, and you will get a good idea of just how famous Wiley really was. Through such resources I have had easy, searchable access to exactly what he said about many of the foods that he fought over. This proved particularly helpful for the period after his resignation from the Department of Agriculture, when his appearance in every town on his lecture tours merited coverage, sometimes both before and after the event. Harvey Wiley was a media sensation, and any failure to account for his many public activities leaves an incomplete picture of both his thinking and the impact of that thinking on American life.

While Harvey Wiley may not be a well-known historical figure, there are nonetheless a few important sources upon which any Wiley biographer must inevitably rely. This is the second book I've written on a subject that Oscar E. Anderson Jr. got to before I was even born. His *The Health of a Nation: Harvey W. Wiley and the Fight for Pure Food* (University of Chicago Press, 1958) remains a remarkable achievement. While overly friendly to its subject and conventionally political in its outlook, Anderson's book is both comprehensive and highly readable. Although we take very different approaches (since food itself was not a common subject of historical study when Anderson wrote that book), I have nonetheless heavily relied on Anderson here. *The Health of a Nation* is better than the chemist's own autobiography for an account of the basic details of Wiley's life. Every other history book that considers Wiley to any significant extent is built upon this foundation.

One other biography, "Harvey W. Wiley: The Formative Years," William Lloyd Fox's 1960 PhD dissertation from the George Washington University, remains unpublished. While this work stops in 1903, it stands on its own as an invaluable examination of Wiley's character and personal life. While I eventually learned to read Harvey Wiley's terrible handwriting in his early letters and the diary he wrote for a few years in his early life, I nonetheless made great use of Fox's extensive excerpts of those records.

Clayton A. Coppin and Jack High's *The Politics of Purity: Harvey Washington Wiley and the Origins of Federal Food Policy* (University of Michigan Press, 1999) is not a biography but covers many of Wiley's struggles over the regulation of particular foods. While I disagree with their overall perspective on the nature of regulation, their research into Wiley's career at the Bureau of Chemistry is thorough and convincing. Their book and many articles leading up to its publication form an essential counterpoint to Anderson's dated and narrow portrayal of Wiley as a progressive hero.

The Poison Squad: One Chemist's Single-Minded Crusade for Food Safety at the Turn of the Twentieth Century by Deborah Blum (Penguin, 2018) came out after I had sent this manuscript to the publisher for peer review but before it was accepted for publication. I used her book to improve many sections of this work, especially my discussions of milk and saccharin. Nevertheless, her perspective on Wiley closely follows the traditional, mostly political perspective on Wiley set out both by Anderson and Wiley himself. It should be obvious from this text that my primary interest in Wiley lies elsewhere.

Finally, while Harvey Levenstein's *Fear of Food: A History of Why We Worry about What We Eat* (University of Chicago Press, 2012) is not a book about Harvey Wiley, its long Wiley section (pp. 62–75) greatly influenced my perspective.

INDEX